Walter Reid is the author of a number of acclaimed works on military and political history, with a focus on British imperial policy. His last book, *Keeping the Jewel in the Crown: Britain's Betrayal of India,* was published in May 2016. He was educated at Oxford and Edinburgh universities. He lives in Scotland but spends several months each year in France.

Gordon Masterton is Professor of Future Infrastructure at the University of Edinburgh and a former president of the Institution of Civil Engineers. He was also a member of the Royal Commission on the Ancient and Historical Monuments of Scotland for 12 years.

Paul Birch is a retired chartered surveyor and professional arbitrator. He is originally from Leeds but has lived in Bridge of Weir since 1982.

SUPREME
SACRIFICE

———

A
SMALL VILLAGE
AND THE
GREAT WAR

———

WALTER REID
GORDON MASTERTON
AND PAUL BIRCH

First published in 2016 by
Birlinn Limited
West Newington House
10 Newington Road
Edinburgh
EH9 1QS

www.birlinn.co.uk

ISBN 978 1 78027 350 1

Any profits received by the authors will be donated to local charities.

British Library Cataloguing-in-Publication Data
A catalogue record for this book is available from the British Library

Typeset by Edderston Book Design

Printed and bound by Grafica Veneta, Italy

This book is dedicated to the memory of the men of Bridge of Weir who died in the Great War, and to the memory of the families who bore their loss.

This book owes much to research carried out by members of the Bridge of Weir Memorial Society, which was formed to renew and preserve the memories of the men whose names are engraved on the village war memorials.

Contents

List of Illustrations

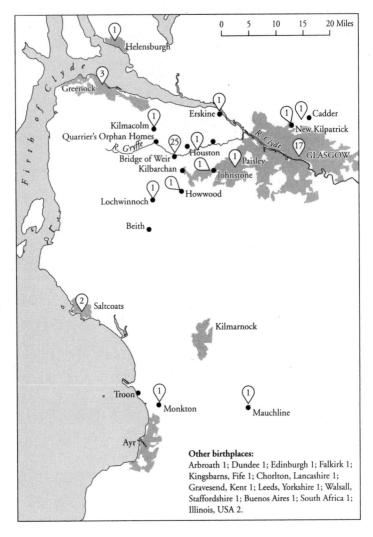

Birthplaces of the Bridge of Weir Fallen

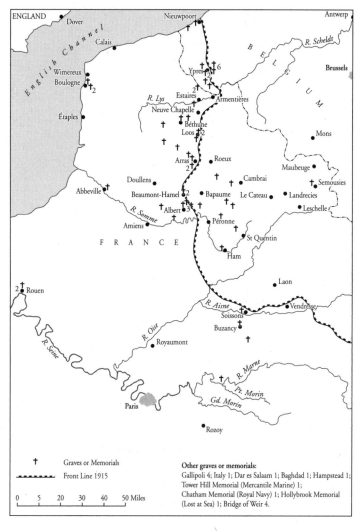

The map shows locations across England, France, and Belgium. Labeled places include:

ENGLAND: Dover

Channel/coast: English Channel, Calais, Wimereux, Boulogne †2, Étaples

BELGIUM: Antwerp, R. Scheldt, Brussels, Nieuwoort, Ypres †2 / 6, Armentières, Mons, Maubeuge, Semousies †, Landrecies, Leschelle

FRANCE: R. Lys, Estaires, Neuve Chapelle, Béthune †, Loos †2, Arras †2, Roeux, Doullens, Cambrai, Abbeville, Beaumont-Hamel †2, Bapaume, Le Cateau, Albert †3, R. Somme, Péronne, Amiens, St Quentin, Ham, Laon, Rouen 2†, R. Aisne, Soissons, Vendresse, Buzancy †, R. Oise, R. Seine, Royaumont, R. Marne, Pt. Morin, Gd. Morin, Paris, Rozoy

Legend:

† Graves or Memorials

▬ ▬ ▬ Front Line 1915

0 5 20 30 40 50 Miles

Other graves or memorials:
Gallipoli 4; Italy 1; Dar es Salaam 1; Baghdad 1; Hampstead 1; Tower Hill Memorial (Mercantile Marine) 1; Chatham Memorial (Royal Navy) 1; Hollybrook Memorial (Lost at Sea) 1; Bridge of Weir 4.

Graves and Memorials of the Bridge of Weir Fallen

xi

Army structure

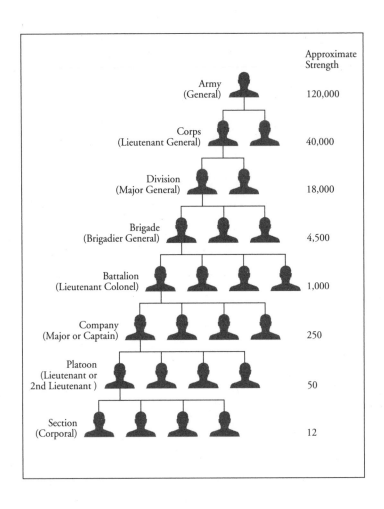

Approximate Strength

Unit	Strength
Army (General)	120,000
Corps (Lieutenant General)	40,000
Division (Major General)	18,000
Brigade (Brigadier General)	4,500
Battalion (Lieutenant Colonel)	1,000
Company (Major or Captain)	250
Platoon (Lieutenant or 2nd Lieutenant)	50
Section (Corporal)	12

The Men of Bridge of Weir
in the order in which they died

Name	Rank	Regiment or Service	Date of Death	Age	Death
James Smellie	Artificer 4th Class	HMS Cressy, Royal Navy	22 Sep. 1914	22	Torpedoed
Thomas Spink	Private	South Wales Borderers	26 Sep. 1914	26	Chivy, after Battle of the Aisne
Frederic Barr	Private	Highland Light Infantry	25 Feb. 1915	26	Near Béthune
Thomas Lawrie	Private	Cameronians	28 Feb. 1915	29	Wounded near Béthune, died Boulogne
Neil McDonald	Piper	Canadian Royal Highlanders	23 Apr. 1915	34	Second Ypres
Peter Houston	Third Engineer	ss Strathnairn Merchant Navy	15 Jun. 1915	30	Torpedoed
James Reston	Lance Sergeant	Argyll & Sutherland Highlanders	20 Jun. 1915	24	Festubert, Pas-de-Calais
Alister Duff	Second Lieutenant	Cameronians	28 Jun. 1915	27	Gallipoli
Andrew Gardiner	Private	NZ Canterbury Rifles	7 Aug. 1915	22	Gallipoli

Name	Rank	Regiment or Service	Date of Death	Age	Death
Robert Milroy	Private	NZ Wellington Regiment	8 Aug. 1915	26	Gallipoli
John Macdougall	Private	Highland Light Infantry	16 Aug. 1915	33	Gallipoli
Walter Brown	Private	Canadian Infantry	9 Sept. 1915	22	Ploegsteert sector
John Clark	Private	King's Own Scottish Borderers	25 Sept. 1915	20	Loos
James Hood	Private	Royal Scots Fusiliers	30 Oct. 1915	26	Wounded Loos, died Aberdeen
Malcolm Brodie	Private	Gordon Highlanders	21 Feb. 1916	33	Ypres
John MacInnes	Private	Cameronians	12 May 1916	36	Loos sector
Peter Higgins	Private	Royal Scots Fusiliers	5 Jun. 1916	30	Béthune
William McKenzie	Private	The Black Watch	27 Jun. 1916	27	Béthune
Lyle Barr	Second Lieutenant	Royal Field Artillery	26 Jul. 1916	26	The Somme
Peter Calligan	Sergeant	Royal Garrison Artillery	16 Aug. 1916	30	The Somme

Name	Rank	Regiment or Service	Date of Death	Age	Death
Hudson Hardman	Lieutenant	Cameron Highlanders	17 Aug. 1916	21	The Somme
George Balfour	Second Lieutenant	Highland Light Infantry	15 Sept. 1916	29	The Somme
David Cummings	Private	Canadian Mounted Rifles	1 Oct. 1916	28	The Somme
James Brooks	Lance Corporal	Royal Scots	29 Oct. 1916	20	The Somme
William McClure	Private	Royal Inniskilling Fusiliers	11 Nov. 1916	34	Messines
Ian Bannatyne	Second Lieutenant	Highland Light Infantry	18 Nov. 1916	19	The Somme
Robert Barr	Private	Highland Light Infantry	18 Nov. 1916	21	The Somme
Robert McDougall	Private	Highland Light Infantry	18 Nov. 1916	21	The Somme
Archibald Fulton	Sergeant	Highland Light Infantry	19 Nov. 1916	21	The Somme
Henry Andrew	Private	Army Service Corps	4 Jan. 1917	39	Salonika, died Paisley
Andrew Jackson	Gunner	Motor Machine Gun Service	27 Jan. 1917	23	Tuberculosis at Banchory

Name	Rank	Regiment or Service	Date of Death	Age	Death
James McGibbon	Gunner	Royal Field Artillery	6 Apr. 1917	30	Arras
David Tod	Sapper	Royal Engineers	6 Apr. 1917	26	Arras
John Holmes	Lance Corporal	Argyll & Sutherland Highlanders	11 Apr. 1917	20	Arras
Hepner Giffen	Private	Royal Scots	28 Apr. 1917	23	Arras
Robert Burns	Private	Lancashire Fusiliers	12 May 1917	20	Arras
Speirs Barr	Captain	Highland Light Infantry	23 May 1917	22	Hindenburg Line
Henry Strang	Private	Highland Light Infantry	6 Jul. 1917	19	Nieuwpoort
Walter McWilliam	Sapper	Royal Engineers	11 Jul 1917	34	Mesopotamia
James Pollock	Private	Highland Light Infantry	15 Jul. 1917	21	Nieuwpoort
David McGregor	Private	King's (Liverpool) Regiment	31 Jul. 1917	19	Third Ypres
William Millar	Gunner	Royal Field Artillery	18 Aug. 1917	23	Third Ypres

Name	Rank	Regiment or Service	Date of Death	Age	Death
Adam McLeod (otherwise Walton)	Private	Argyll & Sutherland Highlanders	22 Aug. 1917	19	Third Ypres
James Woodrow	Private	Seaforth Highlanders	22 Aug. 1917	26	Third Ypres
Richard Arroll	Private	Seaforth Highlanders	24 Aug. 1917	38	Wounded at Arras, died London
William Candlish	Private	Argyll & Sutherland Highlanders	24 Aug. 1917	24	Third Ypres
George Jackson	Captain	Highland Light Infantry	25 Aug. 1917	25	Somme sector
John Begley	Gunner	Royal Field Artillery	26 Sept. 1917	30	Third Ypres
James Burns	Private	Army Service Corps	8 Oct. 1917	23	East Africa
George Fisher	Second Lieutenant	Suffolk Regiment	17 Nov. 1917	26	Third Ypres
Alexander Cameron	Captain	Argyll & Sutherland Highlanders	21 Mar. 1918	42	German Spring Offensive
Charles Morgan	Corporal	Argyll & Sutherland Highlanders	21 Mar. 1918	24	German Spring Offensive

Name	Rank	Regiment or Service	Date of Death	Age	Death
Robert Niven	Lance Corporal	King's (Liverpool) Regiment	9 Apr. 1918	19	German Spring Offensive
John Brown	Private	Argyll & Sutherland Highlanders	17 Apr. 1918	20	German Spring Offensive
Ernest Murray	Private	Cameronians	7 May 1918	25	German Spring Offensive
Edward Shedden	Private	Highland Light Infantry	8 May 1918	28	German Spring Offensive
William Houston	Private	Royal Engineers	14 May 1918	36	German Spring Offensive
Andrew Houston	Gunner	Royal Field Artillery	5 Jun. 1918	36	German Spring Offensive
Robert Sproul	Corporal	Cameron Highlanders	18 Jul. 1918	25	Prelude to the Hundred Days
John Andrew	Lance Corporal	King's Own Scottish Borderers	23 Jul. 1918	28	Prelude to the Hundred Days
William Keith	Private	Argyll & Sutherland Highlanders	23 Jul. 1918	20	Prelude to the Hundred Days
Robert Millar	Private	Argyll & Sutherland Highlanders	1 Aug. 1918	24	Prelude to the Hundred Days

Name	Rank	Regiment or Service	Date of Death	Age	Death
Ritchie Johnstone	Lieutenant	Royal Air Force	14 Aug. 1918	20	Anti-U-boat patrol off Bangor
William Kerr	Private	The Black Watch	29 Aug. 1918	23	The Hundred Days
Robert Browning	Signaller	Royal Garrison Artillery	13 Sept. 1918	32	The Hundred Days
John Gray	Captain	Argyll & Sutherland Highlanders	21 Sept. 1918	27	The Hundred Days
William Blackley	Signaller	Highland Light Infantry	4 Oct. 1918	33	The Hundred Days
Hugh Fulton	Second Lieutenant	Highland Light Infantry	9 Oct. 1918	20	The Hundred Days
John Higgins	Lance Corporal	King's Own Yorkshire Light Infantry	28 Oct. 1918	27	Italian Front
William Neil	Lance Sergeant	The Black Watch	8 Nov. 1918	25	The Hundred Days
Robert Jackson	Sapper	Royal Engineers	16 Nov. 1918	40	Spanish influenza, Rouen
William Cairns	Private	King's Own Scottish Borderers	11 Aug. 1919	28	Septicaemia, Wimereux

Puppets and Puppet-masters

In the course of the First World War, both sides applied a great deal of ingenuity in the attempt to mislead the other side and deduce its intentions. The British fabricated models, 'full size flat images of soldiers, painted in England by women who had once painted bone china, with realistic faces, with moustaches and glasses under their tin hats. These were puppets. They had flat strings snaking over the mud, operated by puppeteer soldiers hidden in foxholes and craters, who made them stretch and turn, stand up and fall. [They were] deployed in hundreds, under a smokescreen, inviting the Germans to fire on them and reveal their own positions. A man in a shell-hole could operate four or five of these "soldiers".' (A.S. Byatt, The Children's Book)

These puppets were dummies, painted boards. But they had their equivalents, flesh and blood figures who danced and fell at the commands of puppet-masters who were far away and fighting a different sort of war.

Prologue

1. THE COUNTRY'S WAR

The sombre flame of tragedy that illuminates the memory of the
First World War is contained within a many-faceted lantern, but
one prism contains a flaw that distorts and misleads, and that
flaw is the notion that the war was futile: an unnecessary war,
not a 'good war' like the Second, not a war that need have been
fought.

In truth the First World War, no less than the Second, was
a war Britain had to fight. If she had stood aside, as she looked
quite likely to do, an aggressive and undemocratic militaristic
power would have dominated the continent with consequences
no less dire for Britain than the rest of Europe. It is to the
nation's credit that without compelling treaty obligations or
threat to her territories she went to war in 1914 and fought on
till victory was achieved without any thought of compromise
or surrender, despite a haemorrhage of blood and a cost that
turned the greatest creditor nation in the world into a debtor.

And victory, victory for Britain and France, victory for the
institutions of freedom and liberal values, would not have
been achieved without Britain's contribution. Her losses were
less than those of her allies, France and until 1917 Russia, but
her contribution on land and at sea was critical. In 1917 and
1918, with Russia no longer in the war, and America not yet
contributing man-power, the war would have been lost without
Britain. In 1918 the war would not have been won without
her. France, drained white by the blood-letting at Verdun, was
exhausted and demoralised. It was an unbroken series of British-

led victories in the last hundred days of the war that brought Germany to request an armistice.

What Britain's commitment required was a transformation which was not asked of the other belligerents. Germany and Russia were military autocracies. Even France, democratic and civilised, had a tradition of militarism and conscription, of a nation in arms. Britain had no such history. There had never been conscription in Britain. The very notion of a standing army in time of peace was anathema. There was not even a national police force. The army was tiny. Wars had been fought cheaply, mostly at sea or, if on land, chiefly by subsidising allies or employing mercenaries.

In Britain in the years immediately ahead of the war there *had* been some vision of a new type of warfare, and plans had been drawn up for it, but they were no more than plans. A massive adaptation had to be made when a sudden decision to fight was made – and to fight not at sea but on land and in huge numbers. The army which fought in France grew from six to sixty battalions. The war which was fought was not one of cavalry-based colonial skirmishes. The army had to adapt to a massive, mechanised confrontation. It did so.

The war saw the fastest learning-curve the British Army has ever undergone, as senior commanders strove to adapt to problems that no army, on either side, could truly have apprehended in their entirety. Every Commander-in-Chief in 1914 was already a grown man when Rudolf Diesel invented the internal combustion engine, and was middle-aged when the Wright brothers flew a heavier-than-air flying machine a few hundred feet.

In 1914 the British Army was prepared for a war not unlike that of the Crimea, with some modifications derived from the American Civil War and the South African War. By 1918 Haig's armies were fighting essentially as the army would fight in 1939–45. In terms of tactics there would be no further substantive changes until the mechanisation of the 1970s.

There was no British tradition of militarism. Further than that, Britain took great pride in individualism, liberty, the lack of state control. There were no identity cards in 1914, and British citizens could travel without a passport. Governments could not pry into the affairs of the citizen. Parliaments were not supposed to do too much legislating, and the notion that powers were balanced to limit the reach of government was prized.

And yet, to win the war, society surrendered much of these sacrosanct liberties. Encountering no resistance, the Government assumed control of almost every detail of national life. State direction of industry, labour, agriculture, feeding and movement was accepted. The changed nature of Government was so marked that, as prime minister, Lloyd George was frequently said – but without any implication of criticism – to have 'dictatorial' powers. But despite all this, despite the fact that in 1917, under the U-boat attacks, Britain risked starving, there was no challenge to social and political cohesion. And nowhere was this heroic cohesion more marked than amongst the men who fought for their country – and the women who stayed at home and suffered there.

This book is intended to do three things. It tells the story of the war – of why it was fought, how it was fought, and why it was fought in that way. That larger picture provides the framework for the second purpose: to tell the stories of seventy-two men who fought and died in it. They fought in a remarkable variety of different roles, and are only linked by one arbitrary fact: they all came from the same village.

Credit for victory must go not to the generals or the politicians, but to men such as those – and to the society that produced these men. The war was not won by the professional soldiers of the original British Expeditionary Force, superlatively professional as it was. By the end of 1915 it no longer existed, its place taken first by volunteers and then by conscripts. These men were, as Shakespeare had put it, 'but warriors for the working day'. Much can be learned from them: not least we learn the awfulness of war. They never questioned the rightness of what they were doing. Some of them were unfortunate in their backgrounds. They might have resented what they were being asked to do. All of them, certainly, were asked to do more than any man should be. But British soldiers, unlike the armies of their allies, never broke collectively: there were no mutinies.

These men were impelled by a sense of duty which brought them to offer their lives for a cause which they could only understand partially: even today, long after the records have been opened, we only have a limited understanding of why the war was fought. Moreover, these warriors for the working day knew nothing of the jealousies, the feuds, the struggles between and amongst politicians and senior commanders. Some of these struggles were between men who were fighting for good reasons, but others were the result of naked ambition. While the men of the village, the puppets, fought battles that cost them their lives, the puppet-masters fought no less intently for their careers. That is the third theme of this book.

How would we, from today's society, emerge from such a test? How would we compare with these seventy-two men? We cannot know. All we can be sure of is that *their* steadfastness, their conviction that their cause was just, that the values they fought for were worth dying for, commands our gratitude, respect and remembrance.

2. The Men's War

Although we deal with the deaths and part of the lives of seventy-two young men from a single village, unusually, the seventy-two did not serve in just a limited number of locally-based regiments or pals' battalions.* What makes the village's

---

* In the early days of the war enthusiastic enlisting often created 'Pals' battalions', which were composed of friends and colleagues from the same background (employment, chamber of commerce, schools and so forth), who

experience unusual is that its men fought in so many theatres of war, joining up and dying at different stages of the conflict. Thus the story of their war, the village's war, is that of the war itself and that of communities throughout Britain.

The story of that war has frequently been told in terms of myth, the myth of lions led by donkeys, unquestioned traditions of men marching in extended line across no man's land. Research in recent years has largely re-evaluated what happened. Generals, fighting a war of which no one had any experience, were far from perfect, but they were not fools. The war, particularly in its later stages, was fought in a very different way from that caricatured in *Oh! What a Lovely War*, or *Blackadder*. The idea of troops crossing no man's land in extended line, for example, was largely the invention of John Buchan, who used it as a poignant example of disciplined courage. In fact troops rarely advanced in this way – they were expected to use fire and movement techniques to take advantage of the geographical features of the battlefield. But in another example of how research confounds expectations, where commanders did use extended line tactics – normally when troops were too inexperienced to deploy in a more sophisticated way – losses were usually lower.

The men from Bridge of Weir fought on the Western Front, Gallipoli, Mesopotamia, Palestine, Salonika, the Italian Front and East Africa, in the British Army, the Royal Navy, the mercantile marine, the Royal Air Force and Canadian and ANZAC forces. The conflicts in which they perished cover the principal military actions from 1914 to 1918. Some were killed in action, some succumbed to tropical disease, and one was a victim of the 1918 influenza epidemic.

In 1914 the tectonic plates of society shifted, creating a chasm

---

joined up and served together. When this happened the result was that these groups of men tended to share the same fate. The same thing happened when regiments recruited from specific parts of the country. For various reasons, the men of Bridge of Weir were not greatly concentrated in particular units, though there were some important exceptions, as will be seen.

that definitively separated the pre-war years from those that followed. It has been said that in some ways those who did not know the earlier years can never wholly understand how different they were. This book is not only the story of those who went; it is also a story of those left behind. The families, the wives, the sweethearts and the children were the most immediately affected. But the deaths left a larger void than that. The book describes how a community was affected.

The germ of this book was born when some members of one of the village churches looked at the memorial to those of that church who had died in the Great War of 1914–18 and reflected on the fact that nothing was now known of these men, beyond surnames and initials. The idea of learning more about just these men grew, to take in those whose names are recorded on the other church memorials and on the memorial erected at the centre of the village. There are seventy-two names in total, and this book records something of each man – there were no women – behind the names.

What was the object behind the research? Essentially commemoration of a sacrifice – made in many cases consciously – for those who would follow. This book and its associated website* are intended to create a faithful remembrance of those who died, in a spirit of respect for their sacrifice. That is a worthwhile objective. If it helps to remind people of what war means, and what the implications of the failure of politics mean, that too will be worthwhile.

When the war ended, the village's first act of communal remembrance was to conceive and construct its memorial. It is that memorial that has inspired this book, not least through the words inscribed in the granite: *Let those who come after see to it that their name be not forgotten.*

---

* See page 245.

1

The Village – Bridge of Weir

The village that our story is about, our village, is Bridge of Weir, a community with a population today of somewhere between four and five thousand, situated about fifteen miles west of Glasgow. The village is in what is still, despite local government changes, referred to as Renfrewshire: the body of land bounded on the north by the River Clyde and on the west by that river's estuary, the Firth of Clyde.

On the east of the historic county (which now consists of smaller administrative divisions) there is fertile agricultural land; to the west elevated moorland. Bridge of Weir lies on the line that separates the two, on a spot where the River Gryffe descends fast from the hills to run more placidly into the Clyde.

Renfrewshire has been peopled from about 5000 BC. There is much evidence of Iron Age forts (*c.* 600 BC–AD 87); the Romans and much later the Normans came; and the mediaeval Church established communities on the rich farmland in the east of the area. The Cluniac Abbey at Paisley was the mother-church for the area. But Bridge of Weir itself is a recent creation. Although the village is surrounded by three older settlements, Kilbarchan and Kilmacolm (whose 'Kil' prefixes refer to a church or the cell of an early saint) and Houston (on the lands of Kilpeter), the pre-First World War census of 1911 failed to recognise Bridge of Weir as an independent village and listed its streets and residents under the neighbouring villages of Kilbarchan and Houston.

1

That was a little unfair. The emergence of the River Gryffe from the hills of west Renfrewshire attracted the establishment of a community quite early in the eighteenth century. Before a bridge was thrown across the Gryffe around 1770, the hamlet was known as Port (or crossing) o' Weir. The weir that gives the village its name was a salmon weir.

Change came fast after the establishment of the salmon weir and the bridge, as the industrial revolution altered the face of central Scotland. The Gryffe was a power source for the new industries. By the mid-1790s, Renfrewshire had half the cotton mills in Scotland. The county was a textile Silicon Valley. Water power was initially used to drive cotton mills, but it came to have much wider applications. Mills and factories were built, extended, adapted or converted for grain, lint, spinning, bleaching and tanning. In and around Bridge of Weir were four large mills and four small ones. The cotton mill which opened in 1793 had a huge water wheel powering 18,000 spindles. Linwood Mill, only a few miles from Bridge of Weir, was the largest mill in Scotland. The neighbouring town of Paisley, famous for its pattern, was a major centre for weaving and cotton thread production.

But the Industrial Revolution exemplifies the paradox that capitalism consists in creative destruction, as investment constantly flows to support evolution. The day of the water-based textile industries ended as suddenly as it had arrived. By 1876 all eight mills had closed and empty buildings were left. Evidence of the river's industrial past is visible in the network of weirs and mill-lades along the riverside between Bridge of Weir and Crosslee, the hamlet to the north. The archaeology of these defunct industrial sites follows a ribbon development – not along the line of the roads, but along the rivers and the complex of mill-lades.

2

The Village on the Eve of War

What chiefly reanimated the village after the decline of its early industries was the arrival of the railway. The line which linked it with Paisley and Glasgow to the east and Greenock and the other Clyde ports to the west opened in 1864. The nature of the village changed, as it became not simply a self-sufficient economic unit, but home for many who worked elsewhere. These prosperous incomers, escaping the soot and noise of Glasgow and the Clyde shipyards, built houses, chiefly on Ranfurly Hill, to the south of the old village.

The building of their substantial villas was stimulated by the Greenock and Ayrshire Railway Company, which offered half-price season tickets to anyone building a house in the village. The process reached its peak in the last decade of the old queen's century and the first of the next, until Lloyd George's Budget of 1910 brought an abrupt end to this residential building spree throughout the country. Substantial residential building did not resume until after the Second World War.

But by 1911 the village had largely assumed the character and physical appearance it would have for the next half-century. Its population was about 2,500.* It had a leather industry which had to an extent filled the void left by the decline of the textile mills; it had golf courses; big houses had been built for

---

* A conventional breakdown of Bridge of Weir's population would suggest that in 1914 there were roughly 1,000 men, 1,250 women and 500 children.

its residents to live in and shops to supply their needs. All this created employment for families from the Highlands, Islands, Ireland and other parts of Scotland and beyond.

The main roads of the village have changed little over the years. Shops appeared along Main Street, the old road running from west to east through the village (and over the Bridge itself), but there were dwellings there as well. As in almost all Scottish towns and villages there was an element of substandard housing with overcrowding and inadequate sanitation. Bridge of Weir residents lived on two sides of the Main Street in densely packed, stone-built terraces or tenement buildings, between the tannery and the Pow Burn. There were newer, more spacious tenements on the north side of the street between the Pow Burn and the railway station. Some of those buildings are recognisable today. Towards the east of the Main Street, Ranfurly Hotel opened in 1882. It started out as a forty-bedroom hotel for golfers; as we shall see it played two important roles during the war.

The old Main Street, together with the new railway line, bisected the village physically and socially. The Ordnance Survey mapped Renfrewshire in 1912 and published a twenty-five inch to the mile map in 1914. It shows in effect two adjacent communities, split by the railway line: old Bridge of Weir to the north and Ranfurly to the south. Up the hill, Ranfurly had its villas, new churches, golf clubs, tennis courts and even a curling pond. Ranfurly Castle Golf Club course had been laid out in 1889 around the remains of a fifteenth-century castle motte. In 1905 some of the members broke away, taking the Ranfurly Castle name to create a new course. A new club, confusingly called Old Ranfurly Golf Club, took over the original course and the castle.

There were three Presbyterian churches in the village. Freeland was the oldest, interesting architecturally and as an epitome of the history of the schisms and fusions of the Scottish church from the seventeenth century onwards. Its congregation can trace its history back to open-air worship in the eighteenth century, in the tradition of the earlier Covenanting conventicles, part of the Original Secession Church known as the Associate Presbytery.

The present church building opened in 1826. In 1839 the congregation rejoined the Church of Scotland. Hardly had it done so when the Church of Scotland was rent by the great Disruption of 1843 over the right of landowners to nominate ministers. Freeland then became part of the Free Kirk, one of a number of dissident bodies, some of which, including Freeland, came together in the United Free Church in 1900.

A second United Free Church, Ranfurly Church, was built on Ranfurly Hill in 1890. Bridge of Weir was not an ecclesiastical parish (a parish *quoad sacra*) until 1886 and until then the parish church, the mainstream Church of Scotland church for the village, was in Kilbarchan. A congregation of the Church of Scotland worshipped under its own minister in the village from the 1870s, and built Bridge of Weir Parish Church (later St Machar's and now St Machar's Ranfurly), before the establishment of the ecclesiastical parish.

Most, but not all, of the Scottish Presbyterian churches came together in the unification of 1929 which followed the Church of Scotland Act of 1921. The three Bridge of Weir churches did, and subsequently the congregations of St Machar's and Ranfurly united.

In 1913, St Mary's Episcopalian Church had opened on the south-eastern edge of the village. The nearest Roman Catholic Church was St Fillan's, in Houston.

The village industries and enterprises provided employment for several hundred people in 1914; that prevented the community from being purely a dormitory. The largest employment other perhaps than agriculture was in tanning and leather production.

The Muirhead family, known to have been working in leather in 1758, dominated the tanning scene. In 1905, James Muirhead sold his share in the Gryffe Tanning Company to his brother Roland for £8,292 18s 2d. Roland was an unusual capitalist. He had left school at fifteen. After a four-year apprenticeship in his father's tannery he emigrated to South America, where he worked as a cattlehand. Then he moved north to Washington State and lived in a community based on the teaching of Robert Owen, best remembered today for his progressive experiment at New Lanark. He claimed that his Washington State experience formed his mind for socialism, and although he was later remembered for his commitment to the Scottish National Party – he was one of its founders in 1934 and its president from 1936 until 1950 – he was much involved in the Labour movement. He joined the Independent Labour Party in 1918. He had returned to Britain in 1891 and ran the family business, which he reorganised to give the workers a share in ownership. He introduced a number of changes for the benefit of his workforce, including better working hours and an emphasis on healthy living, with opportunities to swim and play golf. We shall meet Bridge of Weir golfers later.

Although he credited Washington State for altering his views, it has to be said that the rest of his family, untouched by his American experience, also embraced radical opinions. His sister, Alice, was a suffragette and his elder brother, Robert, was a member of the Socialist Land and Labour League, an organisation with direct links to Marx and Engels. It is a disappointment that Roland, this maverick tannery owner, with his colourful gaucho and Red Clydeside background, is described by the *Oxford Dictionary of National Biography* as being dour, austere and serious.

Another member of the family, Arthur, built the Clydesdale Works for his new company, Bridge of Weir Leather, on the site of Laigh Mill. Here tanned hides were dressed, finished and coloured by curriers. The curriers were skilled men and some were recruited from outside Bridge of Weir. The Bridge of Weir Leather Company made leather upholstery for furniture, car seats, ships and railway carriages. It secured orders from the builders of the *Lusitania*, launched in 1906, from the Ford Motor Company with its Model T Fords and from the Scottish car manufacturers Argyll, Albion and Arrol Johnstone.

The Muirhead companies built homes for their workers. Oils used in tanning and leather production were made from the bark of trees, originally oak; later larch, spruce and hemlock were also used, as was mimosa. Thus just off Mill O'Gryffe Road is a workers' tenement dating from 1896 exotically called The Mimosas.

When war came, the Bridge of Weir tannery and leather companies switched production and dedicated their total output to the military campaign. They made leather for army boots and there was an increased demand from the army for equestrian leathers.

This then was the community from which, between 1914 and 1918, seventy-two men went to war and never returned. The village, like the village's war, was a microcosm of the country. In 1914 Britain was the wealthiest country in the world. Many of the residents of Bridge of Weir shared in that prosperity. The cotton mills had gone, but the leather works and tannery were thriving, and the Ranfurly villas had brought new money to the old village. In Bridge of Weir, as throughout Britain, there was confidence in the future. Only a minority of intellectuals worried about a relative decline in prosperity or Darwinian notions of decay. Most people were confident about the future. The village's belief in the inevitability of progress would die in the conflict that killed her sons.

A poem written at Christmas 1914 captures rather well the spirit of the village at that point in the war – the smug confidence of a privileged, close community which had yet to feel the full force of the tempest that would blow away, perhaps for ever, the self-assurance of nineteenth-century Britain:

The Boys of Bridge-of-Weir
Christmas, 1914

Old Bridge-of-Weir! of wind and wet!
Your charms, how can I e'er forget?
The Golf Course, clad in snowy white!
The sledging on a starry night!
The cross-roads, frozen after rain!
The 'Trotters' for the morning train!
The Station, where the gossips chat,
With paper, pipe and Homburg hat!
The Sabbath bells, the Sunday dress,
The Monday shrieking Coast express,
And Gilbert's sweets, and ginger pop!
And Mary Morgan's cookie shop!
Bright stars in Scotland's cloudy sky!
All near and dear to memory's eye!

Of all the gallant lads and brave,
Gone forth their fellow-men to save,
None better than the boys so dear,
The Bonnie Boys of Bridge-of-Weir!
. . .
And whether you're in drouth or drench,
In hut, or hole, or tent, or trench,
In firing line, or sodden camp,
At sea, or on the weary tramp,
We know each lad will do his part,
With love and honour in his heart,
And on the Holy Christmas night,
We'll wish this wish with all our might,
'Or far, or near, you there, we here,
God bless the boys of Bridge-of-Weir.'

3

The War

Before we look at the fate of the men of the village, let us look briefly at the war in which they fought.

Right up to the declaration of war on 4 August 1914 it was far from clear that Britain would go to war. Arguably, if the Central Powers, Austria-Hungary and particularly Germany, had known for sure that Britain *would* fight, war might have been averted. Some cabinet members were against fighting. Even the position of Lloyd George, later prime minister and often called the man who won the war, was uncertain. Finally he supported the decision to fight, but two of his colleagues resigned.

Equally, the nature of the war that Britain would fight was far from certain. Afterwards, experts like J.F.C. Fuller and Basil Liddell Hart* described the Great War as an aberration from 'the British way of warfare'. That way, the traditional British way of war, had consisted of using the navy partly for large engagements but particularly for raids on the periphery of her enemies' territories, leaving the land war to mercenaries or allies.

The fact that the First World War was an aberration from that way was to an enormous extent due to one man, Henry Wilson, sometimes called the ugliest man in the British Army as the result of a wound he had received from Burmese

---

* Liddell Hart became the most important war theorist of the years between the two wars, but he started his writing career as a tennis correspondent (his collected writings in this genre were published as *The Lawn Tennis Masters Unveiled*).

bandits. Wilson was intelligent, witty, tall and quizzical. He was fascinated by politics, and many in the army distrusted him as a result: Haig, for instance, thought he was more of a politician than a soldier, and regarded him as foxy and unreliable. Others admired him. His lectures at Staff College were spell-binding.

In 1910 Wilson became Director of Military Intelligence, and in the following years he worked closely with the French staff. He liked the French (unusually amongst his brother-officers) and they warmed to him. He spent leaves cycling over that part of France in which Britain fought a few years later, and with the French he evolved detailed plans about where and how Britain would fight alongside the French in the war that everyone expected. These staff talks were unofficial (Asquith, the Prime Minister, and Grey, the Foreign Secretary, kept them secret from most of the cabinet), and in theory bound no one; but because only Wilson was planning in any detail for the war, his plans were accepted by default.

On 5 August 1914, the day after war had been declared, a remarkable Council of War took place at 10 Downing Street. Here was Britain twenty-four hours into a war that had been expected for many years, and no one in a company that included every possible political and military leader, even the eighty-two-year-old hero of the South African war, Field Marshal Lord Roberts, knew what to do. No one except Henry Wilson.

Sir John French was to command the British Expeditionary Force, the BEF, and Sir Douglas Haig would initially command one of the two corps which constituted it. They had been close colleagues. Haig had helped French out of financial difficulties with a loan, and the older man was fond of his young colleague. He gave him a gold flask in 1902, inscribed, 'A very small memento, my dear Douglas, of our long and tried friendship proved "in sunshine and in shadow". JF'. The friendship, although so comprehensively tried, did not survive 1915, when Haig superseded French after machinations in which Haig, at least in part for honourable motives, was closely involved.

Each of them gave possibly unreliable accounts of what the other had done at the Council of War. French was said to have wanted the BEF to go to Antwerp – an entirely novel idea – to liaise with the Belgian Army or possibly that of Holland (which in the event was neutral). Haig was alleged to have wanted to delay landing on the continent for some months until the pattern of warfare became clear.

By contrast Wilson had clear and fully developed plans, and it was these plans, in which the French were involved, that were implemented, placing the BEF in France, to the east of Amiens, to the left of the French. Britain thus from the start departed from the British way of warfare, fighting a land war on the continent in close liaison with her principal ally.

During the pre-war staff talks the French had referred to the British Army as *l'armée Wilson*, Wilson's Army, and the war that Britain fought was Wilson's war. If, without Henry Wilson, Britain had fought in her traditional way, a naval war with a small military element, there would have been far fewer names on Bridge of Weir's War Memorials, but Germany would have won the war.

4

The War at Sea

Thanks then to Henry Wilson, the war that Britain fought was overwhelmingly a land war, but there was of course a war at sea as well, and men of the village fought in it.

In 1914 the Royal Navy was the most powerful navy in the world, ready to fight the sort of war that never took place. The Naval Defence Act of 1889 introduced a two-power standard, requiring a number of battleships at least equal to the combined strength of the next two largest navies.

Naval commanders and politicians on both sides assumed that large warships would have the major part to play in the eventual outcome. 'Dreadnoughts', called after the first of these fearsome monsters, HMS *Dreadnought* commissioned in 1906, were the British expression of this view. At the outbreak of war, British naval ships included eighteen dreadnoughts (with six more under construction). Dreadnoughts had their counterparts in Germany. The Royal Navy also possessed ten battle cruisers, twenty town-class light cruisers, fifteen scout cruisers and more than two hundred destroyers. There were additionally 29 older battleships and 150 aged cruisers, all of which were built before 1907. This huge fleet was the product of an intense naval rivalry with Germany which indeed was a contributory cause of the war.*

---

* In October 1902 the First Lord of the Admiralty (the civilian head of the service) wrote to the Cabinet: 'I am convinced that the German navy is being

The outcome of the war was decided on land and only after four years, but a definitive result at sea would have brought things to a much speedier conclusion. Churchill said that Admiral Jellicoe, the commander of Britain's Grand Fleet from 1914 to 1916, and thereafter First Sea Lord, could have lost the war in an afternoon. Precisely because of this risk, each side was so fearful of naval defeat that there was only one substantial engagement, the inconclusive Battle of Jutland on 31 May 1916. At Jutland Britain had the bigger fleet, with 151 ships to the German ninety-nine, and better trained personnel, but the German ships were generally faster, more modern and better armed. While the British ships were designed for service throughout the world, the German warships were built for action only in the North Sea and their armour could be heavier. German gunnery was better. Had there been a full-scale engagement there is no certainty that the Royal Navy would have won. At Jutland the Royal Navy lost three battle cruisers, three cruisers, eight destroyers and 6,100 men. The German High Seas Fleet lost one battleship, one battle cruiser, four cruisers, five destroyers and 2,550 men.

What was important about the battle was not who won it, but the fact that after it the German High Seas Fleet retreated to its home waters for the duration of the war. As an American observer, said, 'The prisoner is back in his cell, with the jailer still outside'.

The Royal Navy did rather more than act as a jailer, and indeed without it the war could not have been won. By its existence, Britain was protected from invasion. It kept the Channel free for supply. It carried British troops to France. It captured Germany's maritime colonies and kept open the sea

---

carefully built up from the point of view of a war with us. This is the opinion of Sir Frank Lascelles [the Ambassador in Berlin] and he has authorised me to say it. The more the position of the German Fleet is examined, the clearer it becomes that it is designed for a possible conflict with the British Fleet.'

lanes of the British Empire. Above all it enforced the blockade of German ports which finally brought Germany to her knees.

But there is paradox in the fact that the fierce naval competition that was in itself one of the most compelling causes of the war, led not to an outcome at sea, but rather an absence of war at sea. In this sense and in a facetious spirit one could say that the war need never have taken place.

What had more impact on the war was not the fearsome dreadnoughts but craft that had attracted much less interest or pre-war planning – submarines. In the years leading up to the First World War an American naval designer, J.P. Holland, revolutionised the building of submarines, with a double hull construction, air pumped between the hulls to control buoyancy and trim. By 1914, the British and German navies had modern, diesel-powered submarines with a cruising capacity of about 5,000 miles. Winston Churchill coined the name U-boat for these underwater boats (in German, *Unterseeboot*). They were armed with torpedoes which had a maximum range of about five miles, although accurate for only about a tenth of that distance.

German U-boats did huge damage to Britain's trade and her capacity to feed herself. Merchant ships were always an easy target. Nearly half the British merchant marine fleet was sunk: U-boats accounted for a total of 2,189 ships and more than 5 million tons of shipping. Royal Navy losses to submarines included two dreadnoughts, three battleships, three battle cruisers, fifty-four submarines and sixty-four destroyers.

Containing the U-boat threat was vital to British survival. By the end of 1916, Britain's blockade defence included anti-submarine nets, deep mines, air patrols, Q-ships (warships unsportingly disguised as tramp steamers), regular Royal Navy patrols and mine barrages in British coastal waters including the English Channel. But the damage to Britain's supplies very seriously threatened her ability to feed herself in 1917, and it was not until the second half of that year, and after naval resistance to the convoy system had been overcome, that supplies and troops could be transported with confidence. U-boats for the Germans and the blockade for the British were the significant naval elements in the war. Britain was nearly defeated by the former, and the Germans were in part defeated by the latter.

5

Bridge of Weir's Sea War

James Smellie
Engine Room Artificer 4th Class, Royal Navy

Peter Houston
Third Engineer, Mercantile Marine

The First World War started at 23.00 GMT (midnight by German time) on 4 August 1914. Almost immediately the first British shot was fired by the destroyer HMS *Lance*. *Lance* was on patrol in the North Sea when it came upon a German mine-laying ship in the act of deploying mines. *Lance* fired a shell from its four-inch gun. The German captain realised too late that escape was impossible and scuttled his ship. (There is a suggestion that a Bridge of Weir man, James Smellie, whom we shall meet shortly, served on HMS *Lance* but this is not supported by his service record.)

For a short period U-boats respected pre-war conventions and attacked only enemy warships. Then in October 1914, *U17* stopped a British merchant vessel, ss *Giltra*, bound from Grangemouth to Stavanger in Norway. The crew of *Giltra* were allowed to take to the lifeboats before the Germans sank their ship by opening the sea cocks. On 26 October, *U24* torpedoed an unarmed merchant ship with 2,500 Belgian refugees on board. The ship did not sink, but forty people were killed.

In 1914 a total of fifteen ships were sunk by U-boats, including the Royal Navy cruisers *Cressy, Hogue, Aboukir* and *Hawke*, which were all torpedoed by *U9* under the command of Otto Weddigen. The German crew became national heroes and Captain Weddigen was much decorated for his exploits. He died on 18 March 1915 in the Pentland Firth, when his then submarine *U29* fired a torpedo at HMS *Neptune* only to be caught and rammed on the surface by HMS *Dreadnought*. The U-boat was cut in two, leaving no survivors.

Whether or not Engine Room Artificer 4th Class, **James Smellie,** was on *Lance* when her salvo saluted the outbreak of war, alas he was aboard *Cressy* when Captain Weddigen torpedoed her, and he died with his ship.

James Smellie was born and grew up in Falkirk with two older sisters, Minnie and Lillias. Their father, a shipping clerk in a foundry, died at the age of just forty-one. His widow, Annie, married a Falkirk baker, William Forsyth, but he too died young, only four years into their marriage. Annie, with three children to care for, moved to Bridge of Weir around 1911 to become the village postmistress. Minnie was her assistant, and Lillias a telephone operator.

James had been an engineer before he joined the navy in 1912, signing up for twelve years' service. His record says that he was a fitter and turner, and he became an artificer, Fourth Class, an engineer working with weapons and ships' engines. Fourth Class was the lowest level of artificer, the equivalent of a junior non-commissioned officer in the army.

He served on a total of four ships, three of them battleships, *Lord Nelson, Dominion* and *Russell.* All were big and elderly and predated *Dreadnought*. On 30 July 1914, five days before the declaration of war, he joined his fourth and last ship, HMS *Cressy*. *Cressy* was an armoured cruiser built by Fairfield Shipbuilding and Engineering of Govan and launched on the Clyde on 4 December 1899.

In the first month of the war, *Cressy* with her sister cruisers, *Bacchante, Euryalus, Hogue* and *Aboukir,* was taken out of reserve, crewed to a large extent by Royal Naval Reserve personnel, and assigned to the 7th Cruiser Squadron based at Harwich and patrolling the North Sea in support of destroyers and submarines. These cruisers were unimpressive elderly ships. Before the war it had been decided that they would be kept in the reserve fleet and run down until they were completely worn out. Little or no money was spent on repairs and maintenance.

Cressy and her sister ships each had a complement of about 750 officers and men. Many of the Reserve crews were middle-aged, family men. Each cruiser carried nine cadets from the Royal Navy College, most of them under the age of fifteen. The ships had a nominal top speed of fifteen knots but the old engines could not maintain that speed and in bad weather nine knots was about as fast as they could go: their nickname was 'the live-bait squadron'.

The original battle strategy was to let the smaller and faster destroyers lead the patrol with the cruisers in support. The destroyers were armed with torpedoes and better equipped to detect submarines. Unfortunately, destroyers were less effective in high seas and in severe weather they rolled badly. On 17 September the North Sea was rough and the destroyers were sent back to Harwich. Three days later, HMS *Euryalus* returned for more coal and the patrol was reduced to three cruisers: *Cressy, Aboukir* and *Hogue*.

At 06.20 on 22 September, German U-boat *U9* torpedoed HMS *Aboukir*. The ship sank in thirty-five minutes. Thinking that *Aboukir* had struck a mine, *Hogue* and *Cressy* went to her aid, throwing into the water anything which might help survivors to stay afloat. At 06.55 *Hogue* was struck by two torpedoes and it sank as *U9* dived.

A torpedo track was sighted by HMS *Cressy* at 07.20 but it was too late to take evasive action. A hit on the starboard side lifted the stern of the ship out of the water as a second torpedo passed under. At 07.30 a third torpedo hit *Cressy* on the port beam rupturing tanks in the boiler room and scalding the men. It is likely that Artificer Smellie was in the engine room when at 07.55 *Cressy* rolled onto its starboard side, paused and sank, bottom up.

Cressy's boats had already been launched to rescue survivors from *Aboukir* and *Hogue* and were loaded with men. Other survivors were in the water clinging to planks and life jackets and it was 08.30 before the steamship *Flora* arrived and rescued 286 men. *Titan* picked up 147 more before eight British destroyers arrived to continue the rescue. The survivors were almost all naked and so exhausted that they had to be hauled on board the rescue ships by tackle. A total of 837 men from the three cruisers were rescued but 1,397 died, including James Smellie.

The Admiralty issued new orders for large warships in submarine waters to zigzag at thirteen knots but even that left the old armoured cruisers in jeopardy and when the cruiser HMS *Hawke* was sunk by *U9* on 15 October they were all removed from patrol duties.

On 3 October the local paper, the *Paisley and Renfrewshire Gazette,* announced:

MISSING BRIDGE OF WEIR MAN

When the news came to the village that HMS *Cressy* had been sunk by a submarine, there were grave fears that Mr James Smellie, engine-room artificer, would be amongst the missing. After considerable suspense a wire was received last Saturday to the effect that he was not in the lists of the saved. Deceased was the only son of Mrs Forsyth, postmistress of the village. He was on board HMS *Lance* during the engagement off Heligoland, and stood a good chance of further promotion. He was twenty-two years of age and joined the Navy two years ago. The Rev A. M. Shand very touchingly referred to the sad death last Sunday from the pulpit and much sympathy is felt for the deceased's relatives by all in the village.

James Smellie died in the second month of the war, the first Bridge of Weir man to be killed. Everyone knew Annie Forsyth, their postmistress.

Third Engineer **Peter Whitehill Houston** had also acquired skills in civil life. He grew up in Bridge of Weir as the sixth child of a local joiner and at fifteen he was an apprentice tanner. In his twenties he decided to become a marine engineer. He was thirty and unmarried when he died on 15 June 1915, a merchant seaman on ss *Strathnairn*.

Many British merchant ships were owned by small private companies. Peter Houston was employed by one such company, Burrell and Son, run by two brothers, George and William (later Sir William) Burrell. Their grandfather, George Burrell, had come from Northumberland in the 1830s to be a shipping and forwarding agent on the Forth and Clyde Canal. He expanded his interests into coastal shipping and brought his son into the family firm.

His grandsons, George and William, were not purely agents. They were also ship-owners. They played the market by selling their ships when the trade was good and buying replacements when it was bad. At their height, Burrell and Son owned seventy-seven ships, fifty-six of which had names beginning with the prefix *Strath* and ten more beginning *Fitz*.

In 1916 the Burrell brothers sold all their fleet, including vessels still on the stocks. Sir William shrewdly invested his share of the proceeds and devoted the rest of his long life to his passion for collecting art, antiques and ancient artefacts. When he died he bequeathed his collection to the City of Glasgow.

Peter Houston was third engineer on the ss *Strathnairn,* a nine-year-old steamer of over 4,000 tons built on the Clyde.

Early in 1915 German naval policy moved up a gear: Britain was to be starved of supplies, every ship a target for U-boats. Thus, on 30 January 1915 three British steamers were torpedoed and sunk without warning and two days later a clearly marked hospital ship was fired at though not hit. U-boats were no longer required to identify their targets and they concentrated on unarmed merchantmen, including those from neutral countries.

By such standards *Strathnairn* was fair game. She was loaded with coal from Penarth in South Wales and bound for Archangel in the northern part of Russia when she was torpedoed in the Bristol Channel. She was one of 124 ships sunk by German U-boats during a terrible month.

U22 under the command of Bruno Hoppe fired the torpedo that sank her. When *U22* surrendered on 1 December 1918, it had sunk forty-three ships, damaged a further three and captured one. *Kapitänleutnant* Hoppe died off the west coast of Ireland on 17 February 1917, commanding *U86*.

On 26 June 1915 the *Paisley and Renfrewshire Gazette* published its account of Peter's death:

ANOTHER FATALITY

Another sad death has taken place in connection with the war, through the drowning of Peter Houston, Morton-terrace [in Bridge of Weir] and third engineer in the ss *Strathnairn*, which was torpedoed by the enemy off the Scilly Isles on 15th inst. It appears that the vessel was bound from Cardiff to Archangel with a cargo of coal and was torpedoed without any warning, only twelve being saved out of a crew of thirty-two. Peter Houston, it is thought, managed to get into one of the life boats, which was swamped by the sinking vessel. He was a promising young man, of a genial disposition and quite a favourite in the village. Much sympathy is felt for his relatives.

6

The Puppet-masters' Plans

We move from the sea war to the land war, but before looking at the fate of individuals we shall cast a more general view in this and the following chapter over the course of the first months of that war. The events of 1914 established the framework for the rest of the war, and explain what followed. Additionally, we shall introduce some of those senior British officers who would direct events on the Western Front. These were the puppet-masters, and their prejudices and peculiarities determined the fate of puppets in their millions.

The British Expeditionary Force, the army that went to France in August 1914 thanks to Henry Wilson's planning and despite the indecision at the Council of War on 5 August, was a professional force, more highly trained than any other that Britain had sent to war, but a tiny one of just four divisions of infantry and one (soon two) divisions of cavalry.

Wilson himself had known how irrelevant this little force was. When he was Commandant of the Staff College he made his point with typical provocation: 'There is no problem in European politics to which the answer is six British infantry divisions and a cavalry division'. At the end of the war Haig would command not six but sixty divisions.

The enduring perception of the war on the Western Front is of opposing armies dug in to fortified trenches separated by the killing field of no man's land, with artillery bombardments preceding occasional 'big pushes' to gain a few yards of territory at a huge cost of human capital. This was indeed the pattern from the end of 1914 until the spring of 1918, but in its first months the war was one of movement.

In August 1914 the little country of Belgium, created as recently as 1830, assumed great significance in Britain. When, after her hesitation, Britain finally decided to go to war, she did so ostensibly because Germany violated Belgian neutrality, in breach of the Treaty of London of 1839, in terms of which that neutrality was guaranteed by Britain and, strange to recall, the precursor of Germany.

The German sovereign, the Kaiser, dismissed the treaty as 'a scrap of paper' and the British cabinet agreed with him. They were advised that the treaty did not bind them to go to war, and not one Cabinet member, not even Churchill, thought it worth going to war over Belgium. The real reason for going to war was more practical, and based on cold self-interest. The Foreign Secretary, Sir Edward Grey, set it out in his important speech to the Commons on 3 August, using words of Gladstone: Britain could not stand by and watch the unchecked aggrandisement of any one European country. Just as in the time of Napoleon, the balance of power on the continent had to be maintained. Britain went to war as a result of policy not principle, though defending brave little Belgium was good for public relations.

If the kind of war that the men of the village fought, the kind of war that the words 'the Great War' conjure up for us, was the personal achievement of Henry Wilson and his secret deliberations with the French, the fact that Britain fought at all in the war was largely the personal achievement of Edward Grey, this short-sighted ornithologist and country-man who only went abroad once in his life but was his country's Foreign Secretary for eleven years, longer than anyone else has held the office. It was his interventionist arguments in Cabinet, culminating in a threat to resign if he did not get his way, that brought the bulk of his colleagues to support the war, and his speech in the House on 3 August that rallied his party's waverers on the back benches.

So Britain would have gone to war against Germany, Belgium or no Belgium. But the Kaiser did not know that; so why did he take the risk of attacking France through the Low Countries, rather than frontally? For three reasons. First, correctly, he did not think Britain would bother about a long-forgotten treaty. Secondly, even if Britain did enter the war, he was confident that France would be defeated long before Britain could do anything with her tiny army. And thirdly, he did what he had been told to do by Alfred von Schlieffen, who had retired from military service on New Year's Day, 1906, after being kicked by a fellow-officer's horse.

On the eve of emerging as the nucleus of the new German Empire, Prussia had defeated France in the war of 1870–71. France, the France of Louis XIV and of Napoleon, was ignominiously treated. She was compelled to pay heavy reparations for a war she had not started. She was stripped of two of her provinces, Alsace and Lorraine. The statues of these provinces in the Place de la Concorde were draped in black crêpe. The lost provinces were the focus of bitter resentment: 'Think of them always,' the French were enjoined, 'speak of them never.'

Almost immediately after the humiliation of France in the Hall of Mirrors at Versailles, where the King of Prussia chose to have himself proclaimed Emperor of Germany, France was gripped by *revanchisme*, desire for retribution: it was only a question of time before a retaliatory war broke out. In preparation for that war, Germany prepared a series of plans based on refinements of what had originally been prepared by Schlieffen. Precisely what he argued for is now a matter of some scholarly debate, but the consensus remains that it was what was long accepted: recognising the strength of French defensive positions on the line of a direct attack from Germany, he advocated a huge, scythe-like swing by the right wing of the German Army, sweeping through Belgium, and then coming back eastwards to envelop the French armies. Some of his comments – 'Let the man on the right touch the channel with his hand'; and his alleged dying injunction, 'Keep the right wing strong' – are probably apocryphal, but they convey the thinking behind his plan.

The French preparation for an inevitable war was, characteristically, more philosophical than that of the practical Germans. France was ashamed of the defeat of 1871, and wanted to atone for it by aspiring to the highest levels of courage and dash. Her plans, like the Germans', went through a series of refinements, finally distilled by Joffre, who would command the French Army in 1914, into his Plan XVII of 1913. Plan XVII was more an attitude of mind than a military strategy. It predicated a very strong force sitting close to the German frontier. What the force would do was far from certain. What was essential was how it would do it. It would do it with *élan*, with dash, above all with an exhibition of offensive spirit. There would be no repetition of 1870.

In the event Germany only partially implemented Schlieffen. Perhaps even he was only sketching an idea. The classical notion of the Plan involved huge German resources, greater than the armies available in 1914, and they had to move huge distances, very fast, encumbered by impedimenta of war that were double in volume those of 1870. Logistical feats that might have been possible with light, Napoleonic armies or the mechanised troops of 1945 were unrealistic in 1914. Moreover, the enemy, with the advantage of interior lines of communication, could move much faster to regroup and reinforce.

Joffre did what Schlieffen had not wanted to do, and struck at the enemy where she was most heavily defended. French zeal to recover the lost provinces almost cost them the rest of France: instead of confronting the oncoming German armies to the north, France punched further south. Joffre came close to destroying his armies in these early encounters, the Battles of the Frontiers, and was lucky not to have been dismissed. But his failings were mitigated, indeed deserve to be forgotten, for the sake of his steadfastness. He never wavered in defeat; he waited and prepared; he judged the right moment and then attacked on the Marne and the Aisne. By then Germany, having failed to achieve the scythe-sweep, had drawn her line in towards Paris, and both armies locked together, destined to face each other for four years.

Schlieffen knew that Germany's war on the Eastern Front against Russia would be a long campaign. To avoid fighting on two fronts the war in the west had therefore to be a knock-out offensive. His judgement was sound. Whether Germany would have won if his Plan had been fully implemented we shall never know – perhaps it never *could* have been implemented. What we do know is that the attempt to implement it caused the violation of Belgian neutrality, thus providing Britain with a just plausible *casus belli*.

This then was how the Grand Masters, including the dead Schlieffen, had set out long in advance the chessboard for the game that Europe was to play for over four years. There have been few wars where the players and their playthings were so separated. Let us turn from the players to the pawns.

7

How the Little BEF Fitted In

1. The Great Retreat

Bridge of Weir had one man in the British Expeditionary Force, the BEF, Thomas Spink. He, like most of the BEF, had little idea of how the British Army fitted in to what was happening in France in the last five months of 1914. This chapter will explain what happened in the months of advance, retreat and confusion, which finally synthesised into the grim rictus of confrontation that prevailed until the spring of 1918.

At the start of the war, 1,077 German battalions were faced by 1,108 French and 120 Belgian battalions. The British Expeditionary Force, the BEF, amounted to around 3 per cent of the Allied Forces in France. Britain's role in the land war was not intended to be critical. Indeed when Grey spoke to the French ambassador on 3 August, forgetting what Henry Wilson had been up to, he told him that it was unlikely that there would be a land contribution at all. Even Wilson's handful of divisions had a mostly political significance and Britain's main contribution was expected to be to the war at sea. In the event her contribution to the land war did matter, though not, in numerical terms, in 1914 or 1915.

Field Marshal Sir John French, Commander-in-Chief of the BEF, gave every indication that he did not appreciate the wider political import of his token force. He did very little to endear himself to his French allies. He hardly spoke a word of their language. For a long time the French and British armies did not even share a common time-system. His army consisted initially of two corps. Sir Douglas Haig, competent, well-connected and ambitious, commanded I Corps. Sir Horace Smith-Dorrien, 'Doreen' to the troops but 'Smithereens' to those who knew his unpredictable temper, commanded II Corps. French detested Smith-Dorrien and had not wanted him. Smith-Dorrien was imposed on him by Lord Kitchener, the strong, silent military hero of the Sudan, the newly appointed civilian Minister of War (also not much liked by French) after the initial commander of II Corps, Sir James Grierson, died suddenly very soon after landing in France.

Haig had hitched his wagon to French's star before the South African War, but he unhitched it pretty speedily after the outbreak of war in 1914. As early as 11 August, before the Commander-in-Chief had even been tested in battle, Haig wrote, 'I know that French is quite unfit for this great Command at a time of crisis in our Nation's History.'

The Chief of Staff in France was Sir Archibald Murray. A Chief of Staff in the field, as opposed to the Chief of the Imperial General Staff in London who was the professional head of the army, was a sort of second-in-command, with very loosely defined powers and functions. Murray said of French, 'I knew better than anyone how his health, temper and temperament rendered him unfit for the crisis we had to face'. The Sub-Chief of Staff (a title created as a sop after he was passed over for Chief of Staff) was Henry Wilson. As a Francophile and friend of General Joffre he was almost unique amongst the higher command. Haig had a low opinion of both Murray and Wilson. Thus the BEF set off to war with a dysfunctional leadership team that had scant confidence in each other's abilities, in particular those of their chief.

By the time the first British shot was fired near the Mons–

Condé canal, the French were already fighting the Battle of the Frontiers in Alsace and Verdun. In the course of these awful engagements she lost almost 250,000 men, 70,000 of them dead. Daily losses exceeded those of Britain on the first day of the Somme in 1916. In open, Napoleonic warfare – not the war of the trenches – in the whole of the five months from August to December 1914, France suffered well over a million casualties. Germany suffered 800,000. It is astounding that France, with a smaller population and a lower birthrate than Germany, was able to accept punishment on this scale and to go on to sustain the conflict throughout the years that followed.

Britain's first engagement was at Mons. At the time Mons was hailed a great victory. It was neither that nor really a set-piece battle at all. It resulted from an encounter by von Kluck, who commanded Germany's formidable First Army. The encounter was followed, so far as Britain was concerned, by a series of uncoordinated actions, controlled neither by French at GHQ nor by the corps commanders. It delayed the German advance by no more than a day, for British losses of 1,600 men, many of them taken prisoner. German losses were slightly higher, as would be expected of the attacker. Elsewhere that day the French were engaged in far greater battles with far larger casualty counts at Charleroi and in the Ardennes.

Mons was a comparative side-show, but its consequences were serious. Sir John lost such confidence as he may have had in his allies and in particular General Lanrezac on his right who was withdrawing his Fifth Army, forcing the BEF to retreat or risk exposing a flank. Retreat was pretty well inevitable in the face of von Kluck's well-supplied juggernaut, but the British commander blamed the French. He felt betrayed by a nation which he did not regard as a reliable ally with whom he could continue fighting a war.

In reality the French were commanded by a man of solid judgement in 'Papa' Joffre, a strong, imperturbable man of the south, whose nerve never failed in these disastrous opening manoeuvres which saw the German right wing push through Belgium and into France, threatening to take Paris and end the war as speedily as Prussia had won in 1870–71. But the French Army had been recreated since the Franco–Prussian War. It was strong in morale and *materiél*, and Joffre never wavered. His plan was to allow the German Front to extend itself and then counter-attack on the Marne.

By contrast French appeared irresolute and nervous, hesitant to commit his army, always looking to his rear and a fall-back to rest and recuperate. He rarely actively supported the French and then only under pressure from London or in the face of emotional appeals from Joffre. Already his method of command was seen to be flawed. He did not remain at GHQ. He liked to get out and put heart into his troops (which he was good at). The consequence was that the corps commanders found it difficult to obtain instructions. As often as not, the closest they could get to the Commander-in-Chief was Henry Wilson, whose insouciant reaction was usually cheery *laissez-faire*: 'Good luck. You're the man on the spot.' When French *was* in the loop he was unpredictable, and could give even Haig a severe dressing-down for supplying his French neighbouring commander with assistance which strengthened his own flank.

GHQ's staff work was appalling. Intelligence appraisals of the situation of the enemy – even of the position of the various British units – were not shared with the two corps. Orders were issued very late, so that they came down to Brigade level after they should have been implemented. When Lieutenant-General Sir Thomas D'Oyly Snow ('Snowball' or 'Polar Bear' – he was a huge man) arrived at the Front from England with his Fourth Division on 25 August he was horrified by the extent to which he was expected to operate without orders or intelligence.

In these circumstances the retreat from Mons, which is still referred to as 'the Great Retreat', was rapid and verged on panic. It consisted of a parallel but not coordinated movement by the two corps, I Corps under Haig and II Corps under Smith-

Dorrien, the two corps separated by the Forest of Mormal. Haig's retreat started at Landrecies, where his Headquarters were pitched too far forward and the Coldstream Guards came under attack from a small German raiding party. The surprise was exacerbated by confusions of identity and stories of Germans putting on French uniforms.

In the event the clash was a small one, with a few hundred casualties on each side, but Haig misread the situation. He told French that he was under serious attack, and he asked Smith-Dorrien for support. Haig was not on top form at Landrecies. He had dramatic food poisoning, now thought to have been caused by eating fruit that had been treated with fungicide. His medical officer, Micky Ryan, prescribed something which Haig's Intelligence Officer, John Charteris, always entertaining and not always truthful, described, from its 'volcanic' results, as having been designed for an elephant. Even so, on the following morning Haig had to be carried downstairs by his batman. It's perhaps not surprising that his judgement wobbled.

Smith-Dorrien did not respond to Haig's request for help; he was too preoccupied with his own problems. He had always questioned the wisdom of withdrawing while his front was already engaged, and now exercised his right, as the man on the spot, to stand and fight, rather than obey French's order to withdraw. On 26 August II Corps made its stand at Le Cateau. The news of this precipitated something like physical and mental collapse on the part of Murray, the Chief of Staff, who had received a serious stomach wound in the South African war, and should arguably not have been sent out with the BEF. A colleague, 'Fido' Childs, said, 'Do not call a doctor – I have a pint of champagne'. This was poured into Murray. Thereafter he was distrusted and ignored at GHQ; but GHQ itself was collectively in a state of panic, collapse and defeatism.

They fought stubbornly but II Corps had some 5,000 casualties, 700 of them fatalities, before they disengaged in an orderly fashion. Meantime Haig continued to retreat, pausing to send a telegram to GHQ, 'No news of II Corps except sound of guns from direction of Le Cateau and Beaumont. Can I Corps be of any assistance?' Smith-Dorrien did not have time to respond.

Smith-Dorrien was probably right to stand and fight, rather than retreating when he was already engaged with the enemy's forward units. Haig has been criticised for not supporting II Corps, but the situation can be read in different ways and the real failure was French's for failing to make a true appraisal, for risking the integrity of the BEF, for only grudgingly approving Smith-Dorrien's stand, and for leaving Haig under orders to withdraw.

2. WULLY ROBERTSON

The Great Retreat was a gruelling ordeal, performed by an increasingly exhausted army in great heat. Much equipment was lost and morale suffered greatly. It saved the BEF, but only failed to result in a rout because of the grit of the men and the skill of their officers, including Haig and particularly the Quarter-Master General, Sir 'Wully' Robertson, one of the few top brass to come out of this episode with credit, who was prepared to discard caution to ensure that the retreating army was properly fed and supplied.

Robertson had entered the army as a private and he retired as a Field-Marshal. In January 1915 he became Murray's successor as Chief of Staff in France (over the head of Henry Wilson, still distrusted by the Liberal Government for his involvement in the Curragh Mutiny, the incident which had taken place in March 1914 when a number of senior army officers threatened to refuse to take action against Protestant Irish Unionists). Later in the year he moved to London to become Chief of the Imperial General Staff. In this capacity he worked closely with Haig, who was by then Commander-in-Chief of the Armies in France.

Robertson, who had begun life as a footman, spoke no fewer than five Indian languages but he never lost his strong regional accent. It was for this reason that he was widely known as 'Wully', rather than 'Willy' (except when the press baron, Northcliffe, turned against him and called him 'Woolly'). When in 1915 he told Horace Smith-Dorrien that he was to be relieved of the command of Second Army, he's famously said to have announced, "Orace, yer for 'ome.' Another version, much too good to be true was 'Well, 'Orace, I'm afraid you 'ave to 'op it'.

He was not incommoded by his background, although he rarely spoke of it. He was an outstandingly effective Chief of the Imperial General Staff, although not hugely imaginative. Churchill said, 'He had no ideas of his own, but a sensible judgement negative in bias'; incessant attacks from Lloyd George left him little opportunity to exercise his imagination.

Wilson and Haig were closely associated with the attritional war on the Western Front to which Lloyd George, as prime minister, was increasingly opposed. As a result, in February 1918 Lloyd George succeeded in manoeuvring Robertson out of office. These events lay ahead, but in studying the events of 1914 and the years that followed, the tensions within the army and particularly between the soldiers and the politicians should be kept in mind. There were always two wars being fought.

3. Sir John French rallies

Following the Great Retreat Joffre's liaison officer at French's GHQ reported that the BEF 'has lost all cohesion', was finished as a fighting force for the time being and could not be relied on. That was pretty much French's view too. He could see no option other than escape to the Seine, or preferably the coast, there to rest and regroup.

French never adapted to, never understood, the war he found himself fighting. He was likeable, cheerful, impecunious, a spender, an indiscreet womaniser, a good regimental commander. Even as Commander-in-Chief he took time to visit wounded men. Their plight and the deaths of so many caused him anguish. But he was never more than a good regimental commander. His career before 1914 was not remarkable, and he came to popular attention largely as the result of a successful but small engagement at Elandslaagte in the South African War. He got the command in 1914 distinctly *faute de mieux*. Though he was widely assumed to be destined for the appointment (despite the Curragh Incident, of which he too was a casualty), the circumstances of his hearing the news speak eloquently of the confusion in preparations for war. Years later Ramsay MacDonald reported that on the night of 2 August 1914 he was at the house of Sir George Riddell, the newspaper proprietor. 'After supper they went upstairs to Riddell's smoking room. The telephone bell rang and Riddell picked up the receiver. All they heard was: "That you Johnnie? How are you? . . . Oh yes, it's going to be war. Oh yes. Fancy you not having heard. You're to command it all right."' Thus the Commander-in-Chief was told of his appointment by the owner of the *News of the World*.

One of French's telegrams to the War Cabinet raised such alarm that Kitchener was sent out on 1 September to stiffen his backbone and order him not to desert his French allies but to support Joffre. Kitchener and French had never got on, and French was particularly angry that Kitchener, here in his civilian capacity, as Secretary of State, and not as French's superior officer, chose to come out wearing his Field-Marshal's uniform (as he did throughout the war). French told Kitchener that, while he 'valued highly his advice and assistance which he would gladly accept as such . . . I would not tolerate any interference with my executive command and authority so long as His Majesty's Government chose to retain me in my present position.'

Joffre chose to make his stand at the River Marne to the east of Paris. The German lines were now very extended, supply routes were not functioning, horses and men were short of food, and von Kluck, believing he faced a broken army on the run, had departed from the Plan to enter Paris and instead wheeled to the east to deliver the final blow to the main French and British forces, enveloping them between the German armies.

In doing so von Kluck made a potentially fatal mistake. He left his right flank exposed to a counter-attack from the south. Despite this opportunity, and his directions from Kitchener, French remained obdurate. Finally, on 5 September, Joffre called in person on his British comrade to persuade him to keep his forces in the field in support of the French stand. The encounter was emotional and pivotal. Joffre gave an utterly convincing picture of how he could turn back the Germans, and passionately appealed to Sir John's honour. French rose to the occasion. He attempted to reply in French, failed, and said to an aide. 'Damn it, I cannot explain. Tell him that all that men can do, our fellows will do.'

The opportunity was taken: a new French division was brought in from reserve to attack von Kluck's flank, some of them famously taken to the front in Parisian taxi cabs, and the tide was turned in the 'Miracle of the Marne'. The BEF spent the next eight days pursuing the retreating German Armies, albeit at a judicious distance behind the French, on the same route they had so recently marched in the opposite direction. This was what Joffre had been waiting for. Although he failed to break the German Army, he had broken its advance. The Schlieffen Plan had failed. There would be no swift victory in the west. Schlieffen had said that without such a victory the war would be lost. The German commander, Moltke, resigned, a broken man after just six weeks' fighting.

Finally the Germans stopped and turned. A pursuit became a confrontation on the River Aisne and the armies fought themselves to a standstill and dug in. From the start of the war the BEF had routinely scraped shallow trenches for shelter; now they started digging deep in preparation for the defensive siege warfare that returned Europe to the time of the Thirty Years' War.

The war of movement was over. Trench warfare began at the Aisne and by the end of the year was extended to the Swiss border in one direction and the English Channel in the other. The pattern was set and although some territory exchanged hands after hard-won battles, the opposing lines would not change much until the spring of 1918. By the end of 1914, the BEF had suffered more than 90,000 casualties, more than the original seven divisions sent to France.

Having outlined the way in which the shape of the war was formed by the puppet-masters, we now look at the fate of Thomas Spink, our man in the BEF, and then at the war's impact on Belgium and the particular consequences for Bridge of Weir.

8

Bridge of Weir's Man in the BEF

Thomas James Spink
Private, 1st Battalion, South Wales Borderers

Before the war, the French General Foch was once asked, 'What is the smallest number of British soldiers that you would require?' He replied, 'One – and we shall make sure that he is killed.' For Bridge of Weir, **Thomas Spink** was that man.

Most of Bridge of Weir's soldiers volunteered or were conscripted after the outbreak of war. Only one of those who died was a professional pre-war soldier. Thomas Spink was in the army in South Africa at the time of the 1911 Census – he may have fought in the South African War. Thomas was an Englishman, born in Walsall, another centre for leather production, from where his father John Spink, a currier, moved to Bridge of Weir round about 1902. Thomas does not appear to have lived in the village although his family became well known there. He probably enlisted into the army from Walsall.

When war was declared, he and the 1st Battalion, South Wales Borderers were billeted at Bordon Camp, Hampshire and attached to 3rd Brigade, 1 Division, in Haig's I Corps.* A week later, they received orders to move early on the following morning and proceed as part of the Expeditionary Force. They entrained for Southampton, embarked on the *Gloucester Castle*

* See Appendix and diagram on p. xii for organisation of army units.

at 14.00 and, escorted by destroyers, arrived at Le Havre at midnight. The battalion's morning train took them to Étreux from where they marched seven miles in very hot weather to Leschelle, Picardy, about twenty miles from the Belgian border. The men had difficulty with the weight of their packs. 'They could not fight after a long march with present weight and certainly could not double', the battalion's war diary recorded. By 18 August 'several boots have given out. Leather seems bad.'

On 20 August, the battalion was on the move northwards and heard distant guns for the first time. They also learned of cavalry engagements. They dug in for the night of 22 August 'expecting a scrap tomorrow'. They did not get their scrap. But they did hear a 'good deal of firing on the left at the Battle of Mons'.

At 03.00 on 24 August, they received orders to retire 'to lead the Germans on', the tactical device that would be embraced with enthusiasm by Sir John French for the next two weeks. On the first night after a twenty-mile march the battalion scared itself into believing there were Uhlans (crack lancer regiments) approaching, and deployed its defences along the hedgerows, 'shots flying in all directions'. But it was a false alarm. The only casualty was a man who accidentally wounded himself with his bayonet.

On 25 August the battalion diarist recorded the landing of an aircraft, the pilot borrowing a pony from the CO and galloping off with news for Haig. Hasty orders were soon received to retire to Étreux, abandoning the freshly-dug trenches. In the retreat, a German aeroplane dropped a bomb on a transport field – and missed. The battalion had thus already seen evidence of two features of modern warfare – airborne reconnaissance and bombing. That night the battalion bivouacked in a field, dead tired after a thirty-mile march.

The retreat continued. 'The men are getting disheartened by this constant retirement and desire above everything to have a dig at the Huns, but they do not understand the strategy of the campaign.' Well might they not. This was much less of a strategic rearguard action than flight, quite orderly but unmistakeable, in the face of superior numbers and firepower. Twenty-ninth August was supposed to be a rest day, but at 23.00, the 'sickening news' was received that the retirement was to continue. The weather was very hot next day and the troops made improvised sunshades by cutting off the bottom part of a trouser leg and sewing it into the rim of their caps. In one week Thomas Spink and the 1st South Wales Borderers had marched 100 miles in sweltering heat from near Mons to Soissons.

By 5 September the battalion had retreated beyond the Marne and was in Rozoy. Orders came for a further retirement, but these were later rescinded. This was the day of the historic meeting between Sir John French and General Joffre that prefaced the Battle of the Marne, and the battalion was ordered to assume the offensive. 'Everybody is pleased.'

The following day the battalion made its first tentative advance, although there was no engagement with the enemy and there were several protracted halts. The French were bearing the brunt of the offensive. The BEF protected the flanks of adjacent French armies, but saw little direct action.

Eight days later, on 14 September, the battalion crossed the Aisne without casualties and took up a position on a ridge to the north of Bourg about twelve miles north-west of Reims. But this was where the Germans decided to make their stand. After a war that had consisted of forced marches from Belgium to Paris then half way back again, the 1st South Wales Borderers saw their first serious action.

The battalion, at the head of 3rd Brigade, between Moulin and Vendresse, was sent to assist 2nd Brigade. It reached its first objective – a high wooded ridge. In heavy fire many men were killed on both sides. Germans were swarming on the ridge opposite, and artillery was opening up. The battalion war diary: 'One can see a nasty sight through one's glasses. Bunches of Germans blown to pieces.' But the exchanges were inconclusive and the battalion had to retire and entrench for the night.

On the following morning there was a brutalising encounter. At dawn a force of enemy was seen advancing. Captain Paterson, Adjutant, whose personal account is appended to the war diary, noted: 'One of the [German] officers called up to us that he wished to speak to an officer, but after the episode at Landrecies with the Guards, we were not having any of that. I have no doubt that they really did wish to surrender but they must do it properly as one man did this morning and march up with his hands above his head and no arms upon him. So we opened fire, and although we lost some men we wiped them out at 200 yards, and there they lie in front of us. Poor devils.'

But the Borderers had troubles of their own. Their trenches were in an exposed location and they were sniped at and enfiladed. 'Every now and then a man knocked out and nothing to shoot at. One does not mind losing men when one is doing something, but to sit still and be knocked over one by one without seeing a soul is trying.'

After enduring this for three days at the cost of thirty-five killed and 131 wounded, the battalion was permitted to withdraw to a less exposed position. On 26 September, Captain Paterson, wrote:

> The most ghastly day of my life and yet one of the proudest because my Regiment did its job and held on against heavy odds. At 4.15am Germans attacked. Main attack apparently against my regiment, which is the left of our line. D and A Companies in the trenches. B and C hustled up to support, and soon the whole place alive with bullets. News comes that they are trying to work round our left. The CO asked the Welsh Regiment to deal with this, which it did. Poor D Company had to face the music more than anyone else . . .
>
> We are now left with three Officers each in three companies, and only two in the fourth, instead of six in each. A sad, sad business, but everyone played up, and

as the French say, '*Qui perd, gagne*'. ['Losses are the price of gains'.] We have lost men and officers, but have again won a name for doing what it is our duty to do and in this case we held a very important line without giving a yard.

The cost of holding that line was ninety dead, including Private Thomas James Spink, the first of the Bridge of Weir fallen to die in the land war.

As the war developed and casualties rose, the Roll of Honour published in the newspapers grew longer. The principal national paper in the west of Scotland was the *Glasgow Herald* and every day it carried its sombre tally of deaths. The list touched many households, directly or indirectly, and in some homes scrutiny of the paper was postponed until breakfast had been eaten.

Notification of deaths on active service was by Army Form B101–82, a pre-printed form of regrets with appropriate blanks for the Officer in Charge of Records to add by hand the deceased's Number, Rank, Name, Regiment, place of death (often omitted), date of death and cause of death (usually 'Killed in Action'). Later a personal letter was usually received from a battalion officer. From memoirs and diaries it's clear that officers took the painful duty of communicating with next of kin very seriously and attended to it as a matter of priority as soon as they were back in their dugouts. The officer who took the responsibility for this heart-breaking task was normally the company commander. In some cases (mostly in relation to junior officers with whom he'd worked) the regimental colonel also wrote, and so also did the chaplain. There are also poignant letters from comrades, struggling to bring support and sympathy to wives and mothers.

Most soldiers wrote their wills before they went into action. Military wills enjoy a special dispensation and need not comply with the usual technical formalities. In the case of other ranks they were usually written in the soldier's paybook, and were very brief indeed. Handwritten, and often with endearing spelling mistakes, many can be examined online, and they are poignant documents. Interestingly, the great majority of wills left the whole estate to the soldier's mother – not father, or even the parents jointly. In this period it was very unusual for women to hold money or other property in their own right – indeed until recently a married woman could not do so. And yet in those Bridge of Weir wills which have been examined, where the estate was left to a parent, rather than a wife, in six out of seven cases it went to the mother – and in the seventh case the mother had predeceased her son. The reason may have been as simple as a desire to conform to the specimen form of will that appeared at page twelve of men's pay books: 'I give the whole of my property to my mother, Mrs Mary Atkins, 899, High Street, Aldershot. (Signature) Thomas Atkins.' None of the Bridge of Weir men left his property to Mrs Atkins.

9

Brave Little Belgium and Bridge of Weir

In 1914 grand strategy impinged on a peaceful neutral with just 7.6m inhabitants. Belgium enjoyed the instant sympathy of the allied nations, and its tiny army earned great respect for its attempt to stop the mighty German force.

It slowed the German advance, even if only by a few days. The Germans had to bring up the world's biggest guns, 42-centimetre howitzers from the Krupps factory, to bombard the Belgian forts at Liège and Namur. The Germans saw resistance, particularly from civilian saboteurs, as illegal guerrilla activity. Their response, even after discounting some exaggerated propaganda, was brutal and disproportionate. In the autumn of 1914 in Belgium there were three civilian casualties to every military one. The university city of Louvain was overrun and the university library burned down. Belgian resistance and the atrocity stories commended Belgium to Britain, and the wave of sympathy towards brave, little Belgium had practical results even in Bridge of Weir.

Belgium's plight was underlined by the stream of refugees and the stories of ill-treatment, particularly of women and children, that they brought with them. The refugees needed help. A Belgian Relief Committee was formed in London based at the Belgian Embassy, and throughout Britain local committees were established.

By October 1914 there were already around 3,000 Belgian

refugees in Glasgow. On 1 October 1914 the first meeting of the Paisley Belgian Relief Committee took place just seven miles from Bridge of Weir. It was intended at first that the main focus would be on the collection of clothing and money to be sent either directly or via the Glasgow Committee to Belgium. An advertisement was placed in the *Paisley Daily Express* appealing for funds. A similar one was shown on the screen at the Paisley Picture Theatre. This was the emotional appeal:

A BRAVE PEOPLE IN RAGS!

There are three or four hundred thousand helpless old men and women and little children almost destitute of necessary warm clothing. Many are without boots, and without blankets to sleep in, and all are in pitiful plight.

Parcels of clothing were to be sent to the local committee at the YMCA Buildings in Paisley. Flag days and concerts were also planned to raise money.

By late October the Paisley Committee had moved on to making plans to house Belgian refugees, initially at Barshaw House in Paisley, which had been made available by the owners, the Arthur family. The committee received donations of money and of local houses where refugees could either lodge or set up home. Within a day Barshaw House had enough offers of furniture to equip it fully for the forty-six refugees who came to live there.

Further refugees arrived. Alongside the committee, a Paisley Roman Catholic priest, Dean Ooghe, himself of Belgian origin, was finding homes for Belgian refugees. He sought financial support through the Belgian Relief Committee. By November 1914 it was reported there were 112 refugees under the care of the committee, eighty-four at Barshaw and twenty-eight elsewhere, with forty-two others expected. At the same time the committee was sending money for food for the people in Belgium as well as clothing. Arrival and death records of Belgians in Paisley during the war show that most arrived in family groups. The breadwinners had a wide range of occupations. There were merchants, clerks, carpenters, fishermen and industrial workers.

Bridge of Weir found its own way to help the refugees. The Ranfurly Hotel, which had opened in 1882 aiming, quaintly, to 'provide facilities for country gentlemen with a bent for sport' was by the turn of the century in the ownership of Fritz Rupprecht, of whom nothing is known although he does sound interestingly German.

In 1914 the building was sold, and in January of the following year the new owners gave consent for its use as a hostel for Belgian refugees. A local Bridge of Weir committee was established, under the secretaryship of a Mr A.J.H. Moffat. The Glasgow Belgian Committee gave its support, offering financial and any other help required. Once the County Public Health Department had checked the drains, the accommodation could be made ready.

The *Paisley and Renfrewshire Gazette* of 16 January 1915 reported that:

> The proposal by the Glasgow Committee, which meets with local acceptance, as being both suited to the place to be occupied and the locality, is to reserve the hostel for Belgians of the better class, many of whom by a turn of fortune's wheel, have been reduced from affluence to penury, from comfort to untold hardships, with, in some cases loss of family, fortune, relatives and friends at one fell swoop.

The Glasgow Committee felt that at least ninety refugees could be accommodated but the local view was that forty to fifty would be a more appropriate number. The motive for keeping the numbers down is not recorded. Simply furnished rooms for the guests were envisaged, plus a dining room and sitting rooms with 'as far as possible comfortable couches and chairs, and a few small tables'. A piano was also suggested as 'the Belgians are a musical race'.

An appeal was made in all the local churches for furnishings. The Roman Catholics offered their help to deliver the furniture, and the Boy Scouts assisted. Weekly financial contributions were also sought. The leather workers in the village had already been subscribing weekly sums of sixpence or more for the Central Fund for Belgian Relief. They decided that for three months ten shillings a week of their collection would go to the local Belgian hostel. The neighbouring villages of Kilmacolm, Houston, Kilbarchan and Brookfield were also asked for financial assistance.

By 20 February the hostel was more or less decorated and furnished. Donations of £308 had been received and subscriptions of £19 11s 6d weekly had been pledged, plus a blank cheque of up to £150. Some time later the newspaper reported contributions of £246 2s 6d plus £24 1s 11d per week from Kilmacolm. A 'sick ward' funded by Mr McNab of Howwood was prepared under the supervision of Mrs Fullerton of The Grange, a leader in local charitable ventures and a member of the Red Cross Committee. The local medical practitioners, Doctors Graham and Sandeman, were appointed visiting physicians at the hostel. Miss Romanes of Edinburgh was engaged as Matron.

The hostel admitted its first sixteen guests on 1 March 1915, and by May sixty to seventy residents are mentioned in the *Gazette*. Within a short time arrangements were made for the education of the Belgian children, with three classes at the hostel under the direction of four teachers. The Kilbarchan and Houston School Board agreed to supply spare desks for the hostel. The Leather Company made their swimming baths available for both men's and women's swimming classes on Wednesdays.

The Belgians were not the only people in the villagers'

thoughts. By now there was an increasing awareness of the needs of servicemen. Local women and church groups knitted and sewed, and money was collected for comforts for the troops. The Belgians helped with local flag days and played their part by raising money to provide Christmas presents for Belgian soldiers at a concert at the hostel in November 1915. The programme included solos, duets, choruses, a comedy and children's marches. One of the residents, a M. Reuland, gave a speech in English thanking the kind people of Bridge of Weir. The women at the hostel made pyjamas and socks and the children knitted mufflers for British soldiers. In August 1916 the *Paisley and Renfrewshire Gazette* reported that the Belgian women and girls at the hostel were helping the Red Cross. Mme Massart, a mother of seven, was 'cutting and supervising the making of shirts, etc. for our wounded'.

Some of the Belgian residents aimed to be self-supporting. The bilingual M. Reuland gave French lessons and also welcomed pupils anxious to learn the piano. He had been invalided from the Belgian Army, in which he had been a captain. Two residents were delayed in attending a day out in Glasgow arranged for the refugees in January 1916 because they were 'busy making munitions'. Leather Company records show that the company employed Florent Verhaest aged eighteen as a cost clerk in February 1916.

Although public sentiment was generally sympathetic towards the Belgian people there were tensions. Then as now, alas, political refugees did not receive an unequivocal welcome. A letter to the *Paisley and Renfrewshire Gazette* on 13 February 1915 began:

> Sir, I understand we are having another 200 Belgian refugees coming to the town. This information at least has been given from the pulpits of several churches. Would anyone be kind enough to inform me why our striplings and mere boys in many cases are being urged

and almost shamed into these awful trenches and so many able-bodied Belgians skulking about the country. It is only humane that we should shelter women and helpless children of any stricken country, but I fail to see why we should be called upon to support a lot of men who should be in Belgium today fighting for their country . . .

Such sentiments were reinforced by official action. In May 1915 the Government required that all male Belgians in Britain aged between eighteen and twenty-five enrolled as part of the militia levy and reported to their nearest police station by 20 June under the Aliens Restrictions (Belgian Refugees) Order. Hosts could be fined if they did not ensure the order was complied with. The refugees were being required to do something that British residents did not have to. Conscription did not arrive until 1916, and there was no obligation to join the Territorial Army, into which the militia had been subsumed.

Scraps of records provide some glimpses of the refugees. The burial record for Kilbarchan cemetery names Armand Legrand, who died in 1916, as a resident of the hostel. He was a fifty-five-year-old commercial traveller from Namur when he arrived with his wife Marie and eighteen-year-old daughter, Martha, a ladies' hairdresser. Martha remained in Scotland, having married a local historian, William Lyle. Florent Verhaest, whom we met working at the leatherworks, had a brother, Robert Victor Charles Verhaest, a private in the Belgian Army, and he married a Bridge of Weir girl, Frances Becker of St George's Terrace in 1918. So the hostel residents integrated into the local community.

M. and Mme. Massart were both mentioned at various times in newspaper articles. M. Massart was a fifty-year-old farmer from the Waremme area. He and his wife Jeanne had four sons and three daughters aged from three to thirteen and were accompanied to Scotland by an aunt, Flora Dejasse or Dejaiffe. M. Massart left Bridge of Weir to take up a job as a farm overseer in France prior to his family joining him there and the *Paisley and Renfrewshire Gazette* reported their impending departure on 28 April 1917 when the family recorded their wish 'to thank their many Scotch friends for the kindness and hospitality shown them during their stay of two years in Ranfurly Hostel'.

Some of the refugees, then, left to take up employment and life elsewhere and others such as Martha Legrand married locally. However, when the closure of the hostel was announced in February 1918 the *Paisley and Renfrewshire Gazette* reported that the 'remaining Belgians' would transfer to a house in Glasgow where the Bridge of Weir committee and its subscribers would continue to support them. The hostel was to become an auxiliary hospital for wounded soldiers. The same newspaper advertised an auction sale of the hostel's contents on its closure.

Apart from the complaint about able-bodied but skulking Belgians, there is no evidence of tension. Bridge of Weir welcomed its refugees warmly and some of them settled in the area after the war. A reassuring episode in pitiless years.

10

Trench Warfare, 1915

Frederic Train Barr
Private, 9th Battalion, Highland Light Infantry

Thomas Brown Lawrie
Private, 2nd Battalion, Scottish Rifles

James Reston
Lance sergeant, 6th Battalion, Argyll & Sutherland Highlanders

By the end of 1914, soldiers on both sides were learning how to live in rows of parallel trenches four feet wide and eight feet deep, jagged fault lines that crossed Europe. The winter months brought with them the misery of grim weather, but fighting was less fierce: of those from Bridge of Weir who died over the four years of the war, the winter months saw around a third of the deaths of the summer months.

Bridge of Weir men who had been in the Territorial Army before the war had already joined the British Expeditionary Force in France by the end of 1914.

Frederic Train Barr was born in Glasgow in 1899, and was educated at Glasgow Academy, the son of James Barr, a Chartered Surveyor, and Mary Train. The family moved to Rockcliff, Bridge of Weir, where Fred met the girl to whom he became engaged but would never marry, Anna Brown, of Cruachan, Bonar Crescent.

Fred was a marine engineer with Fairfields in Govan when war broke out. He volunteered almost immediately, joining the 9th Highland Light Infantry (Glasgow Highlanders), and as a Territorial was in France by November.

Glasgow Academy is one of four schools that the Bridge of Weir men can be shown to have attended. Its response to the war was impressive. The 1913–14 Rugby 1st XV of its Old Boys' Club, The Glasgow Academical Club, joined up together. Eight were killed, and of the remaining seven, only one returned uninjured. One thousand, three hundred and seventy-five old boys of the school served in the war, and 327 died. The percentage killed, 23.8 per cent, is the highest in Scotland and third highest of all the 193 schools in England, Scotland, Wales and Ireland for which statistics are given in *Public Schools and the Great War*. After the war the school was taken over by a War Memorial Trust, and re-founded as a permanent memorial to its dead.

In February 1915 Fred's battalion was holding the front line just east of Béthune in the Pas-de-Calais when German shells scored a hit on their advanced billets. Fred was killed by falling masonry. He was twenty-six. He left his whole estate, £3,202, 10s 9d, (about £310,594 today*) to his fiancée Anna, who was also his executrix. Anna, like so many others, was never to marry. We will hear more of the Barr family: the deaths of Fred's two brothers are recounted later.

Thomas Brown Lawrie was born in 1885 in Kingsbarns, Fife, the son of David Lawrie, a journeyman mason from England, and Jane Brown from Crail. Some time after 1911 Thomas was working as a mason with John Cumming in Kilmacolm and had found lodgings in Gryffe View, Bridge of Weir.

---

* This comparison, and others that follow, is given subject to the caution that it is impossible to make an accurate comparison of historical monetary values.

Like Fred Barr, he volunteered in September 1914, joining the Cameronians (Scottish Rifles), and after training in Nigg he arrived in France in late December 1914. Thomas was in hospital on 9 February 1915 after being struck by a sniper's bullet while building up trench sandbags in the front line near Estaires, about ten miles north of Béthune. The wounds led to complications and his war lasted only two months. He died of pneumonia in Boulogne Hospital on 28th February 1915. He was twenty-nine.

James Ramsay Farquhar Reston was born in Buenos Aires in 1890 to James Reston, a plumber from Glasgow, and Marion Cowan from Ayrshire. At the time, these geographical circumstances were less surprising than they would be today. Argentina was part of the unofficial British economic empire. The skills of British craftsmen and tradesmen were sought after by this fast-developing nation. The west of Scotland was one of the most industrialised regions of Britain, indeed of the world, and opportunities were available for financial betterment to those with an adventurous outlook.

By 1911, the Reston family were in Bridge of Weir, living in a fairly new tenement block in Windsor Place, and young James was an apprentice iron-moulder. He volunteered early and was recruited into the 6th Battalion, Argyll & Sutherland Highlanders which formed part of the 51st (Highland) Division.

Lance Corporal Reston reached the Western Front on 1 May 1915. Soon afterwards, he was promoted to Lance Sergeant. He was clearly an able soldier, but his war was a brief one. He was shot dead by a sniper on 20 June as he left the firing line in the trenches near Festubert in the Pas-de-Calais, barely seven weeks after he had arrived.

His death inspired an attempt at poetry by 'a comrade', published in the *Paisley and Renfrewshire Gazette*, which closed with an exhortation to those in Bridge of Weir, 'the Brig', who had not yet volunteered.

Swift as a lightning flash the bullet sped,
A treacherous shot, it pierced his head;
We mourn his loss, yet soon may meet,
For death is stalking in our beat.

Ah! who'll be next, God only knows,
We ask with strained voice,
Yet when it comes we will not flinch –
God grant it so, my boys.

Boys of the 'Brig', you that are fit,
Why do not you join the colours?
Come out and do your little bit,
And help with many others.

But if you do not, what will you say
When your children ask, 'Well, Father,
What did you do on that great day
To save us from disaster?'

11

Shells

By May 1915, the demand for bullets and shells was outstripping supply. Some estimates reckoned that British guns could only supply four shells per gun per day to the Germans' 180. The *Daily Mail* fomented a Shells Crisis. Its object was in part – indeed mainly – to precipitate political change, and it was successful.

The *Mail*'s proprietor, Lord Northcliffe, was not alone or (in this case) deluded, in thinking that the Liberal prime minister, Asquith, was a detached figure, far from wholly devoted to prosecution of the war. In 1915 Asquith was accordingly forced to form a coalition with the Conservatives. Part of their price for joining the coalition was to require the resignation of Churchill, who was blamed, a little unfairly as will be suggested when we come to deal with it, for the failure of the Dardanelles campaign. Asquith was no warrior by nature, but in his view, in any case, it was as improper for a prime minister to interfere with the direction of military affairs as to tell the Law Officers what to do in their professional areas. That was not to be Churchill's position in the next war, when he appointed himself Minister of Defence in order to make sure that he could intervene for all he was worth.

It would not be the position, either, of the man who succeeded Asquith as prime minister in 1916, David Lloyd George. But without the base Churchill was to create for himself in 1940, Lloyd George could only snipe at his generals, Haig and

Wully Robertson, not control them. All the same, he brought a dynamism to the political direction of the war that was altogether absent under the torpid 'Squiffy'. Even now, in the 1915 Asquith Coalition, not yet prime minister, but moved from the Treasury, Lloyd George brought the whole weight of the state behind his work as Minister of Munitions. Twelve National Filling Factories were built across the UK to produce high-explosive ordnance.

One of the biggest of those was at Georgetown near Houston, only a few miles from Bridge of Weir, its name derived from that of the Minister. The munitions factory covered 540 acres within a five-mile perimeter fence. It was served by its own railway branch line with two stations. Every week Georgetown produced 40,000 items of quick-firing ammunition, 200,000 pounds of breech-loading cartridges, 160,000 eighteen-pounder shells, 15,000 sixty-pounders, 50,000 4.5-inch and 15,000 six-inch high-explosive shells, and 285,000 fuses.

The factory employed 10,000 workers, mostly women, many of whom had been in domestic service. The work was dangerous. There were frequent accidents, along with the sinister risks that followed exposure to toxic materials including TNT, cordite, black powder and ammonium nitrate. Explosions took place. Local legend recalls – though the memories could come from the Second World War and what has been remembered has been embellished – that after explosions the bomb-proof chambers involved were left closed for some time. When they were opened up the bodies of the workers were never found – they had been vaporised. But the marks of their feet were imprinted on what had been molten metal, and the blast had left an outline of their bodies, like photographic negatives, on the walls. Whatever happened has been exaggerated beyond what is scientifically possible, but it is part of the folk-memory of the place.

One of the overseers in the factory was Anna Rennie. A soldier unpacking one of the shell boxes found her name on a slip of paper and wrote to her. Her reply survives:

Primrose Bank
Rahane
Dunbartonshire
4th May 1917

Dear Mr Hardingham,

Thanks very much for your welcome letter, my name was put in the box and I could not understand who was writing to me. The reason my name happened to be in the box was that we were waiting on fuzes and we had nothing to do, so [an]other two overseers and I thought we would put our names in the boxes, it was not very often we had time for nonsense. It's very interesting work and I enjoyed the work very much at Houston. [An] other nineteen girls and I were at Woolwich training for two months and we had an anxious time wondering if we would pass our examinations. We were in London at the time of the first zepp[elin] being brought down and it was truly a grand and awful sight to see. We were also there at the time of an air raid and I can assure you we were never so happy as when we left London behind and made tracks for home . . . I am now staying with an aunt meantime . . . From where I am sitting I have a splendid view of the Loch and also the hills and everything is so peaceful and quiet it makes one feel as if there was no awful war going on. This is truly a terrible war and there never seems to be a week but we hear of some friend suffering from the effects of war.

I lost one brother who came with the Canadians and he was reported wounded and missing on the 15th Sept. and after six months of uncertainty we received word last week that he was killed. I have also another brother who is in France and I trust he will be spared to come home safe and sound.

Do the 4.5" How[itzers] make much noise when they burst? I have also worked with the 18 pounders and it is a much nicer shell to handle. By and by what makes you think I am English? I am a Scotch lassie and proud of it. But I am not mistaken when I say you are English. Well I think I must stop. I hope you will always have good luck and also that you will be spared to come back. I have a cousin in the Labour Coy. His name is James Weir. I am not sure if it is the 1st or 2nd Platoon he is in. There is a dog sitting beside me and he thinks I have written enough as he is biting my pen.

Yours sincerely,

Anna W. Rennie

This charming insight into a more tranquil life than that which he lived in the trenches was a comfort to Private Hardingham, and he kept the letter, perhaps as a good luck charm. It would have been heart-warming to be able to report that Anna and her Private were to meet and marry. They did not, but at least he survived the war and the letter was found amongst his possessions when he died in 1931.

When the war ended the Georgetown factory was demolished and the site cleared within a year, only to be reincarnated on a bigger scale in the Second World War. So much for the war to end wars.

12

Gallipoli, 1915–16

Andrew Gardiner
Private, Canterbury Regiment, ANZAC

Robert Milroy
Private, Wellington Regiment, ANZAC

Alister Duff
Second Lieutenant, 7th Battalion, Cameronians (Scottish Rifles)

John Macdougall
Private, 6th Battalion, Highland Light Infantry

The Gallipoli campaign was an assault on Turkey by forcing the Narrows which link the Mediterranean with the Sea of Marmara, in order to seize Istanbul and thus attack the Central Powers from the east, rather than on the heavily-defended Western Front. It was a bold move, but ultimately a doomed one. It was ill thought-out and its failure is almost invariably blamed on Winston Churchill.

Whether that judgement is fair or not is a debate that still excites heated argument. This is not the place to attempt a judgement, but those who dislike Churchill should remember that the Commission that was appointed to investigate the issue exonerated him of all blame.

From before the war until his fall in 1915, Churchill was the First Lord of the Admiralty, its political chief. He was frustrated by the stalemate and slaughter of the Western Front, which increasingly he saw as wastefully unimaginative: 'chewing barbed wire'. His thoughts turned to the daring naval initiatives that had formed the staple of the eighteenth-century warfare which had been the subject of so much of his study, and he conceived his obsession with the European soft under-belly which would irritate his American allies in the Second World War.

He was not alone in arguing for the Turkish adventure. Kitchener also pressed for it. Kitchener, however, failed to provide adequate troops, seeing the operation as a naval venture. Churchill believed that it had to be a combined operation, but when he was advised by the Commander of the Mediterranean Squadron, Admiral Carden, that a naval assault alone could force the Straits, he gave way and authorised the naval action of 18 March 1915.

In January of that year the plan might have worked, but by the time Allied ships moved towards their objective and into the Dardanelles in March the Turks and their German advisors had enjoyed the luxury of three months' preparation.

At their narrowest point, the Narrows are only 1,500 yards wide and the Turks had planted 374 mines in ten minefields. Mine-sweepers were sent in ahead of the Allied battleships, but the converted North Sea trawlers employed as mine-sweepers were an easy target for the shore-based howitzers. The civilian captains pulled the mine-sweepers out of range of enemy fire. An Allied fleet of sixteen battleships moved forward. By 19 March the Royal Navy ships *Bouvet*, *Irresistible*, *Inflexible*, *Suffren*, *Ocean* and *Gaulois* were all either sunk or disabled by a combination of mines and accurate shellfire from the shore. The remaining battleships pulled out and did not return to the Narrows.

This ineffective naval performance led to high drama: on 15 May the professional head of the Navy, First Sea Lord Admiral

'Jacky' Fisher, brilliant but flawed and unpredictable, resigned and went into hiding, no one knew where. Churchill's removal, on the orders of the Conservative members of the new Coalition Government, followed. He was shunted into a siding as Chancellor of the Duchy of Lancaster. Although he had a place on the new War Committee, called the Dardanelles Committee, Churchill had no longer any personal authority in the next phase of the operations, the military landings at Gallipoli.

A fleet of ten troop transport ships and four escorts had left New Zealand on 15 October 1914. The Gallipoli campaign is often associated solely with Australia and New Zealand: the ANZAC troops were not the only Allied soldiers at Gallipoli, but they were very important and Gallipoli was indeed the first campaign in the First World War involving the Australia and New Zealand Army Corps. Four Bridge of Weir men died at Gallipoli; two from Scottish infantry regiments and two who had emigrated to New Zealand and fought as ANZACs. Another Bridge of Weir man, Corporal Robert Sproul, served at Gallipoli in the Lovat Scouts. He survived Gallipolli, but not the war.

The fleet reached Alexandria on 3 December. The Antipodean troops did combat training in Egypt, spent some time guarding the Suez Canal and departed from Alexandria on 10 April 1915. After making a brief stop at Mudros Harbour on the island of Lemnos, they continued to what is now known as Anzac Cove, Gallipoli.

Allied landings took place in the early morning of 25 April at Anzac Cove and Cape Helles. British destroyers provided some gunfire support until *Triumph* and *Majestic* were sunk by German submarines. The carnage was terrible. There were no landing craft and most of the invading army was in small boats rowed by British sailors. As soon as they reached the shallows the soldiers climbed out and waded through the waves on to dry land. On one beach an old collier, the *River Clyde,* was grounded and used unsuccessfully as a beaching vessel.

The Turkish resistance was well organised and formidable. The Lancashire Fusiliers won six Victoria Crosses, their men killed in the boats or as they hung on barbed wire. The Hampshires and Munsters were shot down in their hundreds. The Turkish commanding officer reported 'The shore became full of enemy corpses like a shoal of fish'. From the beach to a hundred yards offshore the sea was red with blood. The smell of death was heavy in the hot air.

On 14 June Second Lieutenant **Alister Duff** landed at Cape Helles. He was the first of the four Bridge of Weir men to die at Gallipoli. Alister had been in the Territorial Army before the war and he departed for Gallipoli as an officer in the 7th Battalion of the Scottish Rifles (the Cameronians) as part of the 52nd (Lowland) Division. At Gallipolli he faced the enemy for the first time.

Alister had been born in Bridge of Weir, the only son and youngest of three children who grew up in a large stone house with fine views over the Gryffe Valley. The Duff family had a cook and two domestic servants. The father James Duff was a wine and spirit merchant and proprietor of Macleay Duff & Co. of Renfrew Street, Glasgow.

Alister was educated at Glasgow High School, the second of the schools which men of the village are known to have attended. The High School, founded in 1124, is the oldest school in Scotland. As well as providing two prime ministers, it is the alma mater of Field-Marshal Sir Colin Campbell, finally Lord Clyde, the hero of Balaclava and 'the thin red line' of Highlanders. Its military tradition is reflected in the fact that 2,706 old boys served in the war (a remarkable 1,714 of them officers) and 478 pupils died on service or were killed in action. In October 1915 there were 1,300 former pupils in the armed forces at the same time. The Rector of the school asked the pupils to send each one a gift.

Alister Duff died on 28 June, aged twenty-eight, after spending only two weeks on Turkish soil. His mission had been to lead an attack along Fir Tree Spur against the Ottoman machine-guns overlooking Gully Ravine. Despite fierce resistance and horrendous loss of life, his orders were to press home the attack while the reserve lines came forward in reinforcement. Without artillery support the Cameronians attacked heavily defended Turkish trenches. The Turks were always fierce fighters, respected by the British as 'Johnny Turk'. It was an unequal contest, and the inexperienced Scottish troops were mown down.

Most of the officers and NCOs with 7th and 8th Cameronians were killed and losses in all ranks were so high that the two battalions had to be temporarily merged into one. There is a poignant photograph of eleven Glasgow Academical officers who were all at Gallipoli in the 8th Cameronians. Eight of them died on the morning of 28 June 1915. Most of the four companies were killed in just five minutes, between 11.00 and 11.05.

Andrew Gardiner came ashore at Anzac Cove on 25 April. The weeks passed, with the ANZACs confined to their small beach, the Turks on the hills around them. The men on the beach were an easy target. An Australian wrote that 'the dead have made the sandbags all greasy. The flies hum in a bee-like cloud. A dead man's boots have been dripping grease on my overcoat and the coat will stink forever.' The stench from Anzac Cove carried far out to sea.

Andrew had enlisted at Timuru on 14 August 1914 in the Canterbury Infantry Battalion 2nd (South Canterbury) Company. He must have been one of the first volunteers. Andrew was the son of a Bridge of Weir quarryman and the second of nine children. The oldest was born in West Lothian, the next five in Bridge of Weir and others at Carluke in Lanarkshire in the middle of the Lanarkshire coalfield. Andrew went down the pit and worked underground before he emigrated to New Zealand. When war broke out he was a labourer working for James Grant in Fairlie near Canterbury on the South Island.

Andrew was wounded in the leg at Anzac Cove on 11 May and sent to hospital on Lemnos for treatment. He rejoined his battalion, still at Anzac Cove, on 13 June. An attempt to take the high points was made on the night of 6/7 August by two columns of British, New Zealand and Indian soldiers. At dawn on 7 August the Auckland Battalion got within 200 yards of the summit of Chunuk Bair and Andrew and his Canterbury Infantry Battalion were ordered to support the Aucklands in open fighting. Heavy Turkish rifle and machine-gun fire met the New Zealanders. Andrew was one of those who died. He was only twenty-two.

Robert Milroy volunteered on 13 March 1915 at the Rutland Hotel in Wanganui, which still advertises itself as 'the hotel with heart', and joined the Wellington Infantry Brigade. He embarked for Suez on 17 April. Until he made the voyage to New Zealand, Robert had spent all his life in Bridge of Weir as one of eight children born to a journeyman stone mason from Wigtownshire.

The large family of which he was part grew up in Burnbrae Cottage in Bridge of Weir, where their mother died young and their father remarried. When he finished his schooling Robert started work close to home, in the cotton thread mill of William Shanks. He sailed on the *Rotorua* bound from London to Wellington, New Zealand, on 17 March 1911.

Robert fought in the same action as Andrew Gardiner in the attempt to take Chunuk Bair. On the morning of 8 August, the Wellington Battalion rushed to the summit only to find that it had been abandoned by the Turks, who had moved to higher positions from where they could fire down on Chunuk Bair. It was the evening of that day before reinforcements got through and by then only about seventy of the Wellington Battalion's 760 men were still standing. Malone, the commanding officer, and Private Robert Milroy were amongst those who died in the summit trenches. The Allies held on for two days but on

10 August the Turks launched a massive counter-attack and recaptured Chunuk Bair.

It was 11 September before the *Paisley and Renfrewshire Gazette* caught up with events in Turkey and reported that Robert Milroy's brother, living at Powburn Cottage, had received notification that '10/1922 R. Milroy, Wellington Infantry, NZ Expeditionary Force is missing after action in the Gallipoli Peninsula, Turkey on 8th August and is now believed to have been killed'.

John Macdougall served as a private in the 6th (City of Glasgow) Territorial Battalion of the Highland Light Infantry. The 5th, 6th and 7th Battalions were all formed in Glasgow from men who had been in the Territorial Army and these Highland Light Infantry battalions were also part of 52nd (Lowland) Division which left for Gallipoli from Devonport, Plymouth on 26 May. Their route was the familiar one with stops at Egypt and Mudros Harbour.

Private Macdougall and his comrades landed at Cape Helles on 3 July to be pitched into the thick of the action at Gully Ravine where Alister Duff had fought and died. When the British soldiers were not attacking the Turkish lines they dug trenches. A young sailor from the Royal Naval Division at Helles wrote about the trenches: 'The bottom of the trench was choked with dead bodies, friend or foe, and slippery with their life blood. Corpses had been built into the parapet, the dead thus affording some protection for the living. Wherever one looked there was death in some ghastly form, arms and legs, and decapitated bodies sprawling about.'

John Macdougall died in an offensive on higher ground from Helles Beach. He was posted missing presumed dead on 16 August 1915. His body was never found and he is one of 21,000 named on the Helles Memorial.

John was a thirty-three year old lawyer who seems never to have married. He was born in Greenock on the Lower

Clyde, like his ten siblings, and spent much of his youth there surrounded by ship building, ship repairing, sugar refining and all the traffic of a major port. He became a shipping clerk like his brother Matthew before going into law. The family were obviously intelligent and educated: at least four of the girls became teachers. John's father had come to the mainland from the Isle of Jura and qualified as a doctor. He died before the war, and his widow, Martha, moved her family to a ten-roomed villa in Bridge of Weir. With them went their general servant of more than thirty years, Catherine Taylor from Campbeltown.

There was an unpleasant sequel for his battalion to the events of 15/16 August in which he died. About 100 of the men, exhausted and dispirited by all they had been through, had been ordered to seize 120 yards of trench at a location known as the Vineyard. Command was very weak and no written orders had been issued; indeed oral orders were only given to officers and NCOs immediately before the attack.

Those officers not directly involved in the attack were not much in evidence. Commanders who had watches synchronised them, but many had no watches, and the attack was not coordinated. Artillery fire was badly misdirected. Only about half the 100 men moved forward, and most of them drifted away after a few paces. Those officers who reached the line found themselves quite alone.

It was a disaster for the battalion – particularly tragic for those like John Macdougall who did not shirk their duty. But it was a reflection of broken morale rather than of cowardice and mutiny. The sensible thing would have been to disband and reform. Instead of that, a new, thrusting Corps Commander, Lieutenant-General Davies, issued a blistering statement on 18 August:

> The operation failed for one reason only, namely the misconduct of the men whose duty it was to carry out the attack.

I have not the slightest doubt that if these men had possessed any proper military spirit, the Turkish trench would now be in our possession.

The cowardly behaviour of the men of the 1/6th Highland Light Infantry has brought great discredit on the regiment to which they belong and on the land of their birth.

Out of the confusion of the night no evidence could be brought on which to base a court martial; heavy-handedly an Enquiry was ordered, which lasted three days. The proceedings were not such as to lead to any dramatic outcome. It was recommended that one unfortunate private soldier be brought to trial on a charge of cowardice; but the conduct of the officers, whose loose command was at the root of the problem, was not thought to warrant action, except that 52nd (Lowland) Division's Commanding Officer expressed the opinion that 'Colonel Millar's sphere of usefulness as commanding the battalion has come to an end and that it would be better for himself and for the unit if he were allowed to resign the command'. Better than a firing squad at dawn.

After the failure of the attempts to break out of the narrow coastal strip, the Dominion and British troops made no more attempts to capture the high ground and spent the remainder of the Gallipoli campaign under constant, heavy Turkish fire. Conditions were awful. The nature of the terrain and the close fighting did not allow bodies to be buried and the rotting corpses attracted vermin. There was little fresh water, the heat was terrible and flies, fleas and crawling insects bit until the skin was raw. The autumn and winter brought relief from the heat but only in exchange for gales, blizzards and flooding. Men drowned and froze to death in the trenches and thousands suffered from frostbite. Only 30 per cent of the British fatalities at Gallipoli resulted from action; mostly men succumbed to dysentery, disease and severe weather conditions.

The Commanding Officer, Ian Hamilton, though hugely talented in other ways, had been proved to lack key qualities: judgement and ruthlessness. He was dismissed and Sir Charles Monro appointed in his place. Monro was sent out to decide whether to continue with Gallipoli or to end it. He was a very sound and unflappable officer who had done well on the Western Front. Like most senior officers he believed the war could only be won there, so it was not surprising that he advised withdrawal.

What is surprising is how quickly he reached his decision. He arrived on 27 October and gave his advice to Kitchener on 31 October. Thus Churchill's aphorism: 'He came, he saw, he capitulated'. Some Cabinet members were unhappy and Kitchener himself came out to Gallipoli. He reached the same conclusion, though after longer reflection than he had allowed Monro. Monro had said that evacuation might cost 30 per cent casualties. In the event, not a single man was lost. By 9 January 1916 no troops were left.

Gallipoli nearly cost Churchill his political life, and despite his exoneration by the Gallipoli Commission he never again risked rejecting the advice of his civil servants. Thus his disastrous decision as Chancellor of the Exchequer to return to the Gold Standard in 1925 against his own views and on the advice of officials is the direct result of the Gallipoli campaign.

But it was only Churchill's *political* life that was at stake. The Gallipoli land campaign committed almost half a million British and Dominion troops including 75,000 untested Australians and New Zealanders. By the end Turkish casualties numbered about 250,000, French almost 50,000 and British (including ANZACs) more than 200,000. The Australian dead were over 8,000 and New Zealand lost 2,721.

13

The Scots-Canadians

Neil Watson Macdonald
Private, 13th Battalion (Royal Highlanders) Canadian Infantry

Walter Ian Brown
Private, 3rd Battalion, Canadian Infantry

When Britain declared war on Germany, Canada and the other dominions were as a matter of law carried with the mother-country. If Canada had no say in whether or not she would join the war, she did have a say in what level of support to provide, but there was never any real doubt that her support would be wholehearted. On 4 August, the Governor General cabled the UK Government:

> Great exhibition of genuine patriotism here. When inevitable fact transpires that considerable period of training will be necessary before Canadian troops will be fit for European war, this ardour is bound to be damped somewhat. In order to minimise this, I would suggest that any proposal from you should be accompanied by the assurance that Canadian troops will go to the front as soon as they have reached a sufficient standard of training.

Canada's response to a war half a world away was Herculean. On 4 August she had virtually no army: just 3,110 regular troops, armed with a few old machine-guns and artillery pieces. The rest of her resources amounted to territorial forces of about 59,000 men. By the end of the war, Canada had a fighting force of 110,000 in the field, and had suffered 215,000 casualties; her best troops, like the best of those from Australia and New Zealand, were as good as the best British units and played a critical part in the great advance of the last hundred days of the war. They were commanded by a territorial soldier, Sir Arthur Currie, in peacetime a teacher and then a businessman, who rose through the ranks, starting as a humble gunner, and ending as one of the most effective generals in the war. The Australian commander, Sir John Monash, was also a weekend soldier, a civil engineer who like Currie came to master sophisticated techniques better than all but the best of the regular British generals, who tended to look down on what Haig had called 'colonial scallywags'.

Many of the Canadian volunteers in the first years of the war were first or second generation immigrants from Great Britain, with Scotland strongly represented. The patriotic surge swept along three men who had spent much of their lives in Bridge of Weir.

Neil Watson Macdonald was born in 1881 in Leeds, where his father John, originally from Bowmore on Islay, ran the Clarendon Hotel. In the early 1890s the family returned to Scotland and John took over the Wheatsheaf Inn, Burngill, Bridge of Weir. Neil was still of school age and joined the local Boys' Brigade. In 1901, he was a plumber's apprentice in lodgings in Bowmore. By 1912 his parents had retired to Pollokshields in Glasgow. Neil decided to embark on a new life in Canada.

In Canada, Neil was the first of the three Bridge of Weir Canadians to sign his Attestation Papers for the Canadian Expeditionary Force. He enlisted in the 13th Battalion (Royal Highlanders) which sailed for England as part of the First

Contingent of 33,000 Canadians. It took over three hours for the flotilla of over thirty troopships, escorted by four cruisers, to leave the Gulf of St Lawrence on 3 October 1914. Before the end of the month the troops were in training at Bustard Camp on Salisbury Plain. It was the beginning of a period of abnormally heavy rain, which fell on eighty-nine of the next 123 days. The Canadians were initially under canvas and had to endure permanent damp, mud and overnight sub-zero temperatures. It was not until 17 December that Neil's brigade, the 3rd, was finally assigned hutted accommodation.

In early February 1915, the 1st Canadian Division, 17,300 strong, sailed from Avonmouth to St Nazaire, and headed for the Front by troop train (in trucks that were labelled *40 hommes, 8 chevaux,* accommodation for forty men or eight horses). The Canadians played a supporting role in the Battle of Neuve Chapelle. Neil's brigade was in reserve but not used. His first tour on the front line ended on 27 March 1915 and he went into reserve five miles back.

Between 14 and 17 April, the 1st Canadian Division relieved the French 11th Division holding 4,500 yards of the Ypres Salient. The trenches were shallow because of high groundwater, and much of the necessary protective breastwork was flimsy. The Canadians were taken aback by the condition of the trenches: 'in a deplorable state and in a very filthy condition, all the little broken-down side trenches and shell holes apparently being used as latrines and burial places for bodies'.

The Division then saw action in the Second Battle of Ypres. By the morning of 22 April, 3rd Brigade was deployed with the 13th Battalion on the left. That evening would mark the start of the series of German offensives in which gas was used for the first time. At 17.00, the Germans released the valves on 5,730 cylinders of chlorine gas. It formed a green cloud moving at five miles an hour directly into the African Light Infantry, who retreated with despatch, exposing the Canadian left flank.

On 24 April, the eight Canadian battalions holding the apex

of the salient were attacked by three times as many German battalions. Throughout the early hours of that day the left of 3rd Brigade's line was under continual pounding by German artillery. Another gas cloud was released at 04.00. At 08.30, in a lull in the bombardment, the 13th Battalion was ordered back to the Gravenstafel Ridge. Of the exposed company on the right, only a dozen men reached the ridge.

By the time the battle had run its course a month later, some territory had been lost but Ypres had been held. 'The Canadians had many casualties', a War Office *communiqué* reported, 'but their gallantry and determination undoubtedly saved the situation'. That gallantry cost them over 6,000 men, a third of their strength, in only forty-eight hours.

Neil Macdonald was reported missing, presumed dead, in the defence of St Julien, two days after the gas attack when the Canadians had held the line against superior numbers for almost forty hours. Neil was no doubt either a victim of the pounding bombardment on the morning of 24 April, or killed during the fallback to Gravenstafel Ridge.

Walter Ian Brown was born on 21 July 1893 at Pekin, Illinois, USA, the third of a family of six born to Robert Fulton Brown, from Ardrossan in Ayrshire, and Elizabeth Ann McIntyre, from Bridge of Allan, Stirlingshire. Walter was a full cousin of John Gardner Brown, who died in the last year of the war (see Chapter 36). Both their families were to follow an unusually peripatetic life.

The first of Walter's siblings, Grace, was born in Scotland. His parents then sailed to the USA where their first son, Robert, was born. Soon afterwards, they returned to Scotland and in 1891 were living in Falkirk. Between then and the arrival of Walter in 1893, the family had crossed the Atlantic again, returning to Pekin, Illinois, where Edith and Mary were also born.

In November 1898 the Brown family returned yet again to Scotland and by 1901 were living in Houston, close to Bridge of Weir. Robert was now a jobbing gardener. There were five children, including Walter, in the family home. At the time of the 1911 Census, his mother, usually known as Bessie, and three of the family were living in Tigh-na-Fleurs, Bridge of Weir. Walter, then seventeen, was a grocery shop assistant.

On 20 May 1911, Bessie and the family sailed on the ss *Ionian* from Glasgow to Canada, to rejoin Robert, whose wandering had now taken him to Quebec. Once in Canada, Walter continued his career as a grocer.

He volunteered on 10 November 1914, too late for the First Contingent, but sailed for England as part of the 23rd (Reserve) Battalion in early February 1915. He joined 3rd Battalion, 1st Brigade, 1st Canadian Division.

On 15/16 June, the 1st Brigade fought in the Battle of Givenchy. Third Battalion's role was to mount a secondary assault after heavy losses had been incurred. The *Official History* records, 'The assault was made at 16.45 on 16 June, after a two-hour bombardment – all that ammunition stocks would allow. As soon as the barrage lifted the Germans manned the parapet, and 3rd Battalion, unaided by mine or advanced field guns, met such a hail of rifle and machine-gun bullets that its leading waves could not cross no man's land.' Further assaults on Givenchy were abandoned.

On 24 June, the Division was moved to the Ploegsteert sector, three miles north of Armentières, and took responsibility for 4,400 yards of front line from Messines to Ploegsteert. The next three months were comparatively inactive: the Germans were preoccupied on the Eastern Front. The time was spent entrenching, with 2,000 men engaged every night in digging support trenches and strengthening redoubts. The *Official History*: 'From late June to mid-September 1915 a strange tranquillity persisted across the Canadian Front. Apart from the activity of snipers on both sides and one small patrol clash in no man's land, the only hostilities were an occasional exchange of light shelling by the opposing artilleries.'

Generalisations of that sort can be cruel. Despite the 'strange tranquillity', Walter Brown was killed on 9 September, a victim of a sniper's bullet or random shelling.

David Cummings was born and brought up in Bridge of Weir, the son of David Cummings, an Irish tanner and a deacon at Freeland United Free Church. The family first lived in Campbell's Land and then in a three-roomed flat in The Mimosas, that block built by the tannery and named after the tree whose bark was used in processing leather. Young David was a commercial traveller for cotton yarns, probably employed by the thread mill in Bridge of Weir, before he emigrated. He had a dark complexion, hazel eyes, black hair and a scar on one finger.

He volunteered on 27 June 1915 at the Toronto Armories. He was assigned to the 74th Battalion of the Canadian Expeditionary Force and left Canada for England on 29 March 1916. By then, the Canadians had two divisions in the field, with two more soon to be added. There were then 50,000 Canadian troops in the Canadian Corps, part of the British Second Army.

David was transferred to 5th Battalion, Canadian Mounted Rifles. His unit had been redesignated as an infantry battalion at the beginning of that year. Cavalry was now being recognised as unsuited to this highly mechanised war of barbed wire, artillery and machine-guns. The official view was that this was only a temporary situation in anomalous conditions. Regiments were promised that they would be remounted once normal circumstances were re-established. In fairness, the rapid advances in the last Hundred Days of the war, which we shall meet later, could not have taken place without cavalry.

In early September 1916, the Canadian Corps was redeployed from the Ypres Salient to the Somme. The 5th Battalion would soon see action there and the final episode in David's story is told in Chapter 22.

14

Loos, 1915

John Clark
Private, 6th Battalion, King's Own Scottish Borderers

James Hood
Private, 7th Battalion, Royal Scots Fusiliers

John Clark appears in a family photograph with his mother, sister and three younger brothers, all in their Sunday best, with scrubbed, serious faces, chins up, facing the camera. John is in his new army uniform and the other lads are in suits and ties with well brushed hair. It is no doubt the last photograph of the family together and they appear to be a model of respectability. When the photo was taken the father was probably away working in Canada.

Before joining up, John followed his father's trade. His father, also called John, was a stonemason. There was work for masons in the expanding village, where most of the houses and tenements were stone-built, with imposing façades and dressed sills and lintels. Family tradition has it that John Clark senior was involved in building the stone stair in Freeland Church which gave access to the new balcony. When war came the Clark family was living close to the church in a two-roomed flat in Laird's Land on the Main Street. Young John volunteered for active service in December 1914 when he was nineteen and joined the 6th Battalion, King's Own Scottish Borderers.

James Hood had enlisted a few months earlier, joining the 7th Battalion, Royal Scots Fusiliers. James Hood's father was a currier at the leather works and James learned how to put leather grips on golf clubs. The young man was a good golfer. He moved to Fife to work as a professional at St Andrews, the home of golf, where he stayed in the home of William Fairful, a golf-club maker in nearby Kinghorn.

In 1911, at the age of twenty-two, James Hood finished third in the Scottish Professional Championship and the following year he became the professional at the Muskerry Golf Club in County Cork, Ireland. His golf prowess continued and in the army during training at Aldershot James won his brigade's open championship.

The Battle of Loos set records for the British Army in terms of the number of men engaged and the level of casualties suffered. It was a battle which the British – and particularly Haig – did not want to fight, and it was fought on ground which both he and Sir John French thought unsuitable. They were compelled to fight for the sake of the alliance. France's contribution to the war had been far greater than Britain's. To demonstrate Britain's commitment, Sir John agreed to participate in a joint attack, placing his forces on the extreme right of the French First Army. The old professional British Army had been broken at First Ypres in 1914 in a bloodletting which the historian John Terraine described as 'the true beginning of the martyrdom of the British Army'.* Now at Loos its remnants had to stiffen lightly trained and unseasoned Territorials and volunteers.†

---

* Seventy-seven per cent of officers who served with the first seven divisions in the period August–December 1914 were casualties. Detailed research into all ranks of the 2nd Royal Sussex Regiment reveals that 70 per cent of those who landed with the battalion in August 1914 were no longer there in December.

† It was the Territorials, volunteers and conscripts who delivered victory in the end, but it took time before they approached the calibre of the old, superbly professional BEF. Towards the end of 1914 a corporal in the 2nd Royal Irish Rifles wrote of the Special Reservists, who made up the bulk of the initial reinforcements, 'They had not the smartness of Regulars, and I could not take them to my heart. Their habits were unsoldierly and repellent to me.' In fact

On the morning of 25 September 1915 British and French troops attacked the German lines close to the village of Loos-en-Gohelle. In this flat mining area the most significant local landmark was the double pithead shaft known to the men as Tower Bridge.

John Clark and James Hood, like most of the troops at Loos, had volunteered and enlisted in 1914. Clark was in 6th Battalion, King's Own Scottish Borderers, part of 28th Brigade, 9th (Scottish) Division. Hood was in 7th Battalion, the Royal Scots Fusiliers, part of 15th (Scottish) Division, positioned three miles further south. On the morning of 25 September both men prepared to advance at the German trenches.

Haig had sought to postpone the start of the battle, but had been over-ruled. At his headquarters there was debate about whether or not to release gas. Ernest Gold, FRS, a Fellow of Trinity College, Cambridge, had been attached to the headquarters with the rank of captain. Just before midnight on the night before the attack the wind was blowing onto the British lines. At midnight itself there was no wind at all. At 02.00 Haig was wakened to be told that while the weather over the Front was unhelpful, Gold considered that there were indications that a favourable breeze would spring up before dawn.

Haig was imperturbable in situations such as this. He and his staff went out onto a viewing platform. While Gold occupied himself in his calculations, Haig remained silent, only moving from time to time to look at his watch. The tension within this silent tableau must have been unbearable. Then one favourable reading was received, and, as Haig recorded, it was reinforced by more homely evidence than that of Gold and his weather stations:

---

the Special Reservists, as opposed to conscripts, had undergone considerable training, including six months of full-time training, so the Regulars' reaction to the imperfectly trained and often undersized and unfit civilians conscripted from the streets can be imagined.

Alan Fletcher [his ADC] lit a cigarette and the smoke drifted in puffs towards the north-east. Staff Officers of Corps were ordered to stand by in case it were necessary to counter-order the attack. At one time, owing to the calm, I feared the gas might simply hang about *our* trenches. However, at 5.15 I said 'Carry on'. I went to the top of our wooden lookout tower. The wind came gently from south-west. By 5.40 it had increased slightly. The leaves of the poplar trees gently rustled. This seemed satisfactory. But what a risk I must run of gas blowing back on our own dense masses of troops!

At 05.50 gas was released and at 06.30 the British infantry divisions moved out from the front lines and across no man's land. Despite the outcry over Germany's use of gas at Second Ypres, Britain's decision to use the same weapon seems to have been taken without great anguish. Gas did not prove any more war-winning for Britain than it had done for the Germans, and in places it went quite wrong. A war diary reads: 'When the cylinders were opened the gas hung frightfully and many of our men were gassed but I have reason to believe only slightly. The gas had little or no effect on the enemy, behind the northern craters at any rate.' Most of the British troops wore their gas masks in no man's land.

Piper Laidlaw of the 7th King's Own Scottish Borderers found that the men of his battalion were nervous on account of the gas in their trenches. He jumped up on to the parapet and marched up and down, playing *Scotland the Brave* despite the rifle and machine-gun fire that was sweeping the line and despite the gas that threatened to envelop him. He was wounded, but continued to play, encouraging his men forward and over the first two lines of German trenches. It was a heroic cameo and he was deservedly awarded the Victoria Cross.

John Clark, in 28th Brigade, was on the left side of the front allocated to the 9th Division. It ran into serious problems even before the advance began. Gas hung in the trenches, delaying the assault.

A report says that 'between 06.00 and 11.00 our trenches were pretty heavily bombarded with whizbangs' [*sic*]. There was no cover across no man's land and the German artillery was able to target the British lines, which were packed with men. Gas cylinders were destroyed, releasing even more gas into the area. Clark's battalion continued its advance onto the uncut wire. The men were mown down in rows by machine-guns.

The Germans were as impressed as other observers by the bearing of the British troops. They saw 'an entire front covered with the enemy's infantry'. The Germans stood up – some even on their parapets – and fired into the wave of infantrymen approaching over open ground. The machine-guns were able to open up at 1,500 yards' range. 'Never had machine-guns had such straightforward work to do . . . With barrels becoming hot and swimming in oil, they alone fired 12,500 rounds that afternoon. The effect was devastating. The enemy could be seen to be falling literally in hundreds, but they continued their march in good order and without interruption.' Eventually they reached unbroken wire. 'Confronted by this impenetrable obstacle the survivors turned and began to retire.'

The Germans called the battle *Der Leichenfeld von Loos*, the Field of Corpses of Loos. As a fifth British attack failed, and the wounded survivors worked their way back to their own lines, one German regimental diary commented, 'No shot was fired at them from the German trenches for the rest of the day, so great was the feeling of compassion and mercy for the enemy after such a victory.'

Despite that claim, men *were* pinned down and only about seventy soldiers from the rear ranks made it back to cover. By noon, the attack was seen to be a costly failure and all further tasks for 6th King's Own Scottish Borderers were suspended. John Clark was reported missing on 25 September. His body was never recovered. It was almost a full year later that the authorities declared him presumed killed on that day.

Further south, 15th Division enjoyed greater success, despite being subjected to concentrated machine-gun fire and suffering heavy casualties. By 08.00 the village of Loos was entirely in British hands, but the soldiers who advanced were from different units. They were generally without clear objectives and had lost their officers. Eventually 7th Royal Scots Fusiliers reinforced 200 survivors of the 9th Black Watch on Hill 70 to the east of Loos. The Scots dug a trench beyond the crest line. The Germans were so concerned about the advance that they took steps to evacuate Lens.

And yet, by the afternoon, despite having captured Loos and having made the furthest advance of any division since the outbreak of war, the Division was in some difficulty. Scottish infantrymen were helplessly pinned down on the forward slope of Hill 70 as the Germans regrouped and sought to recapture the hill. The position of 7th Royal Scots Fusiliers was untenable. The opportunities for Allied gains that had existed from mid-morning to noon had been lost by nightfall.

James Hood was one of the men wounded in the first two days of the battle. He survived for long enough to be repatriated to the Old Mill Hospital in Aberdeen. Shrapnel and bits of uniform were removed from his chest and arm but by the end of October he was not getting any better. A haemorrhage was identified from a lacerated artery in his right arm and on 30 October the arm was amputated. He never recovered from the operation. He died with one of his sisters at his bedside.

The body of James Hood was transported to Bridge of Weir for the funeral. It was fairly unusual for a British soldier to be buried at home and the *Paisley and Renfrewshire Gazette* reported the event under the headline:

WOUNDED SOLDIER'S DEATH
MILITARY FUNERAL

The body was conveyed to Bridge of Weir last Monday when a most impressive scene took place as the coffin was borne on the shoulders of the soldiers to his parent's home. Several hundreds of people followed the remains on its sad journey, the procession being loyally headed by the Rev. A.M. Shand, who, along with his sisters, has been very kind throughout the bereavement. The funeral was on Wednesday, when a detachment of the Royal Scots Fusiliers came from Greenock to pay tribute to their former comrade's heroic death. A large crowd assembled on the main streets and window blinds were reverently lowered as the hearse with the coffin wrapped in the Union Jack, proceeded through the village to Kilbarchan Cemetery. The mourners included friends from near and far and were led by a pipe band and muffled drums playing the Dead March.

His monument in Kilbarchan Cemetery is inscribed with the words: '13024 Private J. Hood Royal Scots Fusiliers 30th Oct 1915 aged 26. A good soldier of Jesus Christ.'

The Loos Memorial commemorates the names of 20,605 British officers and men who were killed from 25 September 1915 to the end of the war in the battle sector between the River Lys and the village of Grenay, near Lens. The majority of names on the Loos Memorial are those of men who fell during the Battle of Loos in September and October 1915 when seventy-two British battalions took part in the advance, half of them Scottish. Terrible as the total is, it is made up only of those whose bodies were never found.

Personal tragedies extended to countless families. When he died at Loos, Second Lieutenant Jack Kipling was just eighteen, the only son of the writer Rudyard Kipling. Jack Kipling had poor eyesight and failed the medical examinations for the Royal Navy and the army, but the patriotic Rudyard pulled strings to get Jack a commission in the Irish Guards. Jack's body was not found until 1992. His father was devastated by a sense of loss and the awareness of the fact that but for him his son would never have gone to France. His response was to write words of self-reproach: 'If any question why we died/Tell them, because our fathers lied'.

Kipling became a member of the Imperial (now the Commonwealth) War Graves Commission, and it was at his suggestion that the words, 'Their name liveth for evermore' from the Book of Ecclesiasticus were used on so many of the Commission's memorials. It was Kipling, too, who suggested for the graves of unidentified soldiers the words, 'Known Unto God'. Since there is doubt about whether the body identified as Jack's truly is his, it is a poignant thought that these may be the words inscribed on Jack's true memorial.

Some Bridge of Weir men did survive the Battle of Loos and two of them were able to be home in the village for seven days' leave from 8 January 1916. Private Peter Higgins was a comrade of James Hood's in the 7th Battalion of the Royal Scots Fusiliers and Private William McKenzie was in the 9th Battalion of the Black Watch. They were fortunate survivors of fighting on or near Hill 70. They survived the battle, but only for a year (see Chapter 19).

15

A Change of Puppet-masters

Ordinary soldiers were not the only casualties at Loos. The battle marked the end of Johnny French. He lived on until 1925, and even remained Commander-in-Chief until December 1915, but after Loos he was doomed.

In his Despatch after the battle he took a positive view:

> With the exception of the left brigades (just south of the canal), who found themselves confronted with uncut wire, the 1st Corps and the 4th Corps advanced with magnificent dash and captured the whole of the German front line from the Hohenzollern Redoubt southwards, as well as the village of Loos. The German second line was also pierced and before nightfall Hulluch and Haisnes were seriously threatened.

The general view was less positive. Some observers did agree with French and thought that what was significant was how nearly it had been a victory. But more people saw that advantage had not been taken of such successes as there were: that fresh troops had not been available to push on through. With hindsight it can be seen that this concept of a sudden advance was flawed. Repeatedly in the course of the next two years commanders sought to capitalise on local success to achieve the dreamed-of breakthrough that would be followed by decisive cavalry exploitation. The reality was that defensive superiority on the Western Front made old-fashioned breakthrough a chimera until 1918, when Britain had learned how to fight an entirely new sort of war. Even then, success would not have come without economic blockade of Germany and the attritional warfare for which Haig and Robertson were criticised.

But without hindsight, and in the aftermath of a bloody battle, it seemed that an opportunity had been lost. No one was more seized of this view than Haig, who had fought the battle. Although he tended to start off by contemplating coming offensives critically and cautiously, as an engagement got closer he always became sanguine, extravagantly ambitious. He invariably came to believe that, with determination, victory might be round the corner. It was this reaction, when his tail was up, that made him commit his major error, which was not fighting the sort of battles that he did, but carrying them on too long.

Even before Loos opened up, he was critical of French's plans for the retention of reserves. He voiced his objections to the Commander-in-Chief as early as 17 August, and returned with more specific requests on 18 September. He tried to enlist Kitchener's support, but failed to press the point. In view of the importance he subsequently attached to the issue, he should have done so. French was reluctant to transfer a reserve corps to Haig, but he was not gratuitously obstructive: he thought the line was so stretched that he had to keep a strong reserve under his own control. He also feared that Haig, with his reputation as a 'thruster' might ask too much of the inexperienced New Army soldiers.

But if Haig did not press the issue much ahead of the battle, he certainly made much of it immediately afterwards. There was a baffled reaction in London to the outcome of Loos, and Haldane, the former Secretary of State for War, was sent out to see what had gone wrong. Haig told him that the problem had been French's policy with the reserves. He went further. He criticised French generally and the fact that French and his staff had been twenty-five miles apart while the battle was fought. 'Many of us felt that if these conditions continued, it would be difficult for us to win!'

Wully Robertson had been asked to advise the king whether it was time for French to go. He in turn asked Haig what to say. Haig said that he 'had come to the conclusion that it was not fair to the Empire to retain French in command on the main battle front. Moreover none of my officers commanding Corps had a high opinion of Sir J's military ability or military views; in fact, they had no confidence in him'.

A week later, the king visited his army in France. He asked Haig to dine with him. 'After dinner, the King asked me to come to his room and asked me about Sir J. French's leadership.' Haig said that he had thought French should have been dismissed after the Retreat from Mons, because he had 'so mismanaged matters, and shown in the handling of the small Expeditionary Force in the Field a great ignorance of the essential principles of war'. Haig had, however, subsequently come to the conclusion that when the army got larger French would not have scope for bungling, and thus, he recorded, he had loyally sought to stop criticisms of him. But now, after Loos and the matter of the reserves, and 'his obstinacy and deceit . . . I thought strongly, that, for the sake of the Empire, French ought to be removed'. He ended unctuously, 'I, personally, was ready to do my duty in any capacity, and of course would serve under anyone who was chosen for his military skill to be C-in-C.' A sad ending for that long and tried friendship, proved 'in sunshine and in shadow'.

Haig has often been accused of disloyalty and selfish ambition for the way he briefed against French in 1915. He made his views clear to senior officers and politicians and in particular to the king. He and his wife were friends of both the king and the queen, and as well as speaking directly to King George, Haig completed his nightly confidential diary in duplicate and sent one copy home to his wife for onward transmission to the king's secretary. His justification for this was 'the interests of the Empire'.

Haig was serious and ambitious, so unbearably so that when he attended Staff College his fellow officers scrambled to avoid sitting next to him at breakfast. He was also aware that if French went, it would be he who would be the successor. But his ambition was not without honour, and he certainly believed that he would conduct the war better than French could do. As early as '11 August 1914', as has been mentioned, he had recorded in his diary that he did not think French was up to the job, and two days later he returned to the subject, writing that French's military ideas had shocked him when he was French's Chief of Staff in South Africa (though he never said so at the time): 'However, I am determined to behave as I did in the South African War, to be thoroughly loyal and to do my duty as a subordinate should, trying all the time to see Sir John's good qualities and not his weak ones.'

They were certainly very different men. Haig has been called by one of his biographers 'the educated soldier'. An educated soldier, in the jargon of the times, meant an officer who took his career very seriously – there were not many such officers – and is best translated into modern language as 'the professional soldier'. Haig read widely in the studies of the military art – particularly the accounts of the Napoleonic Wars and the American Civil War. His mind was not a critical one, and he accepted all he read, even in the quarterly magazines, as incontrovertible fact, so the lessons he learned were pretty inflexible ones. But at least he learned lessons. There is some doubt about how much French read, but the debate is merely about whether he only read a little or nothing at all. He believed that the art of war lay almost entirely in intuition.

Another of Haig's biographers called him 'the architect of victory', and claimed the essence of his ability was as a manager. He managed the transformation of the army, and this will be discussed later, from a rifle-based force of six divisions in 1914 into the huge all-arms organisation that won the war in 1918, fighting almost exactly as British armies would fight in the Second World War, using tanks, aircraft, sophisticated artillery techniques and a whole range of deceptive devices. By 1918 his armies contained nearly 3 million men and half a million animals. The British military presence in France was the equivalent of a conurbation six times more populous than the city of Birmingham of the time, and only a third less populous than London, then the largest city in Europe. Haig was responsible not only for the fighting, but also for food, supplies, transport, medicine and all else that this huge entity needed. He also had to liaise with his allies and his political masters.

French could not have done this. He was in some ways a more attractive personality. He was more human, with an endearing sense of humour. He would have been more fun to spend an evening with. He was genuinely concerned about his men, and some of his weaknesses stemmed from the fact that he retained a close, paternal link with his troops. Before and during the Retreat part of the problem for his corps officers was that the Chief could never be found: instead of remaining at his headquarters he went off to visit units on the march, cheering his troops. They loved him for it. Haig was respected, not loved.

In the aftermath of Loos it was only a question of time until Haig replaced French. The change was not much delayed: Haig took over in mid-December. On the same day Wully Robertson was appointed Chief of the Imperial General Staff. The combination of the appointments was very important, and would dictate the way the war was fought. Both men very strongly believed that the war could only be won where the Germans were, on the Western Front: there would be no substantial diversion of resources to what they saw as side-shows. They could both stand up to politicians, Haig in France, Robertson in London where he regularly faced down Lloyd George. When the latter said, 'I've heard such and such', Wully just slammed his ruler down on his desk and said, 'Well, I've 'eard different'. Haig and Robertson worked well together, though they were never really friends. When Haig heard of Robertson's appointment, he failed to rise to the level of events: 'He means very well and will succeed I am sure. How much easier, though, it is to work with a gentleman.'

As we describe the rest of the war, it is to be remembered that the military direction, until Robertson was removed in February 1918, was in the hands of these two men who both believed in a concentration of force in France and Flanders in terms of numbers of men and weight of *matériel*, and who both believed that politicians had no business to be interfering in the conduct of war.

It made life no easier for the men at the Front that their commanders were partly engaged on battles among themselves and not wholly on battles against the Germans. Not only were the generals thus distracted; so were the politicians. We shall look at their quarrels and feuds, but first we return to their puppets.

16

Ypres Salient and the Bluff,
Spring 1916

Malcolm Brodie
Private, 1st Battalion, Gordon Highlanders

The name of Ypres echoes through the history of the First World War like the tolling of a melancholy bell. Until 1914 it was a historic and prosperous town with a population of about 18,000. The Cloth Hall, St Jacob's Church and the cathedral were amongst the finest buildings in Flanders. Its misfortune was that it lay in 'the Salient' – the part of the Allied line that protruded into Flanders, at once threatening further advances and yet vulnerable to envelopment.

British troops were in Ypres from almost the start of the war, when Haig and I Corps defended the town magnificently in 1914, displaying huge resolution in stemming a German advance and playing a critical part in Joffre's defensive strategy. That was the first of the three Battles of Ypres. The Second Battle took place in April and May 1915, and the Third Battle, often referred to as the Battle of Passchendaele, after one of its objectives, lasted from 31 July to 6 November 1917.

But the 'Battles' of the First World War are fairly artificial constructs. So ill-defined were they that a Battles Nomenclature Committee had to be formed to apply designations arbitrarily to particular periods of uninterrupted fighting. This is very true of the Salient. Fighting went on in and around Ypres pretty well continuously. After the Second Battle, British Engineers constructed strong-points on the Ypres ramparts and created a third defensive trench behind the front and second lines. Here the Germans launched diversionary attacks between 14 February and 16 April 1916 in what was sometimes described as the Battle of the Bluff.

The Bluff was a mound of material left over from the original excavation of the Ypres–Comines Canal. It formed part of the British line and as one of the few high points in the British Salient provided excellent observation over the German front line only 200 yards away.

On 14 February 1916 the Bluff came under heavy German shellfire and at 17.45 German tunnellers blew three small mines. One under the Bluff buried a platoon of Lancashire Fusiliers. German infantry then launched a determined assault on the British lines, and the Bluff was lost. Over the next few days limited local attempts to recapture it were unsuccessful. On 19 February there was artillery action on both sides and a German *communiqué* reported that '[t]he British again attempted to recapture the position south-east of Ypres but they were repulsed with bloody losses'. The report was accurate: British casualties in the few days after 14 February were indeed heavy.

On 1 March a British artillery bombardment preceded an infantry attack scheduled for the next day. Ralph Hamilton, the officer commanding C Battery, 108th Brigade, Royal Field Artillery, wrote a first-hand account. 'There has been a terrific bombardment – almost worse than Loos, whilst it lasted.' The following day Hamilton was up at 04.00 and heard the bombardment begin 'with an appalling crash, hundreds and probably thousands of guns, from eighteen pounders up to Grandmama, the great fifteen inch howitzer, let fly together'.

Brigadier-General Uniacke, a British general with a Germanic name in command of V Corps artillery, was imaginative and employed unusual tactics. He ordered his sixty-pounder battery to fire salvos at irregular intervals during the night but always with a first salvo followed by another two minutes later. At the start of the attack Uniacke's guns fired only one salvo so that when the 2nd Battalion of the Suffolks reached the enemy line the Germans were still sheltering in dugouts awaiting the second salvo.

The Bluff was back in British control by 05.10 on 2 March, just seventy minutes after Hamilton had got out of bed, despite severe weather, snowfalls and extreme cold. The *Official History* described its recovery as 'an excellent example of a "set piece" operation'.

Hamilton wrote that by 09.00 British infantrymen wounded in the assault began to stream down the road. 'They were principally men who had been hit through the arm or leg by rifle bullets. They told us they had got back our lost trenches and also some old German trenches... The Suffolks and Gordon Highlanders seem to have lost most.'

One of the Gordon Highlanders' casualties who did not tramp back amongst the wounded was **Malcolm Brodie**. He had enlisted in September 1914 despite being over thirty and a married man with a wife and four young children. The family had moved around central Scotland as Malcolm worked on different farms; when war broke out he was a nurseryman living in a three-roomed flat on the Main Street in Bridge of Weir. He enlisted in the 1st Battalion of the Gordon Highlanders and he was on the Western Front from 31 March 1915. After six months he was injured when a trench collapsed, but he recovered in hospital and had two short periods of home leave to share with his wife and children before his death.

The *Paisley and Renfrewshire Gazette* on 4 March 1916:

News has been received by Mrs M. Brodie, Railway-land, that husband Malcolm Brodie (6818) Gordon

Highlanders, has been killed in France. The Chaplain of the regiment conveyed the news to Mrs Brodie in a touching and sympathetic letter. Private Brodie leaves four young children, three of whom have reached school age. Much sympathy is felt for the widow and her children.

That widow lived on for fifty-nine years, surviving all of the other bereaved wives from the village and living through another conflict after the 'war to end wars' in which her husband had given his life. She never re-married, dying in 1975 at the age of ninety-one.

Malcolm Brodie was one of 1,622 British officers and men killed or wounded recapturing the Bluff. He died on 21 February not attacking the enemy trenches but during a period of intensive artillery fire from both sides. The newspaper report went on to say that Private Brodie was killed by a bursting shell but it refrained from reporting that the shell was British. Malcolm Brodie was killed by friendly fire.

17

Political Wars

We have looked at the internal battles amongst the high command, of which the deposition of Johnny French was an example. The civil war amongst the politicians was at least as vicious. It would not do to think that all these vendettas were entirely selfish. For a successful prosecution of the war it was absolutely necessary that French should not remain as Commander-in-Chief, and no less so that Asquith should not remain prime minister. But it would be naive to imagine that jockeying for power was solely motivated by selfless considerations. It is also important to see how much the direction of the war suffered because of the energy diverted into power struggles.

Let's look at the politicians and their role in the remainder of the war. As we saw, Asquith was obliged to go into coalition with the Conservatives in 1915, when Lloyd George became Minister for Munitions. Lloyd George's energy and effectiveness in that position resulted in his appointment as Secretary of State for War in June 1916, when Kitchener went down on HMS *Hampshire* on his way to Russia. Lloyd George was only in that position for six months. There was continuing widespread discontent with Asquith's hands-off conduct of the war, and by the end of the year the scheming and machinations orchestrated by the press barons, particularly Lord Northcliffe, brought Squiffy down. Lloyd George replaced him.

The Welshman, the pacifist who might have resigned in 1914, threw himself even more dynamically into prosecuting the war. He had come to have his own views on how it should be fought. Even before he became prime minister he had advocated 'knocking away the props', eliminating Germany's allies. Now, as prime minister, he increasingly despaired of the stalemate on the Western Front. Originally an admirer of Haig (who, however, preferred the gentlemanly Asquith, who left him alone), he came to see the insistence on attrition as an abdication of imagination, and Haig as a personification of bone-headed obstinacy.

He set out to displace him, but failed for two reasons. First, Haig was powerfully supported by Lloyd George's Conservative allies – and the king. Secondly, he found that Haig was unchallenged in terms of ability. He sent a powerful team out to France to find a replacement for Haig, and they came back to tell him that there was no alternative to be found. Even in his bitter post-war *Memoirs*, Lloyd George had to admit that Haig was the best general in the army.

Lloyd George was therefore stuck with Haig and his emphasis on the Western Front. He did manage to displace Haig's fellow 'Westerner': poor Wully Robertson was manoeuvred out in February 1918. Haig, to his discredit, did not demur. Robertson had supported Haig loyally, but Haig took no steps to protect him: there was no question of resigning – or even threatening to resign. In the aftermath Robertson said that 'he had found that he had more friends than he knew, but fewer on whom he could count'.

Robertson was succeeded as Chief of the Imperial General Staff by Henry Wilson. In some ways Haig was more comfortable with Wilson than he had been with Robertson, and on one occasion after the war he publicly recorded his gratitude to the former, making no reference to Robertson, which greatly offended the man he had worked with much longer. As CIGS, Wilson was mostly supportive of Haig, but never took any risks on his behalf. Wully Robertson had always been a soldier first and a political servant very much second – that is why he was sacked. Wilson, by contrast, was a political animal. He liked politicians and they liked him. He was sympathetic to the prime minister and remained committed to the French and the idea of a French supreme commander. In these respects he was profoundly different from his predecessor.

When he became prime minister, Lloyd George was succeeded as Secretary of State for War by Lord Derby. Haig slightly unkindly and unusually wittily described him as being like a feather cushion, bearing the imprint of the last person who'd sat on him. But Derby was a loyal friend to Haig and Robertson. He resigned over Robertson's dismissal. (He then un-resigned, but was soon sent off sideways to be ambassador in Paris.) He was succeeded by Lord Milner, who was of a more independent mind, and not automatically ready to defend generals.

Beaverbrook, press baron, schemer and observer, has always to be treated with caution. His view of the changes of February 1918 was that 'whatever may have been the influences prompting Haig, it is sufficient to record that he bowed at once to the civilian authority. He deserted his friends without an excuse or apology. He refused Lloyd George's suggestion that Robertson should be given an army in France. Lord Derby he left stranded like a whale on a sandbank.'

Beaverbrook overstated his case, but the result in any event was that Haig was left very exposed for the rest of the war. That was his problem, but the problem for the men who fought in France, the puppets, was that from now on, unable to dispose of the Commander-in-Chief, Lloyd George sought to control him in the only way he could: by denying him reinforcements. The prime minister thought that Haig had wantonly squandered lives in the later stages of the Battle of the Somme in 1916 and at Third Ypres in 1917, conflicts which we shall narrate in due course, and believed that the best thing he could do (not least for his own reputation) was to avoid further losses by starving Haig of recruits. He wanted American lives to win the war, even though that would mean that victory would be delayed. Reduced drafts meant that the BEF was seriously undermanned when Ludendorff launched his offensive in the spring of 1918, and imperilled the advances in the last hundred days of the war which delivered a British victory.

Thus the remainder of the war that we are examining was increasingly fought in France by generals who lacked moral and material support from London, and it is important to be aware of this dimension to the struggle. It touched the lives of the men whose history is being told. We know something of how the strings that made them move were being tugged in different directions. They did not. Now we return to the drama in which they played their parts.

18

Trench Life, 1916

The Western Front stretched for about 450 miles. The trench line, which had stabilised at the end of 1914, was now well established. The front line of trenches was defended with wire and associated with dugouts, deep bunkers, strong points, reinforced concrete gun emplacements and one, two or three separate defensive lines behind the front-line trench.

The German trenches were usually deeper and safer than the British ones, and arranged for a more comfortable existence. Commanders sometimes had underground quarters for their wives. German trenches were defensive, meant to be static. British trenches were intended to be launching points for advance.

Between the 'battles' and for most of the time and on most of the line, there were no significant offensives. That did not mean that nothing was going on. The French tended, perhaps wisely, to adopt a 'live and let live' approach, husbanding lives between their horribly bloody battles, but British commanders were enjoined to keep up the offensive spirit, and men were sent out of the trenches on most nights. Sometimes the object was to repair wire, sometimes to obtain intelligence by bringing back prisoners or identification badges from German corpses. Both sides shelled and sniped the opposing trenches pretty regularly, fired gas canisters, and raided and bombed. Even in the quiet times life in the trenches was not risk-free.

Shells and bombs were not the only inconveniences. Ninety-five per cent of all British soldiers in the line were infested with blood-sucking lice. The lice lived in the seams of clothes, irritated the skin and moved easily between men. Lice were also responsible for infecting soldiers with typhus and trench fever. Add to the lice the rats, which multiplied, feeding on the corpses of the unburied dead. They disturbed sleep, spoilt food and carried disease. Their presence, and the knowledge of what sustained them, did nothing to bolster morale.

Men standing in the cold, wet mud of the trenches suffered from trench foot and frostbite. The farmland of Belgium and northern France carried infection. Over centuries, the soil had been tilled and spread with manure and the manure caused untreated wounds to infect with what at the time was called gas gangrene, sometimes with fatal consequences.

For a long time it was settled military experience that disease kills more men than bullets; but the Western Front was the exception. Machine-guns, shells, rifles and gas did even better than disease. When thousands were wounded in a single day only those most likely to survive were treated. Sulphonamides and antibiotics were undiscovered, and countless numbers died whom a handful of pills would later have saved.

Major-General Henry Shrapnel was a British artillery officer who died in 1842. In his own time and at his own expense he developed a shell which maintained its trajectory and burst open, firing musket balls at enemy soldiers. The purpose of shrapnel was to kill or incapacitate men (more than to damage *matériel*), and an explosion of shrapnel bullets or bits of metal caused serious multiple injuries.

By the 1880s shrapnel shells were being made from forged steel with a timer fuse in the nose. By now the casing was thin but strong and there was space for many more bullets. The shell was effectively a giant shotgun cartridge propelled through the air until it exploded, firing bullets forward from the shell case with increased velocity. This was the type of shell in use in

1914 – although a group of MPs who visited the Front expected to encounter solid cannon-balls of the sort that were fired at Waterloo.

When fired from a normal field gun, shrapnel bullets were typically lethal for about 300 yards after the shell burst. Fired from a heavy field gun another 100 yards could be added.

In the course of the war, shrapnel shells were gradually replaced by high-explosive shells. High-explosive shells had a much greater percussive velocity, and could kill through blast alone. Its victims were frequently found with their bodies quite unmarked. It was thought for a time that shrapnel was better at destroying barbed wire, but that was not the case – certainly not after the Battle of Neuve Chapelle, when the Germans increased the thickness of their wire. High-explosive shells were not filled with the metal contents of a shrapnel shell; the shell casing itself fragmented into a range of different particle sizes. These shells thus did the same job as shrapnel, but a good deal more too. They were effective against men and *matériel* and they were cheaper and easier to produce. They could be fitted with different fuses, which caused them to detonate above ground, on contact or below ground, after penetrating the surface. The last of these could create enormous shell-holes and obstruct progress very effectively.

'Bombs' in the First World War, unless they were dropped out of an aircraft, were what are now called grenades. They too worked on the shrapnel principle. An exploding bomb thrown into a trench could wreak havoc – though it was not without danger to the bombers, who had to get sufficiently close to the enemy to make a throw. The bomb or grenade was held in the hand and delivered as in bowling a cricket ball. It either exploded with a fuse or on impact. In 1916 Britain was producing half a million hand grenades every week.

19

The Loos Front, 1916

Peter Higgins
Private, 7th Battalion, Royal Scots Fusiliers

John Lang MacInnes
Private, 10th Battalion, Cameronians (Scottish Rifles)

William McKenzie
Private, 9th Battalion, Black Watch

Life in the trenches in the Loos sector in May and June 1916 was relatively quiet and as comfortable as life in hell could be. There was no battle going on and the early summer weather was pleasant, particularly after the cold, the wet and the misery of the winter. But it was in this quiet sector that the lives of the next three Bridge of Weir men whose stories we chronicle were lost.

In 1916 the sector was home to many of the battalions that fought there in the previous year, including those in 15th (Scottish) Division. Men of the 9th Battalion of the Black Watch were in the front-line trenches close to Béthune, and 12th Battalion of the Cameronians (Scottish Rifles) was assigned to defend an irregularity in the trench line known as the Kink. The Kink was a salient or protruding element in the British line, close to Béthune. On 11 May the Germans attacked it with a box barrage and effectively took the position by cutting it off from troops to the right and left.

Privates **Peter Higgins** and **William McKenzie,** whom we met briefly at the Battle of Loos itself (see Chapter 14), were two of the first volunteers to join up in 1914. William joined the 9th Battalion, the Black Watch, and Peter the 7th Royal Scots Fusiliers. They did their basic training in Britain and landed at Boulogne within forty-eight hours of each other on 8 and 9 July 1915. In France they were assigned to the same front-line sector near Lens between the rivers Lys in the north and Somme in the south.

Private **John Lang MacInnes** of the 10th Battalion of the Cameronians (Scottish Rifles) enlisted in June 1915. He saw action in the following year. His name is recorded on the Loos Memorial, one of those who died in the sector, but whose body was never found.

The soldiers' fathers were incomers to the expanding village and worked as gardeners. Peter Higgins, senior, from Ireland, John McKenzie from Inverness and Archibald McInnes from the Isle of Iona were typical of many others from the Highlands and Islands or Ireland who moved to central Scotland to work in expanding industries or the houses of the wealthy.

Peter Higgins's Irish father was a Roman Catholic. In 1901 he was working as a jobbing gardener. Peter's mother was a local girl, and the family of two boys and five girls lived in a two-roomed flat in Cameron Place. Young Peter was later employed in the tannery, where he worked alongside his father, who had given up jobbing gardening.

Peter died from shrapnel wounds. He was probably wounded in the Kink sector between 11 and 16 May. On 27 May 1916 a newspaper reported that he had been wounded but was making progress in No. 3 Hospital. He did indeed recover sufficiently to return to Britain, but died in hospital on 5 June, probably in Paisley: he was buried in Kilbarchan Cemetery. A piece of shrapnel had lodged in his back and Peter did not survive a further operation to remove it. The relapse, after news that he was recovering, must have been difficult for his parents to bear.

There was no Catholic church in Bridge of Weir so the Higgins family attended St Fillan's in the neighbouring village of Houston, where the loss not just of Peter, but of his only brother as well, is commemorated in a stained glass window. The inscription reads 'Sacred memory of Peter Higgins RSF who died of wounds received in action on 5th June 1916 and his brother John Higgins who was killed on the Italian Front 28th October 1918'. The story of John's death is told later.

In the course of this narrative, something is said of the four schools which men of the memorial are known to have attended. Although it cannot be proved, some of the Catholic children (like, perhaps, the Higgins brothers) will certainly have attended the school that was associated with St Fillan's Chapel in Houston. Until about 1868 all the children of the village, except those who went to private schools, attended the Parish or Free Church schools* in the village, regardless of denomination. In that year, however, a new priest, Father Small, came to the chapel, and he started a school. It began on a small scale, on an experimental basis, but it flourished and by the end of the nineteenth century it was well established, and the then priest, Father McGhee, was much involved in the administration of education in the county.

As a young man, Archibald, John McInnes's father, worked as a ploughman on the beautiful island of Iona. He moved to Renfrewshire and a life that was perhaps easier, and found work as a gardener. He married Isabella Lang, a girl from a farming family in Kilmacolm. They had six children, three boys and three girls. After moving three miles from Kilmacolm to Bridge of Weir, Archibald and Isabella raised their children at Burnbrae

---

* Education did not become a statutory responsibility in Scotland until 1872.

Cottage.* During the early part of the war all three McInnes brothers volunteered for the army. John never married. In 1915, he was thirty-five and working as a butcher in Dingwall but returned to Bridge of Weir to enlist. Unlike his two brothers he did not come back from the war. On 12 May 1916, he lost his life defending the King.

John McKenzie, William's father, like Archibald, father of the McInnes brothers, was a gardener originally from the Highlands and Islands. But he and his wife Margaret, a girl from Lochalsh, travelled south to find work, met and married in Edinburgh, and then lived in Ayrshire before settling in Bridge of Weir, where John probably tended the gardens of the big new houses. The McKenzies had at least ten children and by 1911 this large family lived in a three-roomed flat at 4, Windsor Place in the Main Street.

When the war came William had found employment as a postman and he had met and married Margaret Cowan. They had a son, John, who was just one year old when the war began. Margaret had been employed as a domestic servant at one of the big houses. It's appealing to imagine that William had met her when he was out delivering letters.

William volunteered in November 1914, joining the 9th Black Watch. In June 1916 he was in the battalion's first large-scale night raid, on a small redoubt near Béthune. An entire company went out after an artillery bombardment. Most lost direction; only one officer and two men reached the enemy trenches. William was one of seventeen casualties, many, like him, the victims of grenade exchanges. He survived long enough to reach hospital but his injuries were serious and he died on 27 June 1916. William McKenzie's younger brother, Roddy, also enlisted, survived shrapnel wounds and served with distinction in the 6th Battalion of the Highland Light Infantry.

On the night when William McKenzie was killed, five

---

* Where Robert Milroy, who died at Gallipoli (see Chapter 12) had lived before emigrating.

Gordon Highlanders died in a failed night raid in the same sector. The commanding officer was damning in his comments and clearly of the opinion that the Gordons had had little prospect of cutting the wire and achieving their mission. He castigated the waste and the loss of some of the most gallant soldiers in the battalion.

20

Women and the War

The outbreak of war brought changes to women's role in society. As the men went off, many of their jobs were filled by women, some of them taking on what was previously regarded as 'men's work', such as driving vehicles. The country depended on this redeployment. For example, at the local Georgetown Filling Factory, mentioned above, which opened in December 1915 and employed 35,386 people in the course of the war, the majority of employees were women. Such a phenomenon would have been unimaginable before 1914.

War had often seemed likely in the years immediately before 1914, when crises in North Africa and the Balkans threatened to flare up into full-scale conflagrations. As early as 1909 it had been decided to form a Voluntary Aid Detachment in which men and women, but mostly women, would be deployed and which would provide medical assistance in time of war. By the summer of 1914 there were over 2,500 VADs in Britain, two-thirds of whom were women and girls. During the next four years 38,000 VADs worked as assistant nurses, ambulance drivers and cooks.

At first the military authorities were unwilling to accept VADs at the Front, but this restriction was lifted in 1915 and volunteers over the age of twenty-three and with more than three months' experience were allowed to go to the Western Front, Mesopotamia and Gallipoli. Some went as nurses; some helped in other ways, such as writing letters for soldiers who were either too ill to write their own letters or were illiterate.

By September 1915 seven Bridge of Weir women had answered Lord Kitchener's call, as the *Paisley and Renfrewshire Gazette* put it, and joined the VADs. Constance Stewart Adam, of Croydon (a house in Prieston Road, Bridge of Weir, not the borough in the south of London), and Janet Spiers Brown, The Linn, served in No. 3 Stobhill Military Hospital. Marjorie Starr, Ranfurly Lodge, was with the French Red Cross at Royaumont. Marion Mann, Redlands, and Ethelyn Bird commenced a three-month course of voluntary service in the Victoria Infirmary, Glasgow, and on 1 July Frieda Buchanan, Endrick, 'despite her youth' was proving a most efficient directress of one of Glasgow's West End Belgium Homes. Bridge of Weir's District Nurse, Ada Weir, who resided at Windsor Place, volunteered for active service as soon as war was declared, enlisting with the Red Cross Society, and in October 1914 she was called away. Being familiar with both French and German, it was presumed that she would be sent to the Front.

The suffrage movement encouraged women to contribute in a practical and active way to the war effort. Elsie Inglis, an Edinburgh woman and one of the first female doctors, was a suffragette. Something of the attitudes she encountered is reflected in the response received from the War Office when she suggested that medical units staffed by females should be allowed to serve on the Western Front: 'My good lady, go home and sit still'.

She did not do anything of the sort. Instead she raised thousands of pounds and worked to set up the Scottish Women's Hospital Unit and with financial help from the National Union of Women's Suffrage Society she formed the Scottish Women's Hospital Committee. By 1915 the Scottish Women's Hospital Unit had established an Auxiliary Hospital with 200 beds in the thirteenth-century Royaumont Abbey, about thirty miles north of Paris.

It is interesting, if surprising, that a village such as Bridge of Weir contained a band of feminist comrades who tended the flame of female dissent. It did, but the coda that qualified their title is significant. The Bridge of Weir Women's Suffrage Society (Non Militant) called a meeting in August 1914, at Norwood, the home of their president, Miss Dalziel, where it was decided to form the society into a branch of the Active Service League, to be added to the 600 branches already formed. A 'strong and enthusiastic' committee was formed with Miss Dalziel as president and Mrs Moffat, of 2 St George's Terrace, as secretary. Membership of the League would be open to any lady or gentleman without their having to join the Women's Suffrage Society.

By December 1915, Ada Weir had spent sixteen months with the Red Cross and returned from nursing at the Front to resume her position as district nurse in the village. On her return she featured regularly in newspaper reports as an active participant in a variety of events to further the war effort. For example, in January 1916 she was helping with the arrangements for an outing for Belgian refugees. She was a woman with drive and ability. She ultimately became a hospital matron, and died unmarried in 1931.

Marjorie Starr, who joined the French Red Cross, was not the only member of her family to respond to the call of duty. Her brother enlisted shortly after the outbreak of war and her sister's husband, Commander Graham Good, was in the Royal Navy. Marjorie was born in Quebec in 1888. Her family came to Scotland and lived in Bridge of Weir, her father working as an electrical engineer for British Aluminium, who were building a new plant at Kinlochleven.

In 1915, at the age of twenty-seven, Marjorie volunteered to nurse in France with the Scottish Women's Hospitals. She was sent to Elsie Inglis' hospital in the Abbaye de Royaumont, a venerable institution, full of bats. She had to put up, too, with the cold, from aching feet, fleas and mud. There was no gentle induction process. Right at the start she had to cope with 'fifteen beds to make myself, perfect stream of bedpans, three horrid dressings to prepare and then bandage up and clear away – and when the other sister came back if she did not get me to scrub lockers and I jolly well had to smile and do it'. When she first attended an operation she saw:

> All tendons and nerves mixed up – agony of dressings so great they gave him chloroform, and it took six of us to hold him while he was going under – got all sprinkled with blood and pus as he was very septic.

Only strength of character allowed her and her like to move unblinkingly from the ostensibly protected lives of middle-class Scotland to realities such as these. Her diaries reveal how astoundingly quickly she and her colleagues had to adapt to a hell of which they could have had no inkling beforehand, how quickly infernal conditions became commonplace:

> I never saw such filth . . . straight from the trenches – all gory. Still they come, the wounded . . . We had two deaths in the night, the poor man who had the wound in his brain, and one of the men from my ward, who had also a head wound and was doing so well that he was soon to be allowed up. Then yesterday morning he had some sort of fit, and they discovered an abscess on the brain: he went quite mad and died at midnight . . . Miller being on night duty had to help carry the body to the Chapel. She says it was rather a gruesome sight. Miss Duncan, the Matron, went first down three flights of steps and through the moonlit cloisters, carrying a lantern, and these three girls carrying a stretcher, draped in a sheet, and a piece of paper pinned on his chest with his name, aged 19 . . .

After two years she returned to Scotland. Her father had made the acquaintance of a young colleague, John Manson, at Kinlochleven. He liked him and even appointed him as his executor. In 1917 Marjorie married John Manson. After the war he worked in Canada in the aluminium industry. Marjorie travelled back and forth and in 1926 finally returned for good to Canada. She died there in 1981. Two of her ninety-three years had been spent in hell.

Other Red Cross workers who had trained in first aid and nursing were serving elsewhere. Jenny Brown, who worked for twelve months at the No. 4 General Hospital, Stobhill, Glasgow, before going to France, is reported to have returned on leave from her 'strenuous duties' in Calais, and to be preparing to return to France later in December 1915. Cissie Gray, of Airlie, a sister of Captain John Gray, whom we shall meet later, had been 'fortunate enough to be given a place on the nursing staff at Gallowhill Convalescence Home, Paisley', while Mrs W.D. Lyell and Mrs Fraser Campbell underwent training as volunteers at Beardmore & Co., the shipbuilders, in order to allow the paid workers a break.

The women who remained at home in the village contributed to the war effort too. Fund-raising took place throughout the war years to help supply items from cigarettes to hospital beds – even an ambulance. One of the many regular fund-raising projects was for Jock's Box. A box was sent to every Bridge of Weir man on active service, filled with various comforts and a letter conveying local good wishes and kind thoughts.

This local link with the national effort had been established as early as October 1914 when 'a small committee of ladies were so desirous of raising funds with the object of providing a bed to be named "the Bridge of Weir bed" in the Scottish section of the British Red Cross Hospital in Paris', that they approached the ministers to make an appeal from the pulpits. The appeal was successful: in addition to the £50 required (about £4,850 today) there was sufficient to provide a second bed in the same hospital which would be named the 'Ranfurly Bed'. The total amount raised was £125.2s.6d (about £12,137 today) and it was agreed that the surplus money would go towards the urgently needed funds for the supply of ambulances in connection with the Scottish Hospital in Paris.

This fundraising for beds, either to purchase or to sponsor one, was not unique. In August 1915, a postcard was received from Private L. McCann (19215) 2nd RDF who explained that he was the occupant of the Bridge of Weir bed at No. 11 Stationary Hospital, Rouen, and that as he was getting better he hoped that he would be back in the firing line soon. An item in the local paper of December 1915 tells the story of a Bridge of Weir lady who was visiting Springburn Red Cross Hospital where she met an Irish Guardsman patient. He told her that he had been in the same Bridge of Weir bed in Rouen and that it was one of the most popular beds in the hospital. (Why?) It was expected, the paper said, that he would soon discover that there was also one in the Hyde Park Ward in the hospital he was in.

A month after the endowment of the bed a cheque for £300 had been sent to Arthur du Cros for the purchase of an ambulance to be named 'The Lass o' Brig o' Weir', with the request that it be given a place in the du Cros fleet of motor ambulances at the Front.

Rarely a week passed when there was not mention in the newspaper of the vast amounts of socks, vests, gloves, pugarees,* mufflers, mitts, blankets, and shirts which were sent to the Front from Bridge of Weir. One woman, the wife of a currier, despite looking after her husband and eight children, found time to make twenty eight shirts for the soldiers. Mrs Bird, Whinfell, requested gifts of helmets, mufflers, gloves, socks, towels and old linen to send to Nurse Tait, who was in charge of the wounded soldiers in one of the Red Cross stations on the La Bassée canal. There was a drinks fund for sending cooling drinks to the troops which was opened by Mrs Barr, of Rockcliff, three of whose sons would be killed before the war ended.

---

* A pugaree is a scarf, hung from the back of a sun helmet.

An article in the local press in January 1916 said that the village had every reason to be proud of its share in providing comforts for the soldiers, both at home and abroad. The contributions that week to the Red Cross HQ do indeed give some idea of the amount of work which was being accomplished. 'Pairs of sox [*sic*] 110, shirts 16, mufflers 20, mittens 30 pairs, pyjamas 3, night shirts 6.' Of these articles schoolgirls contributed quite a large share and it was noticed that almost every sock was packed with soap, candles, boracic powder, sweets and cigarettes, with the usual cheering message on a slip of notepaper. Two scarves knitted by young boys were included in the school collection.

Help was also given in terms of war *materiél*. In April 1918 War Weapons Week took place. There was no sense that the war would end in little more than six months' time. The response to the Week by Bridge of Weir's Savings Association, which had been set up in 1917, was to seek to raise the sum of £2,500 for the purchase of an aeroplane, by investment in War Savings Certificates and National War Bonds. Every local resident was asked to invest something in one of these securities at some point during the Week. A generous donor offered a six-penny stamp to every child who was a member of the association, to be added to their savings book, for every new member he or she recruited. The appeal raised the sum of £8,433, far exceeding the target of £2,500. The total raised was perhaps in the order of £818,000 today. The money was being invested, not given away (and the return on the certificates, for example, was an attractive 29 per cent over five years), but the response was pretty remarkable all the same.

21

The Somme Offensive,
1 July to 18 November 1916

Even amongst those who claim to know little of the history of the First World War, 1 July 1916 is a day graven on the memory. On this, the first day of the Somme Offensive, British casualties were about 20,000 killed and 40,000 wounded, the most grievous losses suffered by Britain (though not, as we have seen, the French) in any war on a single day.

Terrible as the loss of life was on that opening day, the Somme was the outcome of careful and considered planning. It was not the senseless gamble of its modern caricaturisation. On 29 December 1915 Joffre outlined his plan to Haig for a great Allied attack on either side of the River Somme. In this area British and French troops were already fighting side by side and Joffre's plan was to open a front sixty miles wide. Allied artillery bombardment and infantry advances would be sustained until the Germans could take no more. It was the intensity of the artillery bombardment, it was hoped, which would create breakthrough where so many other attempts had failed.

But the purpose of the Somme, and Britain's role in it, changed with the opening of the Battle of Verdun early in 1916. That battle was a huge German offensive on the French line 200 miles to the east. The Battle of Verdun started on 21 February and ended on 18 December 1916, the longest battle of the First World War. At its centre was the fortified town of Verdun situated on the River Meuse and surrounded by a ring of forts. The German commander, Falkenhayn, saw the way to victory as knocking 'England's best sword' out of her hand by 'bleeding France to death' at Verdun. Because of Verdun, Britain's role on the Somme became an attempt to relieve France in her agonies, to force the Germans to divert men and guns from Verdun to the Somme. For tactical and also for very strong symbolic reasons the French had to hold Verdun at all costs. They succeeded, and the price they paid was over half a million casualties. France was indeed bled white. Her morale threatened to crack fatally, but to the enduring credit of the French Army and nation it never did – at least not until 1940.

Between the start of the Battle of Verdun and 1 July (the planned start date for the Somme had been 1 August but France's need caused the date to be advanced by a month) France's losses were so great that she could commit only eight divisions to the Somme offensive. To the north of the river fourteen divisions of British troops attacked on an eighteen-mile front, with support from three infantry and five cavalry divisions. To the south the French Front was only eight miles wide. Joffre's vision of an offensive front extending for sixty miles was unattainable.

The offensive on 1 July began with an early morning mist over the German trenches and a bright and sunny day in prospect. The night before Haig had written in his diary: 'The weather report is favourable for tomorrow. With God's help, I feel hopeful. The men are in splendid spirits. The wire has never been so well cut, nor the Artillery preparation so thorough.'

His plan for the British attack was indeed based on a massive artillery bombardment, followed by an infantry advance. The artillery bombardment, lasting for eight days and heard in England, was massive at the time, but far less than was deployed later in the war. There were many dud shells, and – critically – a preponderance of shrapnel, rather than high-explosive, failed to destroy enemy entanglements or incapacitate troops sheltered deep in their concrete bunkers.

At 07.30 the artillery barrage stopped, whistles blew and 120,000 British infantry climbed out of their trenches. After the eight-day build-up, the Germans were in no doubt that an attack was coming and when the guns stopped they were ready. In the expectation that the wire had been cut by the artillery bombardment and that defence would be minimal, the British infantry advanced, officers as always an obvious target and men encumbered by up to eighty pounds of kit. This included gas mask, groundsheet, field dressings, trench spade, 150 rounds of ammunition and for some soldiers, sandbags or rolled barbed wire. The distance between the British and German lines was 300–600 yards.

Advance in line, 'extended line', was used in part, as has been said, for ease of control of semi-trained troops who were not up to fire-and-movement, storm-trooper tactics. But there was another reason for its use. It was specifically not an *attack* formation. It was a formation for the *occupation* of a battlefield where opposition had been destroyed by bombardment. Misapprehension about the effect of the artillery bombardment was the principal reason that 1 July 1916 is so enshrined in national memory.

And yet, what has been called the 'tyrannical hold' of the first day of the Somme, the mesmerising effect of this one day, diverts attention from the scale of what had been demanded of Britain. This was the first time that Britain engaged the main body of her principal enemy in a continental war. The timing of the battle was not Haig's choice. Two weeks before Verdun, Haig had told Joffre that in principle Britain would relieve the French 10th Army. When Joffre asked him when he would do it, Haig replied 'next winter'. Then Verdun began. Haig responded generously: 'I telephoned to General Joffre that I had arranged to relieve all his 10th Army and that I would come to Chantilly tomorrow to shake him by the hand, and to place myself and troops at his disposition.' Even then, however, Haig did not plan that the battle should be earlier than 15 August. The battle was fought at a place and date and time that had been decided by the French.

Haig was not shaken by the first day. Indeed, by 14 July he was so encouraged by success in the south that he told his wife that cavalry might be pushed through the German lines:

> This morning very early our troops surprised the enemy, and have captured four miles of his *Second Line*. This is indeed a very great success. The best day we have had this war and I feel what a reward it is to have been spared to see our troops so successful! There is no doubt that the results of today will be very far reaching.

Between 2 and 13 July the battle was characterised by day-time narrow-front attacks with little artillery preparation. The 14 July offensive was a night attack. Haig was not the only person who considered its results satisfactory. Charteris, his Intelligence Chief, wrote on 18 July that another stage of the battle was over and that four miles of the crest of the ridge were now held. There were indeed modest British successes during the month of July, including an expensive operation at Pozières which cost one Bridge of Weir man his life.

The next major attack was on 15 September, when tanks were used and in the two weeks that followed there were successes – but they encouraged Haig to become increasingly unrealistic. His diary reflections of 30 September were sanguine and ambitious – so much so that he told Lady Haig (on his instructions routinely copying his diary entries to the palace) not to copy part of that day's entry.

But from the end of September onwards, German reinforcements and bad weather put paid to any chances of major success. It was at this point that Haig's judgement in relation to the Somme failed. Instead of closing down the battle, he told Rawlinson, who commanded Fourth Army on the Somme, that he intended to continue attacking throughout the winter. The battle was not officially closed down until 18 November – far too late for any military good the losses were doing.

What is history to make of the Battle of the Somme, those sombre four months which, with Third Ypres, have formed forever our picture of the First World War? Hardly any ground was gained. British casualties were about 432,000 as against German casualties of 230,000. What we make of it depends on what it was meant to do. Except when he became over-excited, Haig's expectations were limited. His Despatch said that his objectives had been to take pressure off Verdun, to keep the Germans away from the Russian Front and to wear down the German Army. As far as the first objective is concerned, the Germans had already taken troops away from Verdun before the battle really developed. The battle was not effective in pinning down Germans on the Western Front: fifteen German divisions were in fact moved to the Russian Front.

What about wearing down? Here there was some success. One German staff officer described the Somme as 'the muddy grave of the German Field Army and of its faith in the ability of the German leaders'. The official German history recorded that the heavy loss of life affected Germany much more than the Allies. So, in terms of wearing down, the Somme was effective, even if at a colossal price.

At that same price the Somme performed a crucial educational function. *Preliminary Notes of the Tactical Lessons* were issued as early as July, while the battle was still in its early stages. At divisional level and by GHQ itself many series of notes were produced, and more documents followed early in the following year. These publications emphasised the importance of the platoon as a tactical unit, organised into different specialities. These papers, and the thinking they reflect, contain the genesis of the transformation of the British Army which would deliver victory two years later.

Haig's reputation certainly began to suffer as a result of the Somme. Some politicians were already referring to him as 'the butcher'. Robertson, always defensive of Haig, wrote to him in warning tones on 29 July 1916: 'The powers that be are beginning to get a little uneasy in regard to the situation. The casualties are mounting up and they are wondering whether we are likely to get a proper return for them.' Haig's reply was to point out that the July losses were only '120,000 more than they would have been had we not attacked'.

The concern to which Robertson referred was limited to a pretty small number of critics, including restless spirits like Churchill. It's important, indeed, to know that, contrary to the myth that developed later, Haig was not alone in regarding the battle, including its opening day, as having been successful. A year later, as the Battle of Arras opened, *The Times* reported on 10 April 1917 that:

> The Battle of Arras, if that is what it is to be called, may prove no less disastrous to the Germans [than the Battle of the Somme had been]. Such a battle as has begun this morning cannot be fought without heavy casualties. We must be reconciled to that in advance. But the enemy will suffer more than we, and we shall break him here as we broke him on the Somme.

In 1917, then, the Somme was regarded as a successful operation, and was not seen as the disaster which it came to be regarded as fifty years later, in the 1960s. Now, a further fifty years on, the judgement has moved on again. The Somme is no longer seen by military historians as a disaster. It contributed to victory. It can and should be criticised – Haig should be criticised personally, because the decision was personally his – for its cruel prolongation. He is criticised for attritional warfare, which won the war, but his weakness was rather an unrealistic belief in breakthrough. That belief caused him to keep the Somme open too long in 1916; it also kept Third Ypres open far too long in 1917.

The Cross, Bridge of Weir.
RELIABLE SERIES.

The Cross, Main Street, Bridge of Weir, around 1911. Gryffe Place and Gryffe View on the left were home to three of the men killed.

The railway viaduct over the River Gryffe, with one of the village's weirs in the background. The picture is taken from the road bridge – the bridge, combined with a weir, gives the village its name. Part of the Gryffe Tannery is on the right.

Ranfurly, its villas on the hill, and some of its residents appropriately attired for a Sunday stroll before the war.

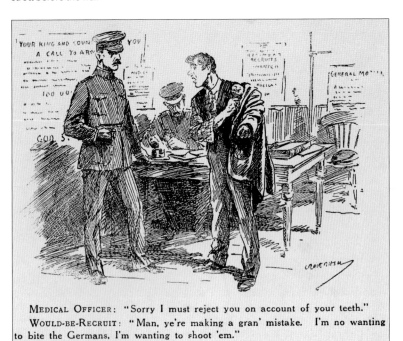

MEDICAL OFFICER: "Sorry I must reject you on account of your teeth."
WOULD-BE-RECRUIT: "Man, ye're making a gran' mistake. I'm no wanting to bite the Germans, I'm wanting to shoot 'em."

A Punch cartoon that echoes the experience of William Blackley, initially rejected for his bad teeth.

Above. John Clark before leaving for the Front, with his mother Annie and siblings.

Left. William Houston, with his wife Elizabeth and children, Andrew and Mary.

The Andrew Family. Back left: John Andrew, killed 23 July 1918 in the attack on Buzancy, next to Henry Andrew, who died in Paisley, 4 January 1917, after contracting fever in Salonika.

British sick and wounded waiting to be taken onto a hospital ship in Salonika Harbour, the first leg of Henry Andrew's long journey home in 1916. *Copyright © Imperial War Museums (Q 31620)*

The remains of New Zealand soldiers killed at Chunuk Bair, Gallipoli, on 7/8 August 1915. The bones of Andrew Gardiner and Robert Milroy may lie amongst them. *Copyright © Imperial War Museums (Q 14340)*

The Scottish Women's Hospital at Royaumont where Marjorie Starr served 1915–17, painted by Norah Neilson-Gray. *Copyright © Imperial War Museums (ART 3090)*

Bobby Barr and Bertie McDougall – two of the Bridge of Weir golfers, both killed in Munich Trench, Beaumont Hamel, on 18 November 1916, and buried four graves apart.

Visit of Churchill to the Georgetown National Shell Filling Factory in July 1918. A roguish WSC is enjoying the female company. *Copyright © Imperial War Museums (Q 84078)*

Left. 2nd Lt Lyle Barr, killed 26 July 1916, the Somme.

Above. 2nd Lt Ian Bannatyne, killed 18 November 1916, the Somme. *Copyright © Imperial War Museums (HU 113286)*

TERRITORIAL OFFICER FALLS

CAPTAIN A. L. CAMERON.

Left. Captain Alexander Cameron, killed 21 March 1918, German Spring Offensive.

Above. Captain John Gray, killed 21 September 1918, in the Hundred Days' Advance.

Dugald Semple, conscientious objector and Simple Lifer, uncompromising and slightly truculent, outside the Wheelhouse.

The Bridge of Weir War Memorial.

Unveiling and dedication of the Memorial on 26 June 1921.

22

Bridge of Weir's Men on the Somme

J Lyle Barr
Second Lieutenant, 157th Brigade, Royal Field Artillery

Peter Calligan
Sergeant, 23rd Heavy Battery, Royal Garrison Artillery

Hudson Hardman
Lieutenant, 7th Battalion, Cameron Highlanders

George Balfour
Second Lieutenant, 6th Battalion, Highland Light Infantry

David Cummings
Private, 5th Battalion, Canadian Mounted Rifles Battalion

James Brooks
Lance corporal, 5th Battalion, Cameronians (Scottish Rifles)

Second Lieutenant **John Lyle Barr** was in C Battery of 157th Brigade of the Royal Field Artillery. He was the first Bridge of Weir man killed on the Somme. He was fatally wounded when acting as a forward artillery observer in support of the 35th Division attacking near the village of Guillemont. His brigade was in continuous and daily action for about six weeks until 11 August.

Lyle Barr was the second of three brothers killed in the war. Fred Barr had died in February 1915 (see Chapter 10). Lyle's brother, Speirs Barr, survived the Somme only to die the following May. The Barr family suffered grievously in their country's cause. The report of Lyle's death in the *Paisley and Renfrewshire Gazette* of 5 August says something about his character.

> Information was received last Friday by Mrs Barr, Rockcliff, Bridge of Weir of the death from wounds of Second-Lieutenant J Lyle Barr, R.F.A., at No. 2 Stationary Hospital, Abbéville, France. He was the third son of the late James Barr, C.E., Glasgow and was employed for eight years with Messrs Agar Cross & Co Ltd, for three years in London, five years in their Buenos Aires office. He was a keen sportsman and belonged to a Rugby team and the Tigre boating club in Buenos Aires. While playing for his team, his knee was badly injured rendering him unfit for Military Service had he not undergone an operation on coming to this country. Lieut. Barr received his commission on March 31st 1915, shortly after his elder brother was killed in Cuinchy, France, while serving with the Glasgow Highlanders and he proceeded to France with his regiment early in February this year. He had only returned from hospital at Havre after a short illness when he received his wounds. Lieut. Barr's sunny disposition made him a favourite amongst his friends by all of whom his death is much regretted.

Sergeant **Peter Calligan** was also an artilleryman. He served with 23rd Heavy Battery, Royal Garrison Artillery, and died of wounds on 16 August 1916. Posthumously he was decorated with the Military Medal which is awarded for acts of gallantry and devotion to duty under fire. Officers were awarded the Military

Cross; the Military Medal was introduced for other ranks on 25 March 1916, although awards were back-dated to 1914. Perhaps surprisingly, out of the seventy-two men from Bridge of Weir who died, Peter Calligan was the only one to be awarded a military decoration for gallantry.

When he died Peter Calligan was thirty and had been married for little more than two months to Euphemia Boyd, a dressmaker from Ayrshire. The wedding was in the Church of Scotland Manse, Stewarton, on 7 June 1916 when Peter was described as a 'gardener, presently Corporal in the Royal Garrison Artillery'. The newly-weds enjoyed only a few days together before Peter was back at the Front in time for the start of the Somme offensive.

He was born and grew up in Dundee, the second in a family of ten children. His father John had a business as a fruit merchant. Peter began work as a greengrocer's message boy but by 1911 he had left his family in Dundee to live at Torr Bothy, Bridge of Weir, and work as a gardener. The link with Dundee was not severed, and it was back to Dundee that he went just a month after the outbreak of war to enlist in the Royal Garrison Artillery. Gunner Calligan achieved rapid promotion and died gallantly, under fire.

Lieutenant **Hudson Hardman** of 7th Battalion, Cameron Highlanders, was killed in action on 17 August fighting to capture Pozières, leading his men in an attack on the switch line in the German trench system in front of Contalmaison. He was twenty-one. Almost exactly three years earlier, on 16 August 1913, at the age of eighteen he had landed on Ellis Island, an immigrant to the USA. He gave his last place of residence as Bridge of Weir, Scotland.

So Hudson did not *have* to fight; but he travelled back to Scotland to volunteer and on 17 April 1915 he was commissioned in the Cameron Highlanders. He was in France on 29 September and was promoted to full lieutenant on 16 December.

Lieutenant Hardman was the grandson of Townley Blackwood Hardman, JP, Dublin, and the son of missionaries to China. The immigration authorities in the USA recorded him as having 'Great British, Irish' ethnicity. His father, Meredith Hardman, was an Irish-born missionary who met his wife, Ella Webber, at the China Inland Mission in Shanghai. They married at Chungking, the commercial capital of Szechwan Province, on 2 March 1892 but returned to Britain for the birth of their two children. Hudson was born in Chorlton, Lancashire and was probably named after Reverend J. Hudson Taylor, who had founded the China Inland Mission in 1865.

The family was remarkably well travelled, having spent time in Canada and Japan in addition to their many years in China. Why Hudson Hardman resided in Bridge of Weir before setting off for the USA is not known; nor is his occupation in peacetime.

Barr, Calligan and Hardman died in the first phases of the Somme. The other Bridge of Weir deaths took place in the later, attritional phase of the battle. Casualties continued at about 4,000 a day as divisions returned to the Front for a second and sometimes a third spell. Increasingly, untested recruits were sent to the Front to fill the gaps in the British lines.

In the later stages of the Somme, many of the recruits were conscripts. Volunteers had dried up and conscription seemed inevitable, but it was no part of the British tradition and was avoided for long as possible. Towards the end of 1915 the first step towards conscription took place. The Derby scheme required men between 18 and 41 to say whether they would 'attest' as being prepared to serve. A man who was prepared to serve was assigned to a group based on his year of birth and then placed in the Reserves without pay and allowances except for one day's pay at infantry rates for the day of attestation. He returned to his home and his employment until such time as his group was called up. He also got an armband to wear to protect him from white feathers. But 38 per cent of single men and 54 per cent of married men refused to attest, and conscription followed in March 1916 for all single men aged between eighteen and forty-one. Just two months later married men were also brought into the conscription net.

At 11.30 on 15 September, British heavy artillery bombarded the north-west corner of a feature known as High Wood, and the Germans began to withdraw. Some were caught in machine-gun fire and others surrendered as the British took the wood yard by yard. Each bite was a small engagement designed to win limited objectives. By 13.00 the enemy had been cleared from the Wood but German shellfire forced the British to abandon the high ground and return to lower-level trenches. The close fighting was so intense that one company came under the command of a corporal when all the officers and senior non-commissioned officers had been killed.

Second Lieutenant **George Balfour** died at High Wood. He had been in the 6th Battalion of the Highland Light Infantry, but such was the loss of life on the Somme that officers and men were moved around and battalions combined. When George died he was serving in the Northumberland Fusiliers. On the morning of 15 September his battalion sent twenty-two officers and 695 men into battle. By the end of the day 500 soldiers, including most of the officers, were dead, wounded or missing.

George was the youngest of the three children of Andrew Balfour, FRIBA, a successful Glasgow architect. The Balfour family lived comfortably in Rostrevor, one of the big houses. At the outbreak of war George Balfour was only seventeen and had recently left the Glasgow High School. He enlisted in the Highland Light Infantry and soon received a commission. A senior officer wrote to George's father:

> I am very sorry that the continuous fighting in which we have been engaged has prevented me writing you

sooner to convey to you my own and the deepest
sympathy of every officer and man in my regiment in
your great loss. Your son fell gallantly leading his men in
an attack in which they did magnificently and it will be
a little consolation to you to know that his life was not
sacrificed in vain. He is buried on the battlefield where
he fell. He was an excellent officer and beloved by all
of us and we shall miss him very much and share your
sorrow.

When the war ended it would be George's father who was called
upon to design the Bridge of Weir War Memorial, a memorial
on which his son's name would appear. But the Balfour family's
sadness did not end with the loss of George. Captain Andrew
Campbell Balfour was his older brother. He had a good war.
He was a captain in the same battalion of the Highland Light
Infantry as Speirs Barr and George Jackson. He was twice
mentioned in despatches, once by Sir Douglas Haig, and
was awarded the Military Cross as well as the Mons Star. He
survived the war but his health was ruined and he died in his
parents' home of bronchitis and pneumonia on 13 April 1925
aged just thirty-four.

Haig ordered a major attack on 12 October. The Canadian
Corps was given the task of capturing and holding Regina
Trench to secure a jumping-off place for the Reserve Army's
impending offensive to the north. We met **David Cummings**,
the commercial traveller with dark complexion, hazel eyes,
black hair and a scar on one finger, in the company of the
other Bridge of Weir Canadians. He now found himself on the
Somme with his corps.

On the night of 30 September his battalion's war diary relates
that all ranks were keyed up and in fine spirits, very eager to
attack. At 15.16 the following day the first wave of Canadians
went over the parapet led by Lieutenants Daubney and

Campbell. When the Canadians reached the trench Campbell was dead, Daubney wounded and many others were casualties. The Germans blew in Regina Trench as they dropped back to their next line. The surviving Canadians had to find shelter as best they could. David Cummings was one of those who died on 1 October, the first day of the attacks on Regina Trench, along with forty-seven officers and men in the 5th Canadian Mounted Rifles.

By 21 October Regina Trench, the capture of which had cost so much blood, was, according to the *Official History* 'no longer a position of strength. Repeated bombardments had reduced it to a mere depression in the chalk, in many places blown twenty feet wide, and for long stretches almost filled with debris and dead bodies'. As in so many cases, had they known this, his relatives would have wondered just what David Cummings had died for and would have struggled to find a purpose and a justification for the sacrifices that were being made on both sides.

James Brooks had lived all his life in Bridge of Weir. His mother Mary McKay was a worker in the cotton mill who met and married William Brooks, an Irish boot-maker and repairer. The family of two adults and eleven children lived in a three-roomed flat at 4 Windsor Place. Unusually, there were two sets of twins in the family, including James and his sister Jane.

James joined the Royal Scots and was on the front line in France on 15 December 1915. When he was killed in action on 29 October 1916 he was a Lance-Corporal serving with the 5th Battalion of the Cameronians (Scottish Rifles) in the 26th Brigade (Highland) of the 9th (Scottish) Division, part of Fourth Army.

James Brooks has no known grave. The great Lutyens Memorial at Thiepval was erected to commemorate 72,000 men who died in that sector prior to 20 March 1918. These 72,000 are not the sum of those who died – *they are only those whose bodies were never found.* James's name appears on the memorial. His body was one of those which were reduced to atoms. He was twenty years old. The scale of the memorial and the losses it commemorates were what inspired Charles Chilton to write what became *Oh, What a Lovely War!*

Other Bridge of Weir men fought on the Somme and survived it, some of them alas to die nonetheless before the war ended. Captain Speirs Barr and Privates Henry Strang and James Pollock of the HLI were in action on the first and last days and survived. Lance Corporal John Andrew was serving in the 17th Battalion of the Highland Light Infantry when he was injured in the leg on 5 July and Private Edward Shedden of 1st Cameronians was shot in the right arm on 15 July. Lance Corporal John Holmes survived uninjured despite having been in action twice. William Houston of the Royal Engineers was exposed to mustard gas and died the following spring. None of these seven men survived the war.

23

The Battle of the Ancre, November 1916

Ian McNiven Bannatyne
Second Lieutenant, 16th Battalion, Highland Light Infantry

Archibald Fulton
Sergeant, 17th Battalion, Highland Light Infantry

Robert Barr
Private, 15th Battalion, Highland Light Infantry

Robert Barr McDougall
Private, 15th Battalion, Highland Light Infantry

As we have seen, the Somme was not just about its now notorious First Day. The majority of those who died did so in its protracted and increasingly unproductive prolongation. The Battle of the Ancre, which lasted from 13 to 18 November, was the last phase of the Somme and ended the offensive. If the losses of the First Day seem terrible, there is perhaps something even more poignant about deaths in the last stages of a now-doomed project.

Fifth Army began its Ancre offensive at 05.45 on 13 November, in darkness and thick fog and accompanied by a tremendous artillery bombardment. By the end of that first day it had secured Beaumont-Hamel, captured St Pierre Divion and advanced to the outskirts of Beaucourt. Many Germans were taken prisoner. British casualties were serious but on the following day more ground was gained when Beaucourt was occupied.

British positions were then consolidated in readiness for a further advance on 18 November. During the night the first snow of the winter fell. When the attack started at 06.10, the snow had turned to sleet, and visibility was poor. A British smoke barrage did not improve matters: advancing troops lost direction and contact with each other.

Thirty-second Division, including 15th, 16th and 17th HLI moved forward on 17 November. On the following morning the task was to attack the Munich and Frankfurt trenches north-east of Beaumont-Hamel. At least six young men from Bridge of Weir were serving in those battalions, of whom four died the following day. The oldest of the four were aged twenty-one. Their comrades, Henry Strang and James Pollock, survived.

Sixteenth Battalion marched to Mailly-Maillet where they stopped for a meal before marching on to Brigade HQ at White City as their assembly position. En route their guides lost their way and the connection between companies broke down. When the assembly position was reached at 02.00 only D Company was in place and it was 06.00 before the whole battalion was assembled in battle positions.

The battalion finally advanced just after 10.00. D Company with part of C Company entered Munich Trench with little opposition. D Company pushed on into Frankfurt Trench, leaving their comrades to mop up behind them in Munich. The enemy then collected in large numbers and 'lively bombing duels' took place before the remnant of the 16th was overwhelmed in Munich, every man a casualty.

With no support, ninety men were left to hang on in Frankfurt. There they remained until 21 November when the forty-five survivors (thirty of them wounded) surrendered.

Sixteenth Battalion suffered more than 400 killed or wounded at the Ancre – and that on top of the losses of early July. Many of them were young men who had been friends in the Boys' Brigade. They enlisted together and they died together. At the end of the war the Roll of Honour for the Glasgow Boys' Brigade Battalion, 16th HLI, recorded the deaths of thirty-six officers and 795 other ranks. Many of those who died on the Somme in 1916 had been amongst the first volunteers to join up.

Second Lieutenant **Ian McNiven Bannatyne** originally enlisted in the 6th Battalion of the HLI in September 1914. He was commissioned into the 9th Battalion and finally transferred to the 16th on 22 October 1916. The war diary records that he died leading his men into Frankfurt Trench.

Ian's name is recorded on the war memorials at Thiepval, Bridge of Weir, Ranfurly Church, Glasgow High School and Ranfurly Castle Golf Club. He was the son of a Glasgow solicitor and one of seven children who lived at Fernhurst in Kilbarchan Road. He enlisted aged seventeen years and three months and he met his death two years later.

Archibald Fulton joined the Glasgow Chamber of Commerce Battalion, 17th HLI, in January 1915, when he was nineteen. The choice of battalion resulted from his employment as a commercial clerk with a foreign merchant and importer. He was on the front line in France from November that year. Archibald was promoted from private to sergeant. He was wounded on 18 November 1916 and died from his wounds the following day. He was twenty-one years old.

Archibald's father, John Fulton, was a house factor with the railway company and the family lived in an eight-room villa in Horsewood Road with three sons, one daughter and a domestic servant. All the sons served in the army and two of them were killed in action. The youngest boy, Hugh, died in the final weeks of the war (see Chapter 42).

The final day of the Somme offensive saw the last coincidence in the lives and deaths of two Bridge of Weir boys. **Robert Barr McDougall** was born on 7 April 1895 and **Robert Barr** sixteen days later. By the time the boys were five years old, both their families lived in The Mimosas. Their fathers, Robert Barr McDougall and Matthew Barr, both worked for the leather company – Robert as a currier and Matthew as a mechanical engineer.

Robert McDougall was 'Bertie' and Robert Barr 'Bobby', Bobby one of eight children and Bertie one of five. They grew up and went to school together. They both had a natural gift for golf, the game that was taking hold in Bridge of Weir, with its four courses in Ranfurly on the other side of the railway track from The Mimosas.

The elite clubs were selective about their membership. Women generally and men from inferior social classes were excluded. The war memorial in Ranfurly Castle Golf Club only records *members* who died in the war and not the professionals who worked at the clubs. (Ranfurly Ladies Golf Club opened in 1897 to allow women to play, at about the same time as the Thistle Course, which provided for artisans. The assumptions of the times are not comfortably recalled.)

Bobby and Bertie made careers out of their game. Bobby became assistant professional at Ranfurly Castle. In the summer of 1913, at the age of eighteen, he went round the course six times in a single day, scoring an aggregate 477, a feat as pointless as it is impressive – the mark of a true sportsman.

Bertie, after serving his apprenticeship as a golf-club maker, became professional at the Old Ranfurly Club. In May 1914, he finished third equal in the Paisley District Professionals' competition and he was good enough to enter the Open Championship that summer, aged nineteen. In that last summer before the war, the two young golfers were in the early stages of what looked likely to be successful sporting careers.

When war intervened, Bertie volunteered. In mid-November

1914 he enlisted in the 15th Battalion (1st Glasgow) HLI, raised mainly from employees of Glasgow Corporation Tramways Department. Bobby volunteered for the same battalion and the same regiment a week later. They trained at Gailes Camp, near Troon in Ayrshire, home to a very élite golf club which would certainly not have accepted them as members. Bertie interrupted his training briefly in February 1915 to marry Agnes Clarke, a domestic servant in one of the Ranfurly villas. For once, Bobby did not follow Bertie's example; he remained single.

After Gailes, the 15th HLI moved to Salisbury for further training, and embarked for France in November 1915. Bobby and Bertie survived to fight on the Somme: the first major engagement for the 15th HLI was the opening day of the battle. They lived through that day and the next four and half months on the Somme; they died on 18 November attacking Munich and Frankfurt trenches. It was a disastrous day for the battalion. The preparatory artillery barrage fell 500 yards behind the front-line trenches. Wintry weather provided a backdrop of snow and frost which showed up the soldiers in stark relief as they emerged from their own trenches. Bobby was killed by shrapnel, Bertie by a sniper's bullet. Their converging lives reached a conclusion on the same day, in the same battle, fighting for a piece of the same German trench. They lie together in a cemetery in northern France, four graves apart, as close in death as they were in life.

24

Ypres, November 1916

William McClure
Private, 7th Battalion, Royal Inniskilling Fusiliers

William McClure was the only Bridge of Weir Memorial man to join an Irish battalion. His paternal grandparents came to Scotland from Northern Ireland and his father David was born in Glasgow in 1855. David was a stonemason who married Jane Beaton from Greenock. They had four sons, twins David and Alfred, William and Stewart. It seems likely that all four brothers enlisted. In particular, Stewart McClure had a distinguished army career and won the Military Medal. He died in 1961 having lived most of his life in Bridge of Weir.

William had been born in Greenock and moved to Bridge of Weir with his family when he was nine. He lived in the village for the next twenty years before going a few miles to Lochwinnoch when he married. He worked as a quarryman, ploughman and probably a coal miner in Lanarkshire, where he enlisted. His wife Annie Clewes was a bleach-field worker; her father was a manager at the bleach-field works in Lochwinnoch. William and Annie had no children. Following William's death Annie remarried twice.

In August 1915, William volunteered and enlisted at Coatbridge. He joined the 7th Service Battalion of the Royal Inniskilling Fusiliers. At the time, that regiment was very keen to sign recruits and it may be assumed that William had no objection to joining a regiment close to his family roots.

In September William started basic training at Aldershot. The first parade each day at 06.00 was followed by a run around the barrack square. Breakfast at 07.30 preceded squad drill and physical training from 09.00 to 12.30. Dinner was at 13.00 and the men had tea when they returned from their afternoon march. A short route march was five or six miles – to the accompaniment, for an Irish regiment, of the fifes and drums. On some nights there were six o'clock lectures in the gymnasium and on other nights the men went out for marches and manoeuvres in the dark.

At 14.00 on 16 February 1916 William and his comrades paraded outside the barracks, marched to the railway station and entrained for Southampton. There they boarded the paddle steamer ss *Mona Queen* and sailed from Southampton Docks to Le Havre with an escort of two destroyers. It was a 'wretched and truly miserable' night's crossing. The *Mona Queen* dived, pitched and rolled through the night and most of the soldiers were sick.

After their arrival in France and a rail journey, the men marched on frozen snow to the Loos Salient not far from Béthune. In the frost and snow, trench foot, frostbite and illness were common. Like all infantry battalions the 7th Inniskillings moved between the front line and billets behind the lines, where there was time to write letters and play football. Some, it is reported, tried to learn French, a scholarly pastime that did not grip the bulk of the BEF.

Later, in April, the battalion moved along the front to the Hulloch sub-sector where they were subjected to a fierce artillery bombardment. William McClure and his comrades defended the part of the line known as the Kink, which was described in the context of the May–June fighting of 1916. There was fierce hand-to-hand fighting in the British trenches. The battalion started one day with 24 officers and 603 other ranks; it finished with 14 officers and 350 other ranks.

The remnants of the battalion, including William McClure, spent time in reserve trenches as the battalion was reformed. At the end of May they were back in the line close to the village of Loos. They moved into the line there for the last time on 20 August, almost six months after crossing the Channel. Five days later they set off by foot and rail to the Somme.

There William experienced all the horrors associated with that battlefield. He and his fellows marched to Arrow Head Copse, the scene of a battle fought two or three days earlier. It was a picture of absolute chaos and utter devastation. Shapeless masses of human beings lay strewn over the ground and the air reeked of putrefying flesh. There was a particularly fierce encounter at Ginchy. By the time they were relieved on the following morning they had lost 5 officers and 184 other ranks.

Finally, William's war took him to Ypres. There, when not in the front line, the battalion moved back to what were known as the Kemmel Shelters on the 'safe side' of Mont Kemmel. A feature of the Shelters – a common one in Flanders – was that the drainage systems could not cope with the floodwaters and the men spent much time digging new drainage trenches in the pouring rain. They were never dry.

On 3 November the battalion moved back into the line in the Kemmel and Bayernwald trenches facing Messines Ridge. It was here, on 11 November, that William McClure was killed. Although casualties were relatively light at this time, Pall Mall trench, where he was, was subjected to regular bombardment by heavy trench mortars. The unit diary says that Suicide Corner was to be avoided.

William McClure had survived six months at Loos and some fierce fighting on the Somme before he died in the Ypres Salient. He is buried in plot E5 at the Kemmel Chateau Military Cemetery. His is the only name that was added to the Bridge of Weir village memorial after its dedication: at the instigation of his great-nephew it was added in 2014.

25

The Mechanisation of War

Andrew Bain Jackson
Gunner, Motor Machine Gun Service

Andrew Bain Jackson was a scion of the Jackson family, sugar merchants in Glasgow. The wealth of Glasgow had been built on its mercantile activities in the eighteenth and nineteenth centuries, particularly on trade with the sugar plantations in the West Indies. The origins of the Jackson business are not now known, but the family was certainly well-to-do and Andrew was educated at Paisley Grammar School and Glasgow Academy.

Paisley Grammar School is the third of the four schools to which the Bridge of Weir men are known to have gone. It was founded in 1576 with a royal charter from James VI, and is consequently one of the older schools in Scotland, even if it is four centuries younger than Glasgow High School. It adherered to a rigorous tradition of education, underlined by a wonderfully uncompromising motto: '*Disce puer aut abi*': 'Learn child, or begone'. There are 109 names on the school's war memorial Roll of Honour.

At the age of seventeen, Andrew was a stockbroker's clerk in Glasgow, making a traditional move from trade to the professions. He enlisted in the Motor Machine Gun Service. The Service was formed in 1914 and incorporated into the Machine Gun Corps in 1915. Motorcycle sidecar combinations were fitted with a Vickers machine-gun. Recruits to the Motor Machine Gun Service had often been members of motor cycle clubs before the war and they were selected for their motorcycling abilities, often taken from other regiments.

The British Army in the Great War is often portrayed as hidebound by convention, averse to change and too attached to its cavalry traditions. The facts prove otherwise. The Motor Machine Gun Service is a good example of early adoption of new technology, also evident in the development of tanks and air warfare. War and weapons had become highly mechanised and the army recognised that a key to success was developing and deploying new technology faster than the enemy. The Motor Machine Gun Service was the twentieth-century equivalent of a troop of cavalry.

From 1916 the nature of this new warfare had been perceived and its needs explored. Infantry no longer consisted simply of riflemen. The platoon worked as a tactical unit, and made use of Lewis guns, trench mortars and grenades as well as rifles. Artillery was being used imaginatively. In 1914 most artillery fire was direct – shells were aimed at targets that could be seen. Now fire was increasingly directed at unseen targets, controlled by new techniques of sound-ranging and pre-calibration, supplemented by direction from aircraft, balloons and forward observation posts. Tanks took their place on the battlefield in 1916. GHQ was not resistant to change. On the contrary, Haig, who has been described as a 'gadget freak', pressed for more machine-guns, and tanks were arguably deployed at a point when their numbers were inadequate and their technology unrefined, at the cost of losing the advantage of surprise. Fortunately, the Germans failed to recognise their potential.

But Andrew Jackson, alas, never had the opportunity to put his training to the test. He died of tuberculosis at Banchory Sanitorium in Aberdeenshire on 27 January 1917 without ever seeing action. His death certificate dates the onset of the disease to April 1914, but only does so with the benefit of hindsight.

The medical officer missed the symptoms. Did Andrew know there was a problem but ignore it in his desire to serve? He was buried in Kilbarchan Cemetery, Bridge of Weir's burial ground. Andrew was the first of two Jackson brothers to die during the war.

26

Arras, 1917: The Big Picture

The Easter offensive of 1917, of which the Battle of Arras was the British component, was a combined Franco–British concept. It had originally been planned at the Chantilly Conference in November 1916, but changes were made when Nivelle took over from Joffre as the French Commander-in-Chief.

Nivelle came with a formidable reputation which he had gained at Verdun by the coordination of artillery and infantry. He was full of confidence: 'Laon in twenty-four hours, and then we break out'. His strategy would result in what he called *rupture*, which means pretty much the same in English as it does in French: the destruction of the German lines. A short artillery barrage – long ones were becoming discredited – would allow his forces to move straight through to open ground to the rear of the German lines. He held out the prospect of more fluid warfare than the Western Front had seen since 1914. He told his Government that he would end the war in two days.

London was at least as charmed by him as was Paris. His mother was English, and he spoke her language fluently – and with a reassuringly upper-class accent, which allowed him entry to London society. Unfortunately, over dinner he openly discussed his preparations in that reassuring upper-class accent and his plans leaked extensively. As a result the German line opposite his front was particularly well built up in anticipation of the offensive.

Haig's Army Commander at the Battle of Arras was Edmund Allenby, who commanded Third Army, of which 15th (Scottish) Division was part. A tense relationship had existed for some time between Haig and Allenby, both cavalrymen. It may have originated in their first meeting, at Staff College, Camberley, when Allenby was elected Master of the Drag Hounds in preference to the reserved and prickly Haig. There was no sign of disloyalty on Allenby's part and both men were meticulously polite in their contacts with each other, although at weekly meetings with the Army Commanders, Haig was inclined to interrupt Allenby's contributions.

Communications between the two cannot have been easy in any case, as they were both outstandingly reticent, even inarticulate. Haig conversed by grunts and half-finished sentences. Allenby was only slightly better. But though he was a man of few words, they were forcefully expressed ones. He was known as 'the Bull'. He made his views clear to superiors and subordinates alike, and his popularity suffered accordingly. He was solicitous for the welfare of his men, but they were less conscious of that than of his outbursts when he came across any breaches of regulations on his forward visits. It was said that a dressing-down from Allenby felt like being blown from the muzzle of a gun, but that when one regained ground, Allenby bore no malice. Only one officer, Sir John Keir of VI Corps, regularly stood up to the Bull: inevitably he was known as 'the Toreador'.

There was a disagreement between the Army Commander and his Chief right at the start. Allenby wanted to give the Germans as little warning of events as possible, limiting shelling to a hurricane bombardment of forty-eight hours, with breaks only to allow barrels to cool down and the men to eat. Haig wanted a more conventional bombardment, lasting five days. Allenby's plan may not have been technically feasible; at any rate Haig's view prevailed. Accordingly, before the British attack began on 9 April 1917, Easter Monday, a week before the French, a huge, five-day artillery bombardment took place, employing 2,800 guns. The period of bombardment was shorter than that on the Somme, but the number of shells delivered on the German defences was twice as great.

The Canadians, north of Arras, took Vimy Ridge, an important geographical feature, after three hours of heavy fighting. Near Arras itself, British Third Army advanced three and a half miles. This was the biggest gain since the trenches had been dug in 1914. To the south of the River Scarpe, 9th Battalion, the Black Watch, advanced less far. The Germans held the village strongpoint of Monchy-le-Preux against repeated British attacks.

In the *Daily Mail* on 10 April 1917, William Beach Thomas reported:

> Near Arras our troops leapt to the attack in the midst of such artillery fire as the world has never seen . . . [I]t is too early to give more than partial news, but the famous divisions directly in front of me . . . went straight through to their goal.

At the end of the first day of Arras the British and Canadian success appeared remarkable. Captain Cyril Falls, an Official Historian, described the Easter Monday attack as 'One of the great days of the war, . . . among the heaviest blows struck by British arms in the western theatre of war'. In the course of the day, Third Army took 5,600 prisoners and the Canadians a further 3,400. Ground had been taken with relatively few casualties and the way seemed open for further advance.

But the weather was appalling. The advance had begun in sleet, and rain and snow succeeded. The terrain was chalk which had been rendered into mud. Additionally, a planned pause of two hours checked the advance. Some further advances were made in the north, but thereafter little happened until 16 April, when the French offensive began.

That offensive was disastrous. On the first day alone the French suffered 40,000 casualties. Nivelle continued the attack on 20 April, before finally abandoning the offensive on 9 May. France had suffered 187,000 casualties compared to a German total of 168,000. Nivelle was swiftly removed and replaced by Pétain. Almost immediately what are known as 'the Mutinies of 1917' began in the French Army. 'Mutiny' is the wrong description for what happened. After the long agony of Verdun, and indeed the bloody course of the whole war for France, ever since she had faced the whole weight of the German onslaught in 1914 almost alone, the confidence of the ordinary French soldier in the High Command had been nearly destroyed. What the troops did was akin to withdrawing their labour in order to show that things must change.

Pétain did change things. He combined stern retribution for the mutineers with an evident concern for the welfare of the troops, a delicate balance cleverly achieved. The army never broke, but the French command was careful for the rest of the war not to ask too much of it. Morale amongst the political classes had been weak long before the soldiers wavered. To understand the course of the rest of the war from the point of view of the British command, it is important to remember that Haig and his Army Commanders were aware that the preponderance of responsibility had moved to their shoulders.

Returning from the politics of grand strategy to Arras itself, on the British Front there had been advances on the second and particularly the first day that were remarkable at this stage in the war; the problem, as always, was an inability to translate gains into movement and manoeuvre. A limited breakthrough had been achieved, but there was no forward momentum. Haig urged Allenby, held up at Monchy, to push forward on the north of the Scarpe and then move south-east behind Monchy, to turn the German flank. Allenby needed no urging. Immediately after the 9 April advance, he ordered further movement. On 10 April his order for the day was charged with adrenalin: 'The

Army Commander wishes all troops to understand that Third Army is pushing a defeated enemy and that risks must be taken'. Four days later he was still for pressing forward, but there was a remarkable 'mutiny' by three of his divisional commanders, who formally represented to General Headquarters that Allenby's attempts at narrow advances left vulnerably exposed flanks. Haig upheld their appeal and ordered a suspension of operations. When the puppet-masters quarrelled amongst themselves, what hope was there for the puppets?

Allenby did not long survive the Battle of Arras: by June he had been, in the jargon of the times, 'degummed', and relieved of his command. The records are opaque, referring to his dismissal as being because of his conduct in command of Third Army 'and many other reasons'.

Haig renewed limited action on the British Front on 3 May in an effort to encourage the French to continue fighting, but the offensive was over by the end of May. The British contribution to the Aisne offensive had been intended as essentially a subordinate one. In the event, the British–Canadian operations demonstrated a potential for success, if not a success which could be translated into victory. The Germans had suffered badly at Vimy and yielded the northern six miles of the Hindenburg line; but by the end of the offensive Britain had lost 150,000 men, against something over 100,000 lost by the Germans. The British Expeditionary Force daily loss rate was 4,076 at Arras compared with 2,963 at the Somme, 2,323 at Third Ypres and 3,605 in the Hundred Days Battles of 1918.

Arras is the forgotten battle of the First World War, but it delivered local success as well as incurring losses as great as in any of the better-known conflicts. How significant was it? At one level, not very. Monchy-le-Preux was eventually taken, at great cost, but the Germans re-took it and held it until 26 August 1918, when it was recaptured by the Canadian Corps during the Hundred Days. There was attrition: the Germans were worn down. With the United States in the war, as they were from April 1917, the Allies could afford larger casualties than the Germans. All the same, winning the war by losing more men than your opponent is not an inspiring achievement. The prolongation of the battle delayed operational planning for Third Ypres: that campaign was fought in dismal autumnal weather rather than the excellent earlier summer weather of 1917.

But Arras contributed to the learning curve that was to result in the radically changed tactics that won the remarkable victories of 1918. The creeping barrage which was developed by Alan Brooke (later to become Lord Alanbrooke, Chief of the Imperial General Staff for most of the Second World War), became a feature of trench warfare from at least 1916, but it was used as a particular tactical element for the first time at Arras. It consisted of moving a pattern of bombardment behind which the infantry advanced. At Arras it only worked moderately well: the barrage could still be too far ahead of the infantry, or indeed too close, causing death by friendly fire. By the following year, it was much refined.

27

Arras: The Picture the Men Saw

James McGibbon
Gunner, Royal Field Artillery

David Tod
Sapper, 51st Signal Company, Royal Engineers

John Holmes
Lance-Corporal, 10th Battalion, Argyll and Sutherland
Highlanders

Hepner Giffen
Private, 16th Battalion, Royal Scots

Robert Burns
Private, 10th Battalion, Lancashire Fusiliers

Richard Arroll
Private, 5th Battalion, Seaforth Highlanders

Arras involved three Scottish divisions, fifty-two Scottish battalions and about 40,000 Scottish soldiers, including six with their names on the Bridge of Weir War Memorial. Two of the Bridge of Weir men, James McGibbon and David Tod, were killed by German shelling ahead of the battle on 6 April, three days before the Allied assault.

James McGibbon was born on 17 June 1886, the son of a farm servant, William McGibbon, and a thread-mill worker, Martha Aitken. Although the names of both parents were on the birth certificate James was born illegitimate, though subsequently legitimated under Scots law, when his parents got round to marrying on 31 October 1893. William and Martha lived much of their lives apart, with William away working on farms until he died from tuberculosis, the scourge of the times, and very common on farms, aged only forty-eight. James McGibbon left school to work in the tannery and by his twenties he was a skilled currier. His choice of occupation put him at risk of dying of the same disease as his father: tuberculosis was common among the tannery workers because they worked with cow hides. He never married and lived most of his life with his mother and a succession of boarders at Campbell's Land and then Riversdale, a tenement on the Main Street in Bridge of Weir.

James joined the artillery soon after the outbreak of war. By July 1915 he was on the Western Front, where he served for twenty-one months. He died near the village of Ste Catherine, aged thirty-one and serving in Z Company, 17th Trench Mortar Battery of the Royal Field Artillery. On 4 April 1920 a William McGibbon from Victoria, Australia, wrote to the army requesting his service medals as James's brother and next-of-kin.

In civilian life **David Tod** had been a joiner, the son of a joiner and the youngest of four children. His parents moved to Bridge of Weir from Falkland in Fife but David was born in Bridge of Weir and lived all his life in the village before joining the army. He was one of the first to enlist, on 15 August 1914, and joined 51st Signals Company of 154 Brigade, Royal Engineers. In the following year he was injured by an exploding shell. On 12 June 1915 the local newspaper reported, 'The extent of his injuries is not known apart from him being deaf.'

He survived for a further twenty-two months. He died

repairing a telephone on the northern outskirts of Arras. Sapper Tod and others were in a dug-out making the repair when they were killed by a direct hit from a shell. The 51st Divisional Signals Company provided communications for the 51st (Highland) Division. Although their work was not glamorous, they maintained telephones, railways, roads, bridges, water supplies and transport without which the army could not function. Even if what they did was not the obvious stuff of heroism, they frequently needed to be heroes to do it.

Lance Corporal **John Holmes** of 10th Battalion, Argyll and Sutherland Highlanders, was part of 26th Brigade and 9th (Scottish) Division which advanced on Easter Monday, 9 April. It had snowed heavily during the night. The 10th Argylls were immediately to the north of the River Scarpe and 11th Argylls to the south. The attack on that first day involved three Scottish divisions: 9th, 15th and 51st.

A Scottish diarist recorded: 'German trenches in a terrible mess – quite unrecognisable'. Progress was slow, and the enemy trenches were only reached at the cost of many deaths and serious injuries. The 10th and 11th Argylls were impeded by a railway embankment which was as high as sixty feet and held by the Germans. British artillery bombarded the top of the embankment but heavy fire was directed down from it, and the Argylls suffered heavy losses, including John Holmes, who died of wounds on 11 April. The diarist described the advance 'in a blinding snowstorm with the thermometer below zero, with no hot food and in the face of the most terrible machine-gun fire which I have ever experienced'.

John Holmes was twenty when he died. He had enlisted in November 1915, soon after his nineteenth birthday. He grew up in Bridge of Weir, the son of a stonemason and the eldest of five children. He was bright and educated. His first job was as a clerk at the leather works. When he enlisted he was living in Glasgow and working as a clerk with the General Electric

Company in Waterloo Street. At the time of his death the army had promoted John to the rank of Lance Corporal (unpaid).

Margaret Holmes, John's mother, acknowledged receipt of her son's personal effects sent on by the army: photographs and correspondence, testament, pocket dictionary, cigarette case, two coins, pipe, prayer book and belt with cap badge and numerals attached. When John died, Margaret's second son, Hugh, aged only nineteen, was away on active service; happily he survived the war.

On that Easter Monday, 16th Battalion, the Royal Scots was part of 101st Brigade, which succeeded in taking three enemy trenches. The Germans then counter-attacked to good effect and 51st (Scottish) Division's determined assault on Roeux on 23 April was repulsed. **Hepner Giffen** died on 28 April when the 101st Brigade tried again to take Roeux.

Hepner Giffen may not have known it, but in only slightly different circumstances he could have been fighting for Germany. His father, Gottfried Hepner, was a German-born musician who married Alma Jacob from Cornwall in 1878. When baby Hepner (at that time Gottfried) was born in Glasgow, Gottfried senior and Alma already had four children, Otto, Frederic, Minna Henrietta and Bertha. Alma Hepner died from internal tumours shortly after the birth and her husband Gottfried was devastated with grief: he too was dead within months.

William Quarrier was a benevolent Scot who created homes for Glasgow orphans in the countryside close to Bridge of Weir, in what is now known as Quarrier's Village but then as the Orphan Homes of Scotland. The Village consisted of a cluster of large houses, each run by house parents. The orphan children of Gottfried and Alma Hepner found their way to Somerville House and the care of house parents Christina and Humphrey Giffen. Mr and Mrs Giffen were then in their fifties.

Most children from the orphan homes were sent to Canada

to find work when they were old enough to be independent, and all of Gottfried's siblings emigrated to Ontario. It was unusual for a Quarrier's orphan to be adopted by house parents; but Gottfried was. His adopting parents took to calling him (as he became) Hepner Godfrey Giffen. Hepner served an apprenticeship as a joiner and met and married a Bridge of Weir girl, Nellie McDougall, who was an assistant in a confectioner's shop. They married on 25 May 1916. By that time Hepner was serving as a private in the 3rd/5th Scottish Rifles and on leave from Catterick Camp in Yorkshire. Nellie was twenty-three, Hepner twenty-two, and their home was the Old Manse in the lane behind Freeland Church.

On 28 April 1917 the British advance at Roeux started at 04.25. The Divisional Commander recorded that 'it began badly, continued badly and ended worse'. The Allied artillery barrage missed its target and the German machine-guns were 'highly active'. Despite that, sixty men from 16th Royal Scots made it to the Chemical Works in Roeux, only to be forced to retreat under the cover of darkness. Hepner Giffen was killed in the course of the day.

Hepner was twenty-three when he died and Nellie had seen little of her new husband in a marriage which lasted less than a year. During those twelve months Nellie also lost her brother, Robert Barr McDougall, the same Bertie McDougall whose death on the last day of the Somme offensive has already been chronicled. Nellie's recently widowed mother, Jane, lived with her in the Old Manse. Nellie received a war widow's pension of thirteen shillings and nine pence per week (about £67 today) to be paid from 31 December 1917. That was the material compensation for her loss.

Robert Burns died on 12 May serving in the 10th Battalion of the Lancashire Fusiliers. The Battle of Arras is usually regarded as ending on 4 May but the big offensive of Third Ypres was coming up and British High Command wanted Germany's attention diverted. Accordingly, on 12 May the 10th Lancashire Fusiliers advanced under orders to take the two German trenches opposing them. The Germans were obviously expecting the attack and opened up with machine-guns, rifles and artillery. Despite heavy losses, some men made it to the German forward trench and fought for a lost cause with bombs and bayonets.

Robert Burns was twenty when he died and his older brother James was killed less than six months later. Although Robert was born in Glasgow he could have been related to his namesake, the poet: both Burns families were from Ayrshire and had links with Mauchline. Our Robert's father, James Burns, was a domestic coachman, who like many coachmen of the period became a chauffeur. After living in the Park area of Glasgow the family settled in Gryffe Castle Cottage, Bridge of Weir. Young Robert could drive a car when he enlisted and he was a driver in the Army Service Corps before transferring to the Lancashire Fusiliers.

Richard Arroll attested under the Derby scheme on 1 December 1915 and in June 1916 he was mobilised into the 3rd/5th Seaforth Highlanders. 'Dickie' Arroll was not only married but established in life when he was called up. His father had originally been a housepainter, but eventually became a landscape artist in oils and watercolours, exhibiting at the Paris Salon. Dickie saw that there was more money to be made in painting houses than in painting canvases. He became a master painter and established a successful business. He was a proponent of physical fitness and taught physical exercise in the Citizens' Training Force in Church Street School in Glasgow from 1914. He had a young wife, Annie, and their three girls Annie, Maymie and Jane were seven, six and three when he left for the war. The family employed a domestic servant and lived in Beaumaris, a stone-built, detached villa on Torr Road with lovely views of the Gryffe Valley.

When he joined the army, Richard was thirty-seven years old, a successful businessman with, it might be thought, leadership qualities. He was not, however, commissioned. During training he served as an acting Lance Corporal but he reverted to private when he went to the Front on 23 December 1916. His battalion served through the Arras offensive, including the First and Second Battles of the Scarpe in April and the capture and defence of Roeux on 13/14 May.

On the following day, 15 May 1917, he received a gunshot wound in the right thigh. He spent some time in a field hospital before being repatriated to the Military Hospital in Hampstead on 28 May. He was three months in hospital but died as a result of complications from his wounds. Dickie is buried in Hampstead Cemetery in North London. It is not known if he was ever reunited with his wife and daughters, even if only for a brief hospital visit.

28

Nieuwpoort, June to July 1917

Henry Strang
Private, 16th Battalion, Highland Light Infantry

James Pollock
Private, 15th Battalion, Highland Light Infantry

Peter and Janet Strang lived in Partick, Glasgow where their children, Alice and **Henry Strang** were born. They moved to 1 St Georges Terrace, Bridge of Weir, before the children started school. Peter was a bank clerk and they could afford to employ a domestic servant. Young Henry appears to have joined the Boys' Brigade Company in Bridge of Weir and it was the 16th HLI, the Boys' Brigade battalion, that he joined, not yet seventeen. He was one of the early volunteers, and was ready to embark for France on 24 November 1915.

James Pollock was the second of three children born to James and Elizabeth Pollock. They were all born in Bridge of Weir although their parents came from Ayrshire. James, the father, was a gardener who found regular work locally and the family were well established in the village. They moved addresses a few times in those pre-war years. By the time of the 1911 Census, two parents, three children, a grandfather and a lodger lived in a two-room tenement flat in Cooperative Terrace on Main Street.

The two brothers, Robert and James, had settled jobs. Robert was an assistant dispensing chemist and James a railway clerk. They both enlisted in 1915. Robert joined the motor section of the Lovat Scouts and survived the war. For James, a railway employee, the Glasgow Tramways Battalion was an obvious choice. He was nineteen when he joined up.

Both Henry Strang and James Pollock had enlisted in the early days, when the war was expected to be over by Christmas, and both entered Pals' Battalions. We've seen already that the 15th, 16th and 17th battalions of the HLI were formed respectively from the Glasgow Tramways, the Boys' Brigade and the Chamber of Commerce. In the regiment they were known as the Boozy First, the Holy Second and the Featherbeds.

After their training in Britain the boys sailed to Boulogne to join the war on 23 November 1915. Most of their comrades who landed on that day did not survive the war or indeed the Somme Offensive.

Henry and James fought in that offensive at its beginning and end and came through unscathed. On the first day, 1 July 1916, twenty-five officers and 755 other ranks of 16th Highland Light Infantry went over the top. Henry Strang was one of just five officers and 221 other ranks who were not killed or wounded. The battalion was reformed and sent back into action on 18 November 1916 (the last day of the offensive) when two-thirds of its men were again casualties.

James Pollock also fought on the first day. His battalion lost almost 500 officers and men. He too was back in action on 18 November.

The 15th and 16th Battalions were in action again in April 1917. James Pollock was with the 15th Battalion, which took prisoners and captured Savy. Henry Strang in the 16th was involved in a successful British action at Fayet near Saint Quentin. Then both battalions marched north to Nieuwpoort and by June the two young men were back on another front line for what would be their last engagement.

Nieuwpoort was established in the twelfth century as a new port to serve the city of Ypres in place of the old port at Lombardssijde. It is on the River Yser only two miles from the North Sea. It was the only Belgian port which was not taken by the Germans in their race to the sea in 1914: Ostend, Zeebrugge and Bruges all became German naval bases and were used to launch attacks by submarines, destroyers and torpedo boats against British shipping and the English coast.

To avoid Nieuwpoort's occupation, the Belgians flooded the town, thus destroying it. The six sluice gates were opened, creating a lake of flood water and an effective defence for the Ypres salient. The destruction of the port was a high price to pay, but it never fell into German hands and was rebuilt after the war.

The British Army and Navy tried many times to bombard Belgian harbours in German occupation but the coastal defences were too strong. By early 1917 Admiral Sir Reginald Bacon had formed a new plan, Operation HUSH. An amphibious Allied landing on the Belgian coast would be supported by a breakout attack from Nieuwpoort and the Yser bridgehead. Four miles of front-line trench ran from the sea to St Georges near Ramscappelle to the south of Nieuwpoort. The French held this sector but in July Dominion forces took over in readiness for HUSH.

And so, on 20 June 32nd Division, including 15th and 16th HLI, relieved the French at the Nieuwpoort bridgehead. Over the next ten days they were joined by four more infantry divisions, 189 heavy guns and IV Corps of the Royal Flying Corps. In England three pontoons were built, each 700 feet long, like the Mulberry Harbours of the Second World War. But the troops which were to land had been trained in secrecy which was less complete than that surrounding the D-day landings and the enemy was well aware of the British plans. The British takeover of the French sector was correctly interpreted as the prelude to a British attack along the coast. The Germans knew that what was to become known as Third Ypres was imminent.

Initially the Third Ypres campaign envisaged a sophisticated combined naval and military assault along the lines of the Normandy operations in 1944. Indeed, the sophisticated nature of Third Ypres as it was planned rather than as it was fought is underlined in that it was to have an air force dimension as well as army and navy ones. In 1917 London was being bombed quite heavily by the standard of the times. Hugh Trenchard, at this time commanding the Royal Flying Corps in France, wanted to counter the bombing campaign by denying the Germans the west European airfields by land occupation following bombing and shooting down enemy aircraft near their bases. Thus he and GHQ saw Third Ypres as playing its part in taking the Germans out of flying range of London.

The Government was less ambitious, and chose to address the bombing threat by pulling aircraft back from the Western Front to south-east England. That element of Third Ypres disappeared. In the end the naval element was also removed: it was delayed to follow the military operation (which it never did) rather than accompanying and reinforcing it. Thus Third Ypres as it was fought was not the operation that had been planned. HUSH was cancelled and no British landing ever took place because the Germans got in first with their Operation *STRANDFEST*, a preemptive strike to eliminate the Yser bridgehead. They moved before most of the British guns and howitzers had arrived and before the tunnellers had done their work.

The German attack began on 6 July, with an artillery bombardment which lasted for three days. The weather was wet, cloudy and foggy and the massed German artillery was relentless. At night, 32nd Division, Strang and Pollock in it, held its section of the line and made a successful counter-attack at night. At the end of *STRANDFEST* only 500 yards of front line was still held by the Germans, but this was achieved at the cost of more than 3,000 British soldiers dead, wounded or missing. The dead included Henry Strang and James Pollock.

Henry and James were both killed as their battalions

attempted to repulse the German offensive on the River Yser. The war diary says that 16th Battalion made a successful raid on enemy trenches on 5 July. On that day two other ranks were killed, one wounded and one missing and another man was wounded the following day. Henry Strang was one of the men who died on 5 July. He was buried in the Ramscappelle Road Military Cemetery which was created in that same month.

James Pollock was probably killed on the front line on 15 July although he is buried in the Coxyde Military Cemetery. The village of Coxyde (now Koksijde) was about seven miles behind the Allied line and was used for rest billets. The cemetery became the most important of the Commonwealth cemeteries on the Belgian coast.

Henry Strang was nineteen when he died at Nieuwpoort and James Pollock was twenty-one. They had survived nearly two years of carnage on the Western Front. Like Bobby Barr and Bertie McDougall, their lives had run in close parallel, and the synchronicity of their deaths is poignant.

29

Young Men from the Hill

William Speirs Barr
Captain, 18th Battalion, Highland Light Infantry

George Jackson
Captain, 18th Battalion, Highland Light Infantry

Bridge of Weir before the war was no less inegalitarian than other parts of British society. Social hierarchy existed in a form that is almost inconceivable today.

Respect was owed to the holder of an office: a judge, a military commander, even a cabinet minister. The office created the need for respect, regardless of the merits of the person who held the office. Today almost the opposite is the case, and there is pretty much an assumption that office-holders are not up to the job, an assumption rebutted only if she or he demonstrates the contrary. That was not so in 1914: to criticise the office-holder was subversive and dangerous. It is interesting that senior military officers were awarded a special celebrity. In the South African War and to an extent in the Great War, their images were collected as cigarette-cards, like those of footballers later in the century.

So, in a desirable and comfortable setting such as Bridge of Weir, there was a system of class distinction on which this narrative has not yet touched in any depth. It is necessary to acknowledge the fact and force of its existence as part of the web of society of the time.

The young men from the big houses up the hill were officer class. They were often educated at Paisley Grammar School or one of the private schools in Glasgow and then Glasgow University. Typically they were in an officer cadet corps at school and joined the Territorial Army before the outbreak of war. The names on the village war memorials include twelve officers.

The Third Statistical Account of Scotland was published in 1962. The entries are written for the most part by the parish ministers, and the entry for Bridge of Weir was written in 1953 and revised in 1959 by the minister of St Machar's, the Reverend William M. McCartney. He commented sadly that despite the beauty of the landscape, where otters compete with man in hunting grayling and trout, there was a division within the village; on the south of the railway line is 'The Hill', wealthy and privileged, whereas '[n]orth of the railway line stands the village . . . united as a proletariat'.

As the minister for the whole of the parish, with his church positioned exactly on the fault-line between the two communities, he would have been well qualified to assess the mood of the village. But he was writing forty years after the end of the Great War, and in the inter-war years consciousness of class developed in Central Scotland. Social divisions were embittered by economic conditions and the consequent political developments. The Liberal party was largely displaced by the Labour Party and militant Red Clydeside.

Happily that sense of division had resolved itself when the present writers first knew the village, and is quite absent today. The village is now much more homogeneous in every way. Similarly, 1914 was not like 1953. Harmony generally prevailed. Before the war class distinction very certainly existed, but it was not necessarily, and certainly not overtly, resented and was moderated by the old Scottish egalitarianism and, in a small village, by a sense of communal responsibility. All the same, in visualising Bridge of Weir in 1914, the significance of class must be remembered, with its sense of hierarchy. It surprises us today that even a modest household would employ a maid, very often another domestic servant, a gardener and even sometimes a chauffeur.

Within the army of the First World War the class structure was pretty immutable. There was an officer class and, with exceptions that became more common as the war went on, one did not join it or get promoted beyond the rank of NCO unless one came from an appropriate background.

There are no officers on the Bridge of Weir memorials from a family which was not professional or wealthy: the fathers of the twelve officers were merchants, businessmen and professionals. That is not to say that the life of an officer was an easy one. Junior officers on the Western Front led by example and were picked out as targets by the enemy in order to leave troops leaderless. Infantry captains and lieutenants had a shorter life expectancy than any other men on the front line. Officers themselves could be treated with condescension. Subalterns – Lieutenants and Second Lieutenants – were often made to feel like schoolboys by more senior officers, not allowed, for instance to speak until spoken to in the mess, not allowed to drink spirits. Pretty intolerable for men who risked their lives for their regiments. There was also an enormous social gulf between the smart regiments and the more ordinary, and perhaps more agreeable, units in which the Bridge of Weir officers served.

Speirs Barr, the brother of Fred and Lyle, who had died in 1915 and 1916 respectively, and **George Jackson,** the brother of Andrew, the young motor-cyclist who died before seeing action, were two of the twelve officers. They had similar backgrounds. Their fathers were successful businessmen. Speirs and George were established in their occupations when war broke out. Speirs did not go into the family surveying business but became an iron broker after serving an apprenticeship with an iron and steel merchant. George went from Glasgow University to work for his sugar-merchant father.

In peacetime both young men were in the Territorial Army and they were accordingly amongst the first non-regular soldiers to be mobilised. By November 1914 both were in France serving initially as privates in the 1st/9th (Glasgow Highland) Battalion Territorial Force of the Highland Light Infantry. They were joined by another Bridge of Weir man, Andrew Balfour, whose brother George's death leading a charge on the Somme in 1916 has already been described. Speirs Barr, George Jackson and Andrew Balfour knew each other well as young men from the same part of the same village, and found themselves in the same battalion of the same regiment. All three became captains in the 18th HLI. In view of their family losses, none of them would have had any illusions about what service in France involved.

George Jackson saw serious active service during the early years of the war but in the months leading up to his death he was a staff officer. Speirs Barr seems to have stayed with the battalion throughout 1916, when he was involved in some of the fiercest fighting on the Somme, including the battles of Albert and Bazelin, the capture of High Wood and the assaults on the Boritska and Dewdrop trenches. Although their battalion had suffered heavy casualties, Speirs Barr and George Jackson survived for more than thirty months on the Western Front.

The 18th Battalion HLI had been established in Glasgow on 26 February 1915 as a bantam battalion. Bantam battalions took their name from the small, tough and aggressive fighting cock. The minimum height for army service was five feet three inches and prior to the establishment of these units, many short volunteers were turned away in the first wave of patriotic fervour in 1914. The Member of Parliament for Birkenhead, Alfred Bigland (history does not record his height) pressed the War Office to form a battalion of men who were smaller than the army's minimum height but otherwise fit for service. The suggestion was approved and a few days later thousands of short men had volunteered. Many of these volunteers had already been rejected as too short. A significant number were coal miners. Even before the battalion reached France the 18th had acquired the nickname 'Devil Dwarfs'. Early in 1917 the bantam battalions were abandoned and those already established ceased to apply any height requirements, though the 18th, like other bantam battalions, retained a core of short men.

The battalion was stationed in the Somme sector. The Germans had fallen back to the strongly fortified Hindenburg Line leaving their old front line to the Allies. Villages, hamlets and farms previously in the German sector were now occupied by the Allies and cemeteries for the German war dead were extended or reconfigured to take British bodies.

Speirs Barr died of wounds in these operations. It is not known how he came to be wounded. War Diaries for the sector report enemy shelling intermittently on most days in the second half of May 1917 and daily patrols by both sides. A few men were killed and wounded by enemy shells and some patrols went out and did not return. Speirs had been home on leave in October 1916 and married Isobel Gilmour, a Bridge of Weir girl, but the following month he was back fighting on the Somme. When he married, Speirs had seen enough of the war to know that his life was fragile: only seven months later his wife was a widow. Speirs Barr is buried in one of the graveyards taken over from the Germans, the Fins British Cemetery at Sorel-le-Grand.

His death was reported in the *Paisley and Renfrewshire Gazette* on 2 June 1917:

A FAMILY'S SACRIFICE –
THREE BROTHERS KILLED

Captain William Speirs Barr, who has died of his wounds, was the fifth son of the late Mr James Barr, C.E., Rockcliff, Bridge of Weir. He was educated at Glasgow Academy and followed the business of iron broker. A private in the H.L.I. when war broke out, he was immediately mobilised and went to France in November 1914 where he has been continuously except for a brief spell in 1915 when home for his commission. In October last he married Isobel Florence daughter of Mr William D. Gilmour, Glencloy, Bridge of Weir. Captain Barr is the third son of the family to make the supreme sacrifice. His brother Mr F. T. Barr also of the Glasgow Highlanders was killed at Cuinchy in February 1915 and his other brother Mr J. L. Barr died of wounds received at the Somme last July. Another brother is at present on service in France. Captain Barr was within a few days of his 23rd birthday when he met his death.

In pitifully rapid succession Mary Barr had lost her husband and three sons; she feared for her fourth. Her response was to throw herself into raising money for the war effort. She did not survive the war and died at Rockcliff on 6 September 1918 aged sixty-six. Had she lost the will to live?

Captain George Jackson had been needed as a staff officer. In the expectation of a short war, the Staff College had been closed soon after the outbreak of hostilities. Because of that, and even more because of the increasing scale of the war, there was throughout a critical lack of staff officers on whom the increasingly complex task of planning depended. Contrary to popular myth many, perhaps most, staff officers, could not help but feel that their duty lay on the front line. Jackson volunteered to go back to his men and rejoined the 18th Battalion at the Front for only a few days before he died on 25 August 1917. He died in the same week as five other Bridge of Weir men were killed further north at Third Ypres.

At the time his own battalion was in the Guillemont Farm trenches due south of a feature known as the Knoll. At 04.00 on 25 August the Guillemont Farm trenches came under fire from artillery and trench mortars. By 04.15 the bombardment became intense. All the Lewis guns were damaged or destroyed and there were heavy casualties. German infantry then attacked the farm and entered the British front line trench. British casualties were seven officers and 153 other ranks. Captain Jackson was one of those officers. He was buried in the Villers-Faucon Communal Cemetery.

The colonel of the regiment wrote to George's parents:

> On the 25th the enemy attacked the position we recently took from him. Your son organised a counter-attack and led it most gallantly and was killed in so doing. He died a soldier's death leading his men. He was a splendid officer and one in whom the men had implicit confidence. Please accept from me, and all our officers and men our most sincere sympathy in the great loss which you have sustained. You have lost a son of whom you may well be proud and the country has lost a brave soldier and a good leader.

George Jackson was twenty-five.

30

Third Ypres, July to November 1917

As we have seen, the Somme did not do Haig's reputation much harm at the time. Terrible as that first day had been, it was regarded as a price that had to be paid. The prolongation of the battle attracted some criticism, and the continuing lack of breakthrough increasingly worried politicians. But though Lloyd George was becoming increasingly sceptical, Haig was able to persuade him that in 1917 one more offensive could win the war.

This offensive was the Third Battle of Ypres. We have seen when we looked at Nieuwpoort that the original plan for this offensive was to have been a sophisticated combined naval, air and military operation, prefiguring in some ways the 1944 invasion of Normandy, but that in the event the naval and air elements were removed, and Haig was left to fight an unsupported army battle.

The flaw in Third Ypres lay in the mistaken belief that Germany was about to crack, a belief which Charteris, Haig's Intelligence Chief, fostered, and which Haig accepted unquestioningly.

The battle started well enough. Second Army was commanded by Sir Herbert Plumer. 'Old Plum and Apple Jam', or 'Daddy' Plumer, looked like a caricature of a music-hall general, an exaggeratedly whiskered Colonel Blimp, but he and his Chief of Staff, Harington, were consummate professionals. They planned meticulously and sought to win limited and attainable objectives by a series of controlled advances which depended on intricate staff work, rather than dash and luck. In the weeks prior to the offensive British tunnellers had buried almost one million pounds of explosive and the assault was announced by an enormous explosion under Messines Ridge, blowing German trenches and men high into the sky. Over 7,000 Germans were taken prisoner as the British secured a foothold on the ridge to the east of Ypres.

Plumer had planned for a series of discrete, achievable advances. His proposal for the follow-up to the assault on the Messines Ridge, for instance, was an advance of only some 1,500 yards. Haig, by contrast, wanted an advance extending to between twenty and thirty miles. Plumer stood up well to Haig, frequently simply by ignoring him. Haig respected but never quite understood him. So Haig entrusted the follow-up to the mining of the Ridge to Hubert Gough, a much simpler and less able man, a 'thrusting commander'.

Under Gough the early stages of Third Ypres were not unsuccessful. The main attack on 31 July, for example, was an example of the learning curve beginning to deliver. There was cooperation between all arms, engineers, artillery and infantry. The artillery tactics were by now elaborate. There was a creeping barrage, plus a standing barrage which lifted to fit in with the advances of the creeping barrage. Fifteenth (Scottish) Division moved forward with Bridge of Weir men in the vanguard. Eight Scottish infantry battalions in the 44th and 45th Brigades took their turns at the Front.

Unfortunately, the Germans had also learned, abandoning linear defence in favour of defence in depth, something of which Britain had not yet formed an appreciation. Their front line was lightly defended and relatively easily taken but the insurgent troops found themselves severely vulnerable, contained in a box by enfilading machine-gun outposts and facing an intimidating second line.

There were nine separate battles, collectively known as Third Ypres, before the capture of the village of Passchendaele, whose name became associated with the whole campaign, on 6 November and the closing down of the battle on 12 November.

Very heavy rain had started to fall on the afternoon of 31 July and with only short breaks it continued for a whole month. This weather was a result of bad luck and not bad planning: the rainfall affecting the first month of the offensive was more than double the average, over five times the amount for the same period in 1915 and in 1916. All the same, heavy bombardment of an area that famously needed a sophisticated drainage system was always going to create problems.

Haig recorded in a Despatch that by mid-August the low-lying, clay soil, torn by shells and flooded by rain, had turned into a succession of vast, muddy pools. The valleys of the choked and overflowing streams were speedily transformed into long stretches of bog, impassable except by a few well-defined tracks, which were pre-registered by the enemy's artillery. To quit these tracks was to risk death by drowning.

It was not only men, horses and mules which struggled. Tanks and guns became immobile as they stuck fast in the mud. When guns were fired the recoil drove them into the mire. Shells came up to the batteries covered in slime which had to be cleaned off. From their high point on Passchendaele Ridge the Germans could observe every movement in the Allied positions. In about two months from 7 June to 4 August the British advanced two miles and were now struggling to move at all in the quagmire. The original plan for a staged leap-frogging infantry assault with artillery support was extinguished by the incessant rain as once well-tilled fields turned to bog.

Plumer's original plan had envisaged that the offensive could be called off if it ran into trouble. But, convinced that Germany was about to collapse, Haig did not call off operations. Rain, mud, mounting casualties, fierce enemy resistance and very slow progress did not deter him.

For the next phase of the battle, Haig switched Plumer and Gough round, Plumer and Second Army in the lead, Gough and Fifth Army in support. The increasing losses persuaded Haig to accept Plumer's step-by-step approach; he even agreed to suspend the fighting so that Plumer could prepare the next advance. The weather improved in September and spirits rose.

A three-week artillery bombardment preceded an infantry attack on 20 September when 65,000 Allied infantry advanced on an eight-mile front, screened by heavy mist and ferocious shelling. The infantry kept close behind the artillery barrage and quickly overran the German outposts. By midday four advanced divisions had taken the Gheluvelt Plateau. Although the Germans counter-attacked, Allied shelling was so accurate and effective that all positions gained were held. Following modest success on the Menin Road, Plumer launched an assault on Polygon Wood six days later. Within the week Polygon Wood and Broodseinde were in Allied hands and with them came control of the ridge east of Ypres.

But the British troops were now close to exhaustion. More-over, Russia's withdrawal from the war released German troops to reinforce the Ypres sector. There were three unsuccessful British assaults on Passchendaele Ridge in late October before it was captured by British and Canadian troops on 6 November. At last Haig closed the battle down.

He never subsequently doubted that the campaign had short-ened the war by wearing down German morale. He also justified it as taking pressure off the French, shaken as they were by Verdun and the 'mutinies'. Later some German commentators did attest to the damage done to their army in Third Ypres.

The original concept of combined land and sea operations had not been without merit, an intelligent way of capitalising on unused British seapower. And Haig can be excused for the prolongation of the campaign to a very limited degree because of the exaggerated stories about imminent German collapse which Charteris fed him (but Charteris fed his Chief only what Haig wanted to hear). All the same, even Haig's loyalist supporters admit that Third Ypres went on far, far too long. And yet there remains a question posed by Tim Harington, Plumer's very able Chief of Staff, that no one has been able to answer. Haig is not seriously criticised for launching the battle. Once it was launched, asked Harington, '*Where,* short of the Ridge, could the offensive have been halted?'

The names of 54,000 unidentified Allied war dead killed before 16 August 1917 are on the Menin Gate. Another 35,000, killed after 16 August, are on the Tyne Cot Memorial at Zonnebeke, marking the furthest point of advance by the Allied army until the last weeks of the war a year later.

British casualties were more than 300,000, Germany's about 260,000. It is estimated that the Third Battle of Ypres cost the lives of thirty-five men for every metre of land gained. Seven Bridge of Weir men died in the battle. Their lives thus bought Britain 200 centimetres of ground. We now tell the tale of their deaths.

31

Third Ypres: The Men

David Anderson McGregor
Private, 18th Battalion, King's Liverpool Regiment

William Millar
Gunner, Royal Field Artillery

Adam McLeod Walton
Private, 11th Battalion, Argyll and Sutherland Highlanders

James Woodrow
Private, 8th Battalion, Seaforth Highlanders

William Candlish
Private, 6th Battalion, Cameron Highlanders

John Begley
Gunner, Royal Field Artillery

George William Fisher
Second Lieutenant, 1/4 Battalion, Suffolk Regiment

David Anderson McGregor was sixteen when war was declared, living in Gryffe View, Bridge of Weir, with his grandmother and aunt. When he was seventeen, he volunteered and joined the

Army Cyclist Corps. At some point later he was transferred to The King's (Liverpool) Regiment. In 1917 his battalion, the 18th, formed part of the 21st Brigade, 30th Division, which took part in the Battle of Pilckem Ridge, the first offensive in the Third Battle of Ypres.

David's body was never recovered and he is assumed to have died on 31 July 1917, the first day of the battle. His name is recorded on the Ypres (Menin Gate) Memorial, one of the 54,000 men whose bodies were vaporised. At the age of nineteen years and two months, David Anderson McGregor is the youngest on the Bridge of Weir War Memorial.

Gunner **William Millar** was twenty-three when he died. He is one of 1,600 men buried in the Bard Cottage Cemetery near Ypres. His father, Robert Millar, was a carting contractor who often took luggage from Bridge of Weir railway station to the big houses up the hill. Many of the better-off in the expanding village were merchants who made regular business trips abroad and young William helped to transport cabin trunks and suitcases. William was the eldest son in a family of nine children. He started working for his father as soon as he was old enough to be useful and when the war came father and son were carting together. When William joined the artillery, he was almost certainly conscripted.

William Millar was killed on 18 August when both sides were engaged in relentless artillery bombardment. He was serving in C Battery, 255th (Highland) Brigade of the Royal Field Artillery. This was a howitzer battery firing some of the biggest and most powerful guns in service in the war. The Mark 1 siege howitzer weighed fifteen tons and took thirty-six hours to dismantle. It could fire a shell of high explosives almost one kilometre.

Privates **Adam McLeod Walton** and **James Woodrow** were both killed on 22 August. They are remembered on the Tyne Cot Memorial. Adam enlisted in Paisley on 23 March 1917 when he was still in his eighteenth year and recruits were badly needed. Volunteers in 1914 and 1915 often spent twelve months on basic training before going to the Western Front, but by 1917 there was an urgent need to fill gaps in the front line. Adam arrived in France on 20 July 1917, just four months after enlisting, and died thirty-three days later. Eleventh Battalion, the Argyll and Sutherland Highlanders, in which he served was involved in some of the fiercest fighting around Hill 35. About a year later the local newspaper reported:

> Private Adam McLeod Walton A & S H who resided at Barngill and was reported missing on 22 August 1917, has now been officially presumed killed on or about that date. Private Walton, who was only nineteen years of age when reported missing, was prior to enlisting in the employment of Mr Hugh Reyburn, Bridge of Weir as an apprentice currier.

Adam's army record says that at his death he had one brother, no sisters, four nieces, four nephews, two uncles and three aunts. He grew up at Ladeside Place with his widowed grandmother, Mary Walton, his mother Jessie, who had been just nineteen when he was born, two aunts and his uncle David, who was his senior by eleven years. The three younger women all worked as factory girls in the thread mill.

There is some confusion about Adam's name in army records, census returns, newspapers and memorials because he was illegitimate. Adam's father appears to have been called McLeod, but the boy used his mother's name of Walton. The newspaper report is uncharacteristic in making no reference to Adam's next of kin. He appears on the village memorial as Adam McLeod.

James Woodrow was the eldest son of a self-employed joiner with two brothers and two younger sisters. All five children were born in Bridge of Weir and the family lived at Burngill before moving to Ladeside Place. James volunteered on 28 August

1915 and he was twenty-six when he was killed serving in the 8th Battalion of the Seaforth Highlanders. The battalion was in some of the fiercest fighting in July and August and led the attack on Frezenberg Ridge where James lost his life. Eighth Seaforth Highlanders lost about two-thirds of their men killed and wounded at Third Ypres.

Henry Woodrow, a younger brother of James, was a butcher to trade who enlisted at the age of eighteen. He suffered multiple gunshot wounds in July 1918 and spent forty days in hospital. Henry survived the war but his army service record includes a medical opinion that he was 'much terrified', a peculiar description of a wholly understandable state. Henry Woodrow must have been one of many survivors who carried the physical and mental scars of war. The Woodrow and Walton families were near neighbours for many years and shared the grief of losing sons on the same day in the same battle.

William Candlish was killed in action with the 6th Battalion of the Cameron Highlanders between Vampir Farm and Beck House on 24 August. His body was never found but his name is on the Tyne Cot Memorial. After a spell in the reserve trenches William's battalion had returned to the line on Frezenberg Ridge on 17 August to sit for five days in torrential rain before attacking continuously for the next two against heavy German resistance. William died in that prolonged attack, his experience of war limited to the almost unimaginable combination of elements that made up the misery of Third Ypres.

William Candlish was almost certainly a 1916 conscript. He was taken from a family that consisted of his parents, his sister Mary and his twin brother James. William was the younger twin. The boys were born either side of midnight and thus unusually had different dates of birth. When he was killed in action William was twenty-four and unmarried. He had already embarked on a career as a shipping clerk.

Life for the Candlish family had been comfortable. William's father, James, was a grain merchant. They lived in a series of large houses – in Helensburgh on the north side of the Clyde, where all three children were born, in Kelvinside in Glasgow and finally the family moved to Bridge of Weir in 1912, when James bought Benvue from his brother George, who emigrated to Canada with his family.

In August 1917 one of the officers in 6th Cameron Highlanders serving with William Candlish, was Captain Philip Christison. He went on to be an outstanding commander in the Burma Campaign in the Second World War, and was finally the senior general in the British Army. He is a rare example of a man who chose to decline a field-marshal's baton, but he was so closely identified with the great commanders of the Second World War, like Slim, that he was known as the 'Last of the Marshals'. He was a soldier's soldier. His diaries of the First World War record something of the awfulness of the conditions that Candlish and his comrades endured at Third Ypres:

> Rain, mud, gas shelling and constant bombardment. I had never seen such a scene nor thought it possible. The whole country was water-logged, small spits of muddy land joined shell holes great and small, full of water; many with dead men and animals, the stench of which made us retch. In the blinding rain in the dark, heavily weighted men would slip into a shell crater and drown in gas-contaminated mud often unheeded by their comrades. I found I lost three in this way when we reached the front line.

Even moving in and out of reserve was ghastly:

> At 01.00 hours we left and marched round the south side of Ypres, crossed the notorious Menin Road and up 'C' track to Cambridge Trench. We had to don respirators from then on as we struggled, heavy laden, along greasy,

slippery duckboards or knee deep in glutinous mud, trying to avoid falling into shell craters filled with water. It was pitch dark that night and, what with wearing respirators and being under continuous shell fire of all kinds, it was one of the worst reliefs remembered. I made each man hold onto the haversack worn on the back of the man in front. As we progressed slowly along some shells fell in our trench causing casualties and confusion. The dead were heaved into shell holes and the wounded lifted out of the trench and left lying on the surface to await the stretcher bearers. One leading NCO slipped off the track into a huge shell crater full of water. He just disappeared and could not be got out as the sides of the crater were just glutinous mud.

Gunner **John Begley** served in 103rd Brigade, part of 23rd Division, Royal Field Artillery, in turn part of Plumer's Second Army. He died of wounds on 26 September. It seems likely that John was injured by German shelling in the lead-up to the attack on the Menin Road or during the five-day artillery shoot-out between 20 and 25 September.

John was the youngest of eight children and the son of a foreman stonemason. He followed his father's trade whilst most of his brothers and sisters worked in the tannery or thread mill. One sister, Ellen, was a schoolteacher. The impression is of a hard-working, close and mutually supportive family. For many years the Begleys lived in a three-roomed flat in Co-operative Terrace. As some children left home, grandchildren filled up the space and by 1911 the widowed mother of John Begley was living with seven children, including her widowed son James and his four children.

John Begley was a bachelor. He volunteered and enlisted in the Royal Field Artillery on 21 November 1914. In July 1915 he was at home on leave having received a nasty kick on the knee from a horse. The local newspaper reported that he was 'making good progress and hopes to proceed to the Front shortly'. Artillerymen worked closely with heavy horses which pulled their guns and a kick from a Clydesdale, Shire or Suffolk Punch could be a serious injury. Heavy horses have a placid nature but subjected to shellfire they could become nervous and skittish.

When he died of wounds on 26 September 1917, John Begley was thirty. John and his family were Roman Catholics and attended St Fillan's Church in Houston. A stained glass window in the church commemorates him.

George Fisher, single, like all the six Bridge of Weir men who died at Third Ypres, and a volunteer, survived the official battle, only to die in Flanders shortly afterwards, in the sporadic exchanges of rifle and shell fire which went on whether or not a battle was underway.

His connection with Bridge of Weir was not as close as some. His father was a stockbroker originally from Paisley who had married a Bridge of Weir girl in 1888. He then emigrated to South Africa, where George and a brother, William, were born.

George came back from South Africa to Scotland to study law at Glasgow University in 1911, and stayed with his mother's sister, a widow named Wilhelmina Brown. The 1911 Census records him as a boarder in her house, Cruachan on Ranfurly Hill. He was then nineteen. In the house was another boarder, Frederick Blair, a clerk in a firm of East India merchants, his aunt, her daughters Mary, twenty-one, Anna, nineteen, Williamina, six, and sons William, twelve, and George, eleven, with their live-in domestic servant, Marion Clayton, twenty. A lively, youthful household.

When he graduated, George went to London to take articles and there he joined the Inns of Court Officers Training Corps in February 1916, being commissioned as second lieutenant in February 1917 in the Suffolk Regiment. The regiment saw action in the First and Second Battles of the Scarpe, which were part of the Arras offensive, in operations on the Flanders coast, and later in the Third Battle of Ypres, in particular the battles of Menin Court Ridge and Polygon Wood in September 1917. George survived all of these, but was killed in November at the very end of Third Ypres. He was buried in the Tyne Cot Cemetery. George Fisher's name is not on the main village war memorial, but it is on the war memorial of the parish church, now St Machar's Ranfurly.

His cousin Anna Brown was the sweetheart of Fred Barr, and as we have seen was the beneficiary of his will, which was made in December 1914, just two months before he was killed. She never married. She inherited Cruachan in 1944 when she was fifty-two.

32

A More Exotic War

Henry Andrew
Private, Army Service Corps

Walter McWilliam
Sapper, Royal Engineers

James Burns
Private, Army Service Corps

The Great War was fought in many theatres. The vast bulk of the British effort was on the Western Front. But Salonika, Gallipoli, Mesopotamia, Palestine and Italy were also significant, and indeed the empires of the combatant nations extended worldwide.

Volunteers and conscripts from home were not exempt from exotic assignments. There, service did not involve the mud of France or Flanders, but it could offer other horrors. Death was less likely from a sniper's bullet or a shrapnel shell than from malaria, cholera, heatstroke or tropical fever. Disease was a daily hazard, and that was what claimed the lives of three young men consigned to far-flung conflict whose names are on the Bridge of Weir memorial.

Henry Andrew was the eldest of a family of seven. His father Henry and mother Janet were natives of Ayrshire, and Henry, senior, was a jobbing gardener who spent his early years working in a number of large houses in Ayrshire and Renfrewshire, finally settling in Bridge of Weir where the Ranfurly villas provided ample work opportunities. Although they lived only a few yards from Freeland Church, Henry and the family were members of Ranfurly Church, the other Bridge of Weir United Free Church.

Young Henry started work at thirteen as a grocer's message boy and later became an ironmonger's assistant in Falkirk. He was thirty-six when the war began but nonetheless he volunteered for active service and was assigned to the Army Service Corps. The ASC provided the food, equipment and ammunition for the fighting soldiers. Their feats of logistics were part of the achievements on which victory would rest. But better pay, conditions and comparative safety did not endear them to the infantry for whom the ASC acronym meant 'Ally Sloper's Cavalry' (Ally Sloper was a hapless, large-nosed comic-strip character of the time, habitually lazy and work-dodging). When the ASC earned its 'Royal' prefix in 1918, the new acronym was immediately translated as 'Run Away, Someone's Coming'. Unfair.

At its peak, the ASC had 10,547 officers and 315,334 men. It also employed tens of thousands of Indian, Egyptian, Chinese and other native labourers, carriers and storemen. This vast organisation gets scant attention in most histories of the war.

Henry was in the Mechanical Transport Reserve. He was given his first overseas posting in 1915, arriving in Egypt in April. Just as Egypt was the springboard for operations at Gallipoli in 1915, so it was for the Franco–British force that landed at Salonika in Greece to reinforce the Serbs in their fight against the Bulgarians.

Henry Andrew was not short of Scottish companions in Salonika (or Thessalonika, and now Thessaloniki). There were eleven Scottish infantry battalions, around 10,000 men, and so many Scots medical staff in the 42nd General Hospital on the outskirts of Thessalonika that Christopher Murray Grieve, then a sergeant in the Royal Army Medical Corps but later better known as the poet Hugh McDiarmid, nicknamed it 'Thistleonica'. There were also volunteer units of Elsie Inglis's Scottish Women's Hospitals. Henry, like Grieve, was to experience care in these hospitals first-hand as a victim of dysentery or malaria. These diseases were endemic in the area and proved difficult to eradicate. Sufferers were prone to re-infection, and the worst cases had to be evacuated. Total British battle casualties in the two years of the Salonika campaign were 18,000. This was dwarfed by the 481,000 that succumbed to illness.

Henry was invalided home. The journey home in late 1916 must have been an appalling experience for sick and dying men. Sea conditions, especially in the Atlantic, were far from benign at that time of year. He had stop-offs in hospitals in Malta and Liverpool before reaching Paisley, and the welcome opportunity for his family to see him. But he was beyond saving. Complications set in, operations were required and in his weakened state he did not survive. He died a few days after the New Year. The loss of the eldest son was to be the first of several hard knocks to the Andrew family.*

Walter McWilliam was the son of an office porter in Glasgow who had been born in Ireland. Walter was brought up in Glasgow, in later childhood by his mother Annie after his father's early death. It appears that Walter's mother took the family to Windsor Place, Bridge of Weir, probably in the latter half of 1916 when she and daughter Janet joined Freeland Church.

Walter, however, remained in Glasgow. He was there in April 1916, when he married Jessie Urquhart. Walter was thirty-three and Jessie thirty-two. Their marriage was made by declaration in presence of witnesses, under warrant by the sheriff, the

---

* See Chapters 37 and 41.

procedure accelerated because Walter was about to be sent abroad.

He had worked as a railway ticket collector but later became an inspector in the National Telephone Company. This civilian background suited him for a Signals Company of the Royal Engineers, and that is where he went.

When Turkey looked certain to enter the war on the side of the Central Powers, Britain sent an expeditionary force from India (Force D) to Mesopotamia (now Iraq). By November 1914 it had secured Basra, and beaten off a Turkish counter-attack. The Force then pressed on in an attempt to take Baghdad. It got within thirty miles of the city by November 1915, but then met superior numbers of Turkish reinforcements transferred from Gallipoli.

A British-Indian force under Major-General Charles Townshend withdrew to Kut-al-Amarah. One hundred and forty-seven days later, Townshend finally surrendered. It had been the longest siege the British Army had endured, easily beating the nearest contender, Ladysmith (121 days, during the South African War). The aftermath was terrible (though not for Townshend, whom the Turks allowed a very comfortable confinement). More than 13,000 British and Indian troops were taken prisoner. They were separated from their officers. Their water bottles and boots were taken from them and they were driven through the desert at bayonet point, stragglers raped or murdered. When they reached Baghdad the American consul tried to come to their aid and was killed.

They were then pushed on to Anatolia, on what one of the men called an extended massacre. When they got there they worked in appalling conditions in chain gangs on the railway. Of 2,592 Britons taken prisoner at Kut, only 837 survived the war. The Indian prisoners were treated better: 7,423 survived out of 10,486.

This was a heavy blow to British prestige in the Middle East, and preparations were put in hand to prepare a British-Indian counter-offensive. Reinforcements, including the Black Watch, Seaforths and HLI, were assembled and a renewed offensive began in December 1916 led by General Sir Frederick Stanley Maude. It seems likely that this was when Walter joined the Mesopotamia campaign.

In February 1917, Kut was recaptured, and Maude pressed onwards up the Tigris. It was the height of the Mesopotamian summer with shade temperatures of 50° Celsius. Baghdad fell on 11 March 1917 and became the base for Maude's army of occupation. Walter was attached to GHQ with the Army Signals Company. As on the Salonika Front, casualties from sickness in Mesopotamia outnumbered those in battle. The excessive heat was hard on British conscripts, exacerbated by a lack of proper guidance and equipment to help deal with it.

It was thought at the time that the spine was vulnerable to the heat, and soldiers in Mesopotamia often had to wear spinal pads, which were uncomfortable and of no value at all. It was heatstroke that claimed Walter's life on 11 July 1917. The telephone inspector from Glasgow ended his days in an unfamiliar city of mosques and minarets. Unlike Henry Andrew, he did not have the comfort of his family around him when he died. He died 6,000 kilometres apart from his young wife and has since lain in Baghdad War Cemetery. Though he may never have lived in Bridge of Weir, his connection with the village meant that his name would be incised on its war memorial.

The war in Mesopotamia continued. Even at the time it received far less attention than the Western Front, and now it is almost forgotten. And yet it was an important war. On the Allied side it was fought almost entirely by the British, by soldiers of the British and Indian armies. If there had been more of the former and fewer of the latter it might have been better known. About 400,000 men fought, sustaining casualties, including those missing and taken prisoner, of about 93,000. It linked to the offensives in Egypt and Palestine, which together culminated in a series of important victories, including the taking of Damascus and Jerusalem. It destroyed the Ottoman Empire and placed Britain in a position of great power in the Middle East. But for it, the state of Israel would not exist.

James Burns, Ayrshire-born and brought up in Glasgow, the brother of Robert Burns who died at Arras, found work as a domestic groom with the Ogilvie family in Houston and later as coachman and chauffeur at Gryffe Castle, Bridge of Weir, which was then let to William Alexander Campbell, the cousin of Sir Henry Campbell Bannerman, prime minister until 1906 and originally from Glasgow. James was living in Gryffe Castle Cottage with his younger brother Robert when the war started. Like Henry Andrew, James was assigned to the Mechanical Transport Reserve of the Army Service Corps. His experience as a chauffeur had obvious relevance. Henry Andrew's travels, exotic as they were, were eclipsed by James's. He was sent to the most distant posting in the army – British East Africa.

German East Africa (now Burundi, Rwanda and mainland Tanzania) marched with British East Africa (Kenya). Hostilities began just a few days after war was declared. The German Askari forces were commanded by Lieutenant-Colonel von Lettow-Vorbeck. Although outnumbered, he fought a campaign of guerrilla warfare, raids and occasional small battles, with the aim of keeping British troops away from the Western Front. His small force kept fighting right through the war, even though it lost control of German East Africa in 1916. General Smuts, a former Boer commander, but now a loyal servant of the Empire, was charged with facing Lettow-Vorbeck and chased him throughout the region, but Lettow-Vorbeck chose to avoid the larger pursuing forces, at the cost of conceding territory. Smuts never caught Lettow-Vorbeck. Instead, he was called to loftier responsibilities and joined the War Cabinet in London.

James Burns played his part in the campaign, probably as a driver/mechanic attached to GHQ in Dar Es Salaam.

The principal danger was exposure to tropical diseases. He succumbed to dysentery on 8th October 1917. News of his death did not reach his church in Bridge of Weir until January 1918 when his name appeared in the Death and Interment Register: *Burns, James; Pte. Motor Transport; Gryfe Castle Cottage; Died in service in East Africa; Jany 1918; aged 24.* Robert had died five months earlier.

33

A Pacifist Interlude: Dugald Semple, Simple Lifer and Conscientious Objector

Not all Bridge of Weir's younger men fought in the war. We have seen how 'attestation' was followed in 1916 by conscription. The conscription legislation allowed exemption for those objecting to service on grounds of conscience.

The provision for 'conscientious objection' was the response to protests against compulsory service from those who disagreed with the 1916 Military Service Acts on political or ideological grounds. A notable west of Scotland leader of such opinion was John Maclean, a Marxist and revolutionary socialist. He was a Glasgow schoolmaster until he was sacked following arrest under the Defence of the Realm Act. Thereafter he became a powerful lecturer and speaker, to the authorities a dangerous agitator. He called for an end to the war, and for a Bolshevik revolution.

The *Paisley and Renfrewshire Gazette* of 8 January 1916 reported on a lecture he gave in the 'Co.[operative] Hall' in Paisley under the auspices of the British Socialist Party. He gave his talk a religious title, 'Peace on Earth, Goodwill Towards Men', but he told his listeners the Church was preaching hate by supporting war. His speech highlighted the differences between Socialists who had supported the Government and the war and those Socialists who held to internationalist ideals:

The introduction of attestation and conscription made the working-classes of this country wonder what the upshot would be. Many believed that conscription was meant to increase industrial slavery, break the backs of the Trades Unions, and introduce cheap and speeded-up labour.

Maclean was arrested and imprisoned in February 1916 and in April was tried on four charges of sedition and sentenced to three years of penal servitude. He was released in July 1917 after demonstrations that followed the Russian February Revolution. In prison those convicted of sedition could expect a rough time at the hands of patriotic wife-beaters and jingoistic murderers.

In 1918 Maclean was again imprisoned for sedition after a trial in Edinburgh, where he conducted his own defence and made a famous speech from the dock. In Peterhead Prison he went on hunger strike and was force-fed. He was released in December, after the Armistice. When he died in 1923 his funeral is said to have been the largest ever held in Glasgow. The fires of pacifist socialism burned bright in the same west of Scotland that supported disproportionately high levels of volunteering and sacrifice.

At an even more local level another important voice against compulsion was that of Roland Muirhead, the odd-ball Red Clydeside tannery proprietor whom we met in Chapter 2.

Appeals by conscientious objectors and by those seeking exemption on practical grounds were adjudicated by local tribunals. The local press regularly reported these cases, although rarely are the applicants named. On 18 March 1916, for instance, several Bridge of Weir men presented their appeals. A local carter requested exemption for his twenty-four year-old son as he had no one else to help with a contract for the gas works, his other two sons already being in military service. This request was refused. A slater and plasterer from the village said that he supported his mother, a cousin and helped a paralysed uncle, aunt and five children financially. This case was continued so that fuller enquiries could be made. However, the case most fully reported was that of Dugald Semple, known locally as 'The Simple Lifer'.

Dugald Semple was born in 1884, the seventh of eleven children. His father, a Johnstone clothier, was related to the Semples of Lochwinnoch and Belltrees, a notable family, active in Scottish life in mediaeval and late modern times. Dugald obtained a bursary to the Grammar School at Paisley, but did not like it. 'I hated school life with its compulsory attendance and rigid discipline.'

From a young age Dugald had a questioning mind. He worked as a draughtsman, developing his own philosophy by listening to his fellow workers and reading widely. He rejected the type of religion which was central to the lives of his parents and became one of the founders of the Johnstone branch of the Independent Labour Party, promoting the socialist cause at public meetings. He had also become a vegetarian in early adulthood, adopting indeed what appears to have been a vegan diet. His ideas on food were linked to his developing concept of a health-enhancing outdoor lifestyle. This thinking was influenced by camping expeditions he took as a young adult with the Reverend Charles A. Hall, a Swedenborgian Paisley minister. These trips helped him establish a knowledge and love of natural history. A further influence on his simple-living philosophy was Thoreau's *Walden*, the mid-nineteenth-century account of an American experiment in living as part of nature.

Dugald's views on most aspects of life clashed with those of his parents and in his early twenties he left home, initially lodging in Brookfield, a village about two miles to the east of Bridge of Weir. However, he wished to live closer to nature and test out his developing philosophy of the simple life. He negotiated a sub-lease of ground on the inhospitable Linwood

Moss and erected a bell-tent there in August 1907. His living conditions were pared down to bare essentials:

> My personal belongings were almost nil; a large tin box for most of my possessions, a waterproof ground sheet for my heather bed, all of which were under neither lock nor key at any hour of the day.

But he continued to work as an engineering draughtsman as well as lecturing and writing reports on his simple lifestyle and philosophy for publication in local newspapers. With the approach of winter he acquired a redundant 'omnibus' which a horse and a band of men pulled to the site at Linwood. This became his 'Wheelhouse'.

Dugald's press articles and publications made him something of a tourist attraction and he had many visitors to his camp site to see this curiosity. Unfortunately, the owner of the land at Linwood Moss became concerned by the disturbance (especially to game birds) caused by the increasing number of callers, and the sage was given notice to leave.

This led to his move to Bridge of Weir, along with the Wheelhouse, a move made possible by the offer of land by Arthur Muirhead, Roland's brother and the owner of another leather works in the village. Dugald wrote articles and short publications about the natural history of Ladeside, a favourite walk for local people, close to the new location of the Wheelhouse. He continued to work, still walking there and back, but then calculated that he could end his life as a wage-slave, and live on five shillings a week by establishing a garden and growing his own food. He earned money from lectures, his writing and selling postcard pictures of his Wheelhouse. 'I began to sell my thoughts both in writing and lecturing in order to earn a livelihood,' he recorded in his memoirs, *Joy in Living*.

By the time the Great War began Dugald had thus been established for several years as an exotic part of the community in Bridge of Weir. He was a member of the local literary society in which several local notables, including his family, were involved. He had also acquired a second wagon, more easily drawn by a horse, to take him on tours of local towns to lecture on his philosophy of life. As his thinking developed, he distanced himself from the socialist movement, presenting the view that individuals needed to reform themselves before society could be changed.

At the beginning of the war Dugald concentrated his writing and lecturing on nutritious eating at a time when the food supply was increasingly restricted. An example appears in a letter to the *Paisley and Renfrewshire Gazette* in December 1915, under the title 'War-Time Economy'. Here he protests against the advice that the peelings of fruit, vegetables and potatoes should be burned. Instead he extols the nutritious value of cooking and eating potatoes in their skins, and the usefulness as stock of the water in which vegetables have been cooked. With the increasing political importance of economy in food as part of the war effort, Dugald's local lecturing role even began to receive official blessing. In January 1916 he lectured on 'Food for Wartime' in Johnstone Town Hall and in February he was engaged as secretary of the London Vegetarian Society, giving lectures at significant events in England as well as writing extensively.

However, Dugald was never destined to enjoy the warmth of official approval. He was summoned to attend a medical for potential war service. He refused to do this and was called to a military tribunal. He applied to be exempted from military service on the grounds that he was a conscientious objector. His appeal was supported by Roland Muirhead. However, despite his influential backers the appeal was refused and Dugald was assigned to non-combatant service. This normally took the form of work supporting the military effort, such as being a stretcher-bearer at the Front. The report in the *Paisley and Renfrewshire Gazette* records the hearing which took place on 1 April 1916:

> He stated on his application form that war was
> inconsistent with Christian teaching, that war was
> contrary to loving one's enemies, that we must obey God
> rather than man, and that God, who gave life, was the
> only one to take it away. He stated that in his writing
> and lectures he had shown he was always opposed
> to war ... While he would not agree to take non-
> combatant service, he considered he was doing national
> service.

Dugald appealed against the tribunal's decision. He was granted a conditional exemption in May on the basis of his intriguing argument that his lecturing work was of national value to the war effort.

As the exemption was conditional, it came up for review in September 1917. Some of his lecturing work on food economy was described at the tribunal and Dugald, adopting a slightly specious patriotic position, stated that 'he felt it to be his duty to give his services to the country in the best way he was capable of in the present crisis'. The military representative, Captain Cochran Patrick, argued not unreasonably that the lecturing could be carried out by someone over military age. Fortunately for Dugald the tribunal shared his view that his lecturing skills were unique; a further exemption was granted on condition that he continued on food economy.

So Dugald remained active throughout the war years promoting the cause of nutrition. In 1917 he lectured at economy exhibitions in London and wrote articles in the national weekly publication *Food*. He returned to Scotland in the autumn of 1917 and continued lecturing locally.

His residence at the Wheelhouse ended during the war. It was ended by matrimony. In *Living in Liberty – The Wheelhouse Philosophy* he set out his typically uncompromising requirements for a wife: 'My primary idea of a wife is not one whose chief qualification consists in being able to wash, sew or bake apple dumplings . . . [A] wife, too, should be able to bake ideas as well as scones . . .'

On 17 April 1916 he married a widow, Catherine Tuckwell. He was 32. She was 47, but Dugald did not know that, because she gave her age as just 40. Her father, James Graham, was a timber merchant who resided in Bridge of Weir up to his death in 1908. She had married John Tuckwell, a civil engineer, in 1896. He died in 1909 leaving £10,916 and an estate abroad. Catherine lived in a villa in Kilmacolm at the time of her marriage to Dugald. Catherine's son John, known as Ian, served in the war and died on 23 March 1918. He is mentioned on memorials at Arras and Kilmacolm. His stepfather wrote 'He had gone over the top with his men at Bapaume and was never seen again'. What John or Catherine thought of Dugald's conscientious objections is not known. The subject must have been a sensitive one. Dugald and John could not both be right.

Dugald married a woman who could offer him financial security. He appears to have negotiated the change from self-sufficiency on the Thoreau model to being a kept man without difficulty. He recorded that Catherine was a soulmate. She shared his love of outdoor living and his interest in wholesome food. During the war they travelled together as he gave lectures, and she helped prepare recipe leaflets. They spent much of the war in London after their marriage, but then returned to Kilmacolm. The Wheelhouse remained at Bridge of Weir until they moved to a small farm near Beith after the war, where it was stored in the garden. Their new home was named The Wheelhouse: he maintained his position to the end. But one still wonders whether Dugald was simply an old rogue.

34

The German Spring Offensive, 1918

Bridge of Weir had had its worst year of the war in 1917. In the course of that year, twenty-one young men from the village were killed or had gone missing in action. In contrast, the first three months of 1918 were relatively quiet. But it was a brief period of winter respite before the war returned to the drama of its opening months, in two great spasms. The first brought the Entente powers, Britain and France (Russia had made her humiliating peace in 1917) to the brink of defeat; the second compelled Germany to sign an armistice and then to submit to the terms of a series of crippling treaties. In the course of these convulsions the suffering of the families of the men of Bridge of Weir would continue.

Peace with Russia after the Bolshevik revolution allowed Germany to transfer divisions to the Western Front. In November 1917 there were 150 German divisions in the west. By the end of March 1918 there were 192. At the same time, Haig's pleas for more manpower in France and Belgium had been resisted by Lloyd George, making the Allied line in France acutely vulnerable.

The United States had joined the war on 6 April 1917 but by March 1918 they still only had four raw and untested divisions in Europe, which their commander, Pershing, was not prepared to incorporate into French or British units.

The German commander, Ludendorff, could see that he

might win the war if he acted now, in the brief window before the Allies' weakness would be repaired by America's involvement. If on the other hand the war went on and American resources in terms of men and industrial power were deployed, Germany and an increasingly fragile Austria-Hungary were bound to lose.

Logic dictated an immense Spring Offensive, the Kaiser's Battle, the *Kaiserschlacht*. It broke down into five separate thrusts: MICHAEL from 21 March to 5 April; GEORGETTE from 9 to 11 April; *BLÜCHER-YORCK* on 27 May; *GNEISENAU* on 9 June; and *MARNE-RHEIMS* from 15 to 17 July. It was a bold and desperate plan. If it failed, Ludendorff knew that the German losses could not be replaced and the war was almost certainly lost.

He planned to concentrate his initial attack (MICHAEL) on the weakest-held stretches of front line on the Somme, with a second blow (GEORGETTE) in Belgium to take Ypres and the Channel ports. On 21 March 1918 MICHAEL began with a 'fire waltz' of high explosives, shrapnel, smoke, tear gas and poison gas thrown against forty-three miles of the Front. The infantry attack was to focus on Gough's British Fifth Army. It was intended to punch a hole in the front line and split the British and French armies.

Everyone knew what was coming. Churchill, with some time to spare before a conference at Saint Omer, decided to visit his old Division, the Ninth, now commanded by General Tudor, a friend of his since his subaltern days in India.

> Before I went to bed in the ruins of Nurlu, Tudor said to me: 'It is certainly coming now. Trench raids this evening have identified no less than eight enemy battalions on a single half mile of the Front'. The night was quiet except for a rumble of artillery fire, mostly distant, and thudding explosions of occasional aeroplane raids. I woke up in a complete silence at a few minutes past four and lay musing. Suddenly, after what seemed about half

an hour, the silence was broken by six or seven very loud and very heavy explosions several miles away. I thought they were our 12-inch guns, but they were probably mines. And then, exactly as a pianist runs his hands across the keyboard from treble to bass, there rose in less than one minute the most tremendous cannonade I shall ever hear ... Among the bursting shells there rose at intervals, but almost continually, the much larger flames of exploding magazines. The weight and intensity of the bombardment surpassed anything which anyone had ever known before.

All the drama of the first year of the war had returned. The Allies could easily have been defeated within a matter of weeks, and defeat would have been all the more bitter after the sacrifices of the previous four years, monstrous and in such an event unavailing. The great danger was that the German advance would separate the French and British Armies. Haig was well aware of the need to keep the armies together and pointed out that if the Germans separated them, then Britain would be thrown back on the coast: what would happen in 1940 at Dunkirk could have happened in 1918.

Haig pressed the French commander, Pétain, to keep close contact. Initially Pétain agreed, but by 24 March pressure on the British and French Front threatened an immediate rupture. Late on the night of that day, at 23.00, Haig, breaking with his usual orderly timetable, drove through the night to see Pétain at his headquarters. Precisely what happened at this crucial meeting may never be known. Pétain, on his side, claimed later that he had held out his hand to Haig, that he had warned Haig of the dangers of separation, and that he feared he had not convinced him. According to Haig, the position was reversed: it was he who recognised the need for keeping in touch, and Pétain did not intend to do so. Haig's account of the meeting varies between the manuscript diary which he kept at the time and the typescript version which he prepared after the war. There are a number of instances of variations of this sort and they are not generally more than an attempt to tidy up a contemporary record. In this case, there may have been more to it: Haig's resolve may have wavered. According to the later, typewritten account, Pétain told Haig that he would fall back to cover Paris, at the cost of abandoning his British ally, but it may have been Haig who wobbled, threatened to let go of Pétain's hand and fall back on the Channel ports and evacuation. The original version hadn't strongly suggested that Pétain was wobbling. The unanswered question is, who was doing the wobbling at this midnight conference?

Haig would have been remiss if he had not made contingency plans, but he was hardly the man to panic. He had awaited the German attack with confidence, almost impatience. In the subsequent retreat, as the German advance continued, his nerve never faltered.

The evidence is very complicated and this is not the place to rehearse it. It would scarcely be surprising if Haig had been rattled. He was politically insecure and expected to be dismissed. In London there was certainly something like panic. On 23 March the War Cabinet did indeed discuss falling back on the Channel ports and evacuating the troops to England.

Having left Pétain in the early hours of the morning of 25 March, Haig got back to his headquarters at 03.00. A telegram was sent to Henry Wilson, the new Chief of the Imperial General Staff, asking him to come to France with Lord Derby. What followed was a series of three meetings between the British and the French in the town of Doullens on 26 March 1918.

The circumstances, as well as the momentous issues at stake, made Doullens dramatic and exceptional. No other conference throughout the war took place so close to the Front Line. Shells were falling nearby and troops fresh from the battle fell back through the town. The setting of this momentous conference has been preserved more or less unchanged. In an anteroom to the Council Chamber of the *mairie*, Haig's chair still sits at the end of the table. A painting and a stained-glass window represent the scene on 26 March 1918. These static representations reveal nothing of the turmoil of events.

No one really knows *exactly* what happened at the meetings. There may not even have been an official record. The proceedings were in French, 'spoken fast', and the conference repeatedly broke up into small groups of people talking simultaneously. But the outcome, at any rate, was clear. At someone's suggestion (Haig claimed it was his, but there can be no certainty) Foch was appointed as what became known later as Supreme Commander.

The reaction of the parties varied: immediately afterwards Haig was said to have looked ten years younger. He had taken immense steps earlier in the war to avoid fighting under a Frenchman, but he was happy to fight under an *Allied* Commander-in-Chief who happened to be French. Pétain looked like a man who had lost his nerve.

The French prime minister, Clemenceau, who did not like Foch, patted him on the head, called him '*un bon garçon*',* and told him sourly: 'Well you've got the job you so much wanted.' Foch replied: 'A fine gift; you give me a lost battle and tell me to win it.' But he rose to the challenge wonderfully and did the essential thing: he looked after the interests of *all* the Allied troops, British, French and Belgian, seeing the Allied effort as a cohesive entity.

But the Germans still had to be checked. Seized by the knowledge that they might win the war now – before the Americans were present in force – and also aware that if they did not do so they would assuredly lose, their onslaught had all the berserk drive of what the Romans called *Furor Teutonicus* when they tried to describe the whirlwind attacks of the Germanic tribes in all their wrath. The Germans brought not only their

---

* 'A good little boy', a patronising mode of address for a generalissimo.

unparalleled martial spirit; like the British, they too had been learning new techniques. On the Russian Front they had been developing the nub of what would become the *Blitzkrieg* of 1940. The best of Ludendorff's troops were in battalions of what were already being called storm troops. No limits were imposed on their objectives. 'Infantry which looks to the left or the right,' they were told, 'soon comes to a stop. Touch with the enemy is the desideratum; a uniform advance must in no case be demanded. The fastest, not the slowest, must set the pace.'

British Fifth Army faced the advance. Britain had adopted the same concept of defence in depth that Germany had been using at Third Ypres in the previous year. Within the battle zone a series of strongly held positions was supposed to be established, supporting one another by flanking fire. The theory was that if the enemy succeeded in breaking the front line they would be funnelled into 'boxes' in which they would be raked from defended positions.

Hubert Gough commanded Fifth Army. 'Goughie' was a favourite of Haig's, the 'thrusting commander' of Third Ypres, but his merits were not very obvious, and he was pulled down by the politicians after Fifth Army's performance in the *Kaiserschlacht*.* To be fair to him, lack of man-power had prevented him from establishing his defensive positions in time. Heavy fog on 21 March did not help. The rear zones had not been completed, and consequently there was a concentration of troops – about a third of the infantry – in the forward zones, which were meant to be held only lightly.

The British Army had fought an attacking war from the start,

---

* Lloyd George secured the dismissal not only of Gough, Haig's friend and an Army Commander, but of Sir Laurence Kiggell, Haig's Chief of Staff, Wully Robertson, the Chief of the Imperial General Staff whose views so often coincided with Haig's, and John Charteris, his Chief of Intelligence and long-time colleague. Robertson's dismissal was inevitable if unjust, and the others were not up to their jobs. But it was a remarkable fact that the Cabinet had so little confidence in the Commander-in-Chief that they would not let him choose his own Chief of Staff or Chief of Intelligence. Puppets and puppet-masters.

as opposed to the Germans, who were trying to hold initial gains, not usually to increase them; and the British lack of defensive experience was costly in March 1918. By the evening of the first day, 21 March, the Germans had made great gains along a front of nineteen miles. Artillery pieces were lost, some 7,000 British soldiers were killed, 10,000 wounded and 21,000 taken prisoner. In fact, Britain resisted the first wave of the offensive in March with some success, though at great cost. Part of that cost was exhaustion of reserves, and consequently the impact of the April offensive was far more serious.

The sheer weight of German superiority of numbers and the force of her reckless push were delivering results. In two weeks the Germans advanced thirty-seven miles, and on 12 April Haig issued a famous Order of the Day. It was an unusually moving piece of writing from a famously restrained man. He was always more effective with the written word than with the spoken one. He wrote his order out in his own hand with scarcely an alteration. It had a powerful effect on opinion at home (though his soldiers, like Nelson's sailors when they saw his 'England expects' message, were less impressed):

> Three weeks ago today the enemy began his terrific attack against us on a fifty mile front. His objects are to separate us from the French, to take the Channel Ports, and destroy the British Army. [. . .] Many amongst us are now tired. To those I would say, that victory will belong to the side which holds out the longest. The French Army is moving rapidly and in great force to our support. There is no other course open to us but to fight it out. Every position must be held to the last man. There must be no retirement. With our backs to the wall and believing in the justice of our cause, each one of us must fight to the end. The safety of our home and the freedom of mankind depend alike upon the conduct of each one of us at this critical moment.

The Germans were to an extent victims of their own success. Their position was the reverse of the British: in the course of the previous three and a half years they had become experts in defence; now, in attack they were in an unfamiliar role. Their lines of supply were extended beyond their railheads. Years of blockaded ports had created shortages of imported materials like brass and rubber. The rate of advance slowed down. And after the initial onslaught they did not achieve a rout. Despite overwhelming pressure, Gough still managed a retreat to positions of strength until reinforcements could be deployed, whilst inflicting heavy losses on the advancing Germans.

Eventually Ludendorff's Spring Offensive would be checked. And it would not be replaced by stasis, but by an amazing unbroken advance to victory which would be led by Britain. But before that lay some of the hardest fighting of the war, which would cost the lives of hundreds of thousands on both sides, amongst them the twelve young men from Bridge of Weir whose fate in the successive phases of the *Kaiserschlacht* we now relate.

35

Operation MICHAEL, *21 March to 5 April*

Alexander Leckie Cameron
Captain, 8th Battalion, Argyll & Sutherland Highlanders

Charles Morgan
Private, 8th Battalion, Argyll & Sutherland Highlanders

William Fulton Houston
Private, Royal Engineers

Alex Cameron was the fifth in a family of six born in Johnstone, a few miles to the west of Bridge of Weir, to Alexander Cameron, a teacher of English, and his wife Margaret Fyfe. Alex was educated at the High School of Glasgow, and became a mercantile clerk with Thomas Wiseman & Co, foreign merchants in Glasgow. In due course he became a partner. In 1910, when he was thirty-three, he married Gertrude Cowan, the daughter of a silk merchant from Uddingston. The couple chose the new settlement of Ranfurly for their home and bought Cintra, half of a double villa in Watt Road. In the next few years, they became part of the social fabric of the village, well known in tennis and golfing circles and members of Ranfurly Church, and they soon had a child.

A photograph of Alex survives. He is handsome, with a roguish moustache, a self-assured, determined gaze, an aura of leadership. His image is that of a successful family man. Alex had been a Territorial before the war. He volunteered right at the start, in August 1914, and was commissioned as a captain. He was not in the first drafts sent to France, but attached to the 6th Argylls, stationed in the south of England until December 1917. Gertrude did not want to be separated, and moved south to Bexhill to be with Alex. They named their house there Cintra too – the home in Ranfurly held happy memories.

In December 1917, when manpower on the Western Front was severely depleted, Alex was finally sent to France, attached to the 8th Argylls, part of the 61st Division. On 21 March 1918 the Division was holding the front line north-west of Saint Quentin, directly in the face of the main German attack. It suffered many casualties as it fought a chaotic but ultimately successful withdrawal back over the Somme. In the initial clash, it faced three enemy divisions. Captain Alex Cameron was one of those killed on the first day of that desperate defence against much larger numbers.

Charlie Morgan was a baker, but not just any baker. He specialised in pastries and won many prizes for his creations during his studies at Glasgow Technical College. He had followed his father's trade in the family bakery and confectionery firm and served his fancy pastries to the ladies of Ranfurly in those carefree years before the war. Charlie was also a keen sportsman, captain of the Kilmacolm football team for two years. He joined up in May 1917 at the age of twenty-three; his age suggests that he was conscripted. His older brother Peter, also a baker, had volunteered in 1914 for the Glasgow Yeomanry. Charlie was essential to the continuation of the business, but the war was hungrier for blood than pastries, and exemptions were increasingly rare. By April 1917, the village had already suffered thirty-four fatalities so Charlie knew the risks he faced. For him, like many a young man on the way to war, impending separation proved a spur to marriage, and he married Ruby

Boyle, a thread-mill worker from Johnstone on 30 April 1917. Within a month he was with the 8th Argylls, the same battalion that Captain Cameron was to join in December.

Charles Morgan's fate was initially to be reported missing and his family could hope that he had been taken prisoner: the Germans did indeed take thousands of prisoners in their Spring Offensive. As time went on, however, and no further word came, Ruby's hopes must have been fading. It was January 1919 before Charlie's parents were sent official intimation of his presumed death on 21 March 1918, the same day as Alex Cameron.

William Fulton Houston was born in Erskine, Renfrewshire, the second of a family of eight born to Robert Houston and Mary Fulton, from Whithorn, Wigtownshire. Robert was variously a warehouse foreman in Liverpool, a general labourer back in Scotland, and a foreman-roadman with Renfrewshire County Council, living in Bridge of Weir. He was also the church officer at the parish church.

Robert continued to be restless, and before 1911 the family moved back to its roots in Wigtownshire where he turned to farming. William was by then a joiner, and he stayed behind in Bridge of Weir, lodging with the Tod family in Ladebank Terrace (David Tod was the young signaller who was deafened by an incoming shell in 1915 and killed at Arras). He had a good reason for staying: he had fallen in love with Elizabeth McIntosh, and they married in July 1911. A daughter, Mary, was born in 1912 and a son, Andrew, in June 1916. By then, conscription had been introduced and was no longer restricted to single men. Three months later William was serving in the Royal Garrison Artillery in Plymouth. By 1918, he was attached to the 9th Prince of Wales's (North Staffordshire) Regiment, which formed the pioneer battalion of the 37th Division.

In April 1918, William was fighting at the Ancre, on the Somme Front, on the final day of Operation MICHAEL. He was exposed to mustard gas. He lingered on for several weeks before succumbing to its effects in No. 9 US Hospital in Rouen on 14 May 1918.

It was a horrible way to die. Tom Green, a soldier who fought on the same front, described the effects of gas in his journal:

> Later that night, very late it was, the nurses came in and several doctors, the beds were turned down and later the convoy arrived. I can see them now, about 30 of them all blindfolded with hands on each others' shoulders filing down the marquee and the nurses and doctors breaking them up as they came to their respective beds, poor devils. I tried to see what was going on at the far end, then the sister said something to one of the nurses, both turned to look in my direction and within minutes I was given a drink from a feeding cup and two tablets. I could not see any more, I was off in a deep sleep, that was my lot.
>
> It must have been early morning when I awoke and remembered the scene of the night before. Every bed was empty and at the foot of each bed was a urine bottle half full of pink urine, yes they had all been gassed, blind and died, but what of the horror never seen.

William Houston's father, Robert, died at his farm in Wigtownshire less than two months later. William's wife and two young children received a pension of 25s 5d a week (about £118 in today's money).

36

Operation GEORGETTE *and the Battle of the Lys: 9 April to 8 May*

Robert Niven
Lance Corporal, 18th Battalion, King's Liverpool Regiment

John Gardner Brown
Private, 2nd Battalion, Argyll & Sutherland Highlanders

Ernest Murray
Private, 9th Battalion, Cameronians (Scottish Rifles)

Edward Shedden
Private, 15th Battalion, Highland Light Infantry

Andrew Houston
Gunner, Royal Field Artillery

Robert Sproul
Corporal, 5th Battalion, Cameron Highlanders

Robert Niven lived in the same tenement as Charlie Morgan, the pastry maker, before the war. He was the eldest son of Robert Niven, a plasterer from Paisley who had settled in Cooperative Terrace. In August 1915 young Robert enlisted at the age of seventeen, a year short of the legal minimum. His forty-year-old father responded equally patriotically to the call of duty. He gave up his plastering business, which had employed a small workforce, and volunteered three months later. Perhaps he could not watch his son go to war while he, still young enough to fight, stayed at home. Young Robert was in the King's Liverpool Regiment in April 1918, part of 30th Division, holding the front line near Ypres.

On 9 April, the first day of GEORGETTE, the battalion War Diaries report a bombardment of enemy trench mortar fire after a quiet few days, with one killed and one wounded. One of those may have been Robert Niven, although his death was not confirmed until October 1919 which suggests he went missing on a day of multiple fatalities and that his body was not found for some time. Robert's name is recorded as one of those interred at the Ham British Cemetery in northern France, 100 miles to the south of Ypres, which adds to the uncertainty. His father survived the war, living with the memory of the eldest son who did not.

For a lad from a semi-rural Renfrewshire village, **John Gardner Brown** had led a remarkably cosmopolitan life. John was born in Boston, USA, to Gardner Brown, a Gardner by name and a gardener by occupation, and Margaret McLoughlin, a parlour maid, originally from Greenock. They had married in Boston in 1891, two Scots in a foreign country. John was their fourth child born in the USA. Unlike most of their fellow emigrants, the family abandoned America and returned to Scotland in 1900, spending a few years in Falkirk, before settling in Bridge of Weir in 1906. John was a full cousin of Walter Brown (see Chapter 13).

John enlisted into the 2nd Battalion Argyll and Sutherland Highlanders which from November 1915 formed part of 98th Brigade, the 33rd Division, and fought at the Somme, Arras and Third Ypres.

In March 1918 the Division was concentrated near Arras but on 8 April it was ordered to entrain for the Ypres Salient in the Meteren area. It was rushed to the front line in response to the build-up of German forces and arrived in time to see the results of GEORGETTE: the stragglers, the wounded and the civilian refugees fleeing the German onslaught. The Divisional History says, tellingly, 'The moral [morale] of many of the British troops at this juncture in the battle cannot be said to have been high.' The understatement does not hide how desperate the situation was. The Division saw fierce fighting around Meteren and Bailleul from 12 April. On the night of 15 April the battalion took its place in the front line. That day had been pivotal. Ground had been conceded; but despite throwing six divisions against a front held by one British brigade, the Germans had failed to break the line. By the morning of 18 April the enemy was exhausted, made no further attacks and the gaps in the British new line were linked and consolidated. The first wave of GEORGETTE had failed; but John Brown had been killed on 17 April, his body never recovered.

The Murray family were also incomers to Bridge of Weir. The father was a leather dresser, or currier, and in his forties moved from Arbroath to work in the Clydesdale Leather Works in Bridge of Weir. **Ernest Murray** was a joiner by trade, aged twenty-one when war was declared. He did not volunteer immediately but attested under the Derby scheme.

In February 1916 he was called up, and posted to 5th Battalion, Scottish Rifles. At some stage he transferred to 9th Battalion of the same regiment, part of 9th (Scottish) Division. In March 1918, the Division was holding about 1,000 yards of the front line near Villers-Guislain on the extreme left flank of Gough's Fifth Army.

After suffering heavy losses and blunting the German thrust between Third and Fifth Armies on the Somme from 21 to 27 March, the Division was reassigned to what was expected to be a quiet sector in the southern part of the Ypres Salient. Its strength was increased by very large drafts chiefly of youths of eighteen and nineteen. It was these untested troops, supplemented by veterans like young Ernest Murray, that bore the brunt of GEORGETTE.

Ernest's Division was involved in the First and Second Battles of Kemmel and the defence of Wytschaete, retreating some two miles in the month of April. Ernest Murray was wounded, taken to hospital in Boulogne but died on 7 May 1918. He is buried in Boulogne Eastern Cemetery. The Division was finally relieved on 26 April. The Germans had gained a few miles but got no further. The new line held.

Robert Shedden was a journeyman currier from Kilmarnock in Ayrshire who moved his family to Bridge of Weir in the early 1900s. One of his sons followed him into the leather trade, and another became a cartwright, but **Edward Shedden** had a different talent – golf. By 1914 Edward was living at 1 Windsor Place, and was professional at Ralston Golf Club in Paisley, having been assistant professional at Old Ranfurly Golf Club, Bridge of Weir between 1905 and 1907. He had been fourth in the Glasgow & District Professional Golf Association Championship in 1910, runner-up in the Autumn Competition in 1911 and winner in 1913 at Cochrane Castle. He was good enough to enter the 1914 Open Championship, like Bertie McDougall who died on the Ancre in 1916. In that summer of 1914 he must have been enjoying the most fulfilling year of his life.

Then came the war. Edward volunteered in November 1914 and enlisted into 10th Battalion, the Highland Light Infantry. At some time during his army service he transferred to the 1st Battalion of the Cameronians (Scottish Rifles) 19th Brigade, 33rd Division. He fought in the Battle of the Somme. On 15 July 1916 he was shot and wounded in the right arm, which would probably have put paid to his golfing prospects at the highest level. But he was fit enough to fight, and after a period of recuperation he returned to active service.

Edward Shedden survived Meteren, unlike John Brown in the same Division, and the Division was relieved by the 1st Australian and 34th French Divisions on 20 April. On 6 May Edward was back in the front line, closer to Ypres, on the line running through Ridge Wood and Scottish Wood. At 07.30 on 8 May the Germans launched an attack preceded by heavy bombardment. In the fighting that followed, the Cameronians in particular suffered very heavy casualties, becoming detached from the rest of the Division for a time. Ignominiously, their commanding officer was captured. Ridge Wood was retaken that evening in a counter-attack but Edward's body was never found. His army record is one of many that simply records a man as 'missing'.

Andrew Houston was born in the Wheatsheaf Inn in Bridge of Weir to Alexander Houston, the innkeeper, and his wife Ann McNaughton from Kilmichael in Argyll. His mother produced boys: Andrew was her seventh son. By 1901 Andrew was a butcher and, with his brother William, a grocer's assistant, was boarding with the family of Robert Millar in Gryffe Place.* Andrew was an early volunteer on 12 September 1914, when he was thirty-two. He enlisted into the Royal Field Artillery. By July 1915 he was in France. He survived the war for almost three years, and he enjoyed at least one return home on leave when he was based at Armentières in France in January 1916. In March 1918, his brigade, the 58th, formed part of the 11th (Northern) Division. He was killed on 5 June in the Pas-de-Calais.

Robert Sproul, whom we met briefly at Gallipoli, had been a spirits salesman. He married Anne Ferguson in September 1914

---

* Intricate family connections are woven through the fabric of a small community. Robert Millar is the grandfather of the Millar cousins: William (Chapter 31) and Robert (whom we'll meet in Chapter 37).

in Glasgow's registry office. He may have been planning to volunteer and wanted to share a few months with Anne. In any event by February 1915 he had volunteered for service and was a private in the Lovat Scouts. He served, as we saw, at Gallipoli in September 1915, was wounded at Suvla Bay in October, but survived and returned home on leave in January 1916. He was then transferred to the 5th Battalion Cameron Highlanders, the Lovat Scouts' 'parent' regiment, part of 26th Brigade, 9th (Scottish) Division, and was promoted to corporal, serving with Ernest Murray. The Division, regarded as one of the most effective fighting formations in the war, had been on the Western Front since 10th May 1915 and was to see action in the tough later battles, including the Battle of the Lys in April 1918.

The battalion spent most of May 1918 resting near St Omer. When it returned to the front line near Meteren it was 'largely composed of youths little more than eighteen years of age'. An experienced corporal like Robert Sproul was rare and valuable. The Division settled into a pattern of sending out daily raiding parties to harass the enemy and capture prisoners for intelligence. On 18 July, Corporal Robert Sproul appears to have been one of five other ranks reported missing after an unsuccessful raid on a machine-gun post. After almost three years in active theatres of war, a survivor of Gallipoli, the Somme, Arras and Third Ypres, Robert had run out of luck.

37

Further Phases of the Spring Offensive

1. Operation *Blücher-Yorck* and the Battle of the Aisne

William Robertson Keith
Private, 8th Battalion, Argyll & Sutherland Highlanders

John Andrew
Lance Corporal, 7th/8th Battalion, King's Own Scottish Borderers

William Robertson Keith, a farm labourer from Kaimhill on the outskirts of Bridge of Weir, enlisted at Paisley on 14 February 1917 when he was still eighteen. William expressed a preference for the Cameron Highlanders but another regiment had a greater need, and he became a private in the 5th (Reserve) Battalion, Argyll and Sutherland Highlanders. On 4 July 1917 he was posted to the 1st/8th Battalion of the Argylls and joined the British Expeditionary Force in France; two weeks later he was posted to the 11th (Service) Battalion, Argylls. Between March and June 1918 he had been treated in hospital variously for dermatitis, scabies and gastro-enteritis, typical hazards of life in the trenches.

On 9 June 1918 he rejoined the 1st/8th Battalion, Argylls, now part of the 15th (Scottish) Division. The Division was sent to replace battle-weary American forces on the night of 22/23 July under the command of the French 10th Army, a result of the supreme command structure now in place. Their first task was to bury American dead. They were in action the following day at 05.00 in a counter-attack near Buzancy on the River Aisne. Eighth Argylls were to capture Le Sucrerie and nearby bridges but according to the battalion war diary 'met with bad luck. Owing to heavy shelling, and the short notice given to them' they lost contact with their neighbours for a while then had to cover the left flank of the Division, exposed after its advance. The enemy counter-attacked at 18.00. Private Keith was killed on 23 July 1918 in a 'gallant attempt to bring in a wounded man'. Officers writing to grieving parents rarely reported anything other than a brave and gallant death, but this narrative is specific enough to carry credibility. Learning that one's dear one had died in such an endeavour was perhaps slightly less painful than the grim void of 'missing, presumed dead'.

John Andrew, youngest of a family of six, the brother of Henry Andrew who was invalided home from Salonika in 1916, was a bright child who began his education at Bridge of Weir School and then went on to Paisley Grammar School.

Bridge of Weir School is the fourth school that we know the men memorialised in the village attended. Initially the responsibility for educating the children of the village lay with the Church. Latterly it was entrusted to a series of statutory authorities. It cannot be said with certainty how many of those who died were pupils of the school, but it must have been the cradle of many, some moving on to further education, others leaving to go into the world. The school continued the tradition of uncompromising instruction in the essential skills of reading, writing and reckoning that had been the staples of Scottish education since John Knox had said that there should be a school in every parish.

We do not know how many of the school's boys fought or died in the war, but the influences that took so many young Scotsmen into the army were certainly strong in Bridge of Weir. In 1871 a presentation was made to Matthew Gemmill, who had been schoolmaster since 1840. In the course of his reply Mr Gemmill spoke about the number of boys of the school who had fought all over the globe in the army and the navy. He mentioned the Crimea, where his pupils had fought. Several had been at Alma, the first battle of that war, one had died at Inkerman, and one, Alex Tonner, from George's Square, Bridge of Weir, had charged with the Heavy Brigade, Tennyson's Three Hundred,* at Balaclava. Other boys fought in the Indian Mutiny, taking part in the relief of the sieges of Cawnpore and Lucknow. The influence of history and tradition was heavy on the shoulders of the schoolboys of 1914–18.

By 1914 John was a teacher at Mossvale School in Paisley. He volunteered in early November of that year and was drafted to the Glasgow Chamber of Commerce 17th Battalion (3rd Glasgow) of the Highland Light Infantry. He was in France on 22 November 1915. On 5 July 1916 he was injured in the leg during a British offensive. He recovered, returned to active service and was later promoted lance-corporal and transferred to the King's Own Scottish Borderers. By March 1918 his battalion formed part of the 15th (Scottish) Division.

The battalion's objective was the village of Rozières. They advanced a few hundred yards before stopping due to heavy losses and lack of artillery support. They later had to cover the right flank of the division while it waited for the neighbouring French divisions to join. John Andrew was on the right flank, William Keith on the left. Corporal Andrew was killed on 23 July 1918, the same day as Private Keith near Buzancy, just a mile or so apart. John was the second of the two Andrew brothers to fall. The French commander was so impressed by 15th Division's fighting spirit in the battle that he ordered a memorial to be

---

* As opposed to the Six Hundred, who were the Light Brigade.

built immediately, the only one built during the war by a French unit and dedicated to a British one:

> *Here will flourish forever the glorious thistle of Scotland*
> *among the roses of France*
> *– the 17th French Infantry Division to the 15th Scottish*
> *Infantry Division.*

2. Operation *Marne-Rheims* and the Second Battle of the Marne

Robert Millar
Private, 5th Battalion, Argyll & Sutherland Highlanders

The Millar family clan has been mentioned already. They were to become a well-known business family in the village, with interests in haulage, coal and transport. By the outbreak of war the patriarch, Robert Millar, was living in Gryffe View. One of his sons, John Millar, a ploughman, worked for many years on Loanhead Farm in nearby Houston, supported by his wife Mary, younger than him by eight years. They had five girls, Elizabeth, Mary, Margaret, Agnes and Jane aged between three and twelve years old when a son, **Robert Millar**, was born. In his early years Robert was pampered and pestered by his sisters.

John left his farming sometime between 1901 and 1911, and, like his brother Robert, became a carting contractor. It was a natural progression for a man who knew horses well. John's son, Robert, was of an age to help by then, and indeed Robert was part of his father's business by the time he was seventeen. When war broke out John was sixty, and Robert was twenty-one and an important part of the business. But the case for exemptions had become ever harder to make, and Robert was conscripted in January 1917 and joined the Argyll & Sutherland Highlanders.

By March 1918 he was in the 5th Argylls, part of the

34th Division. He was killed on 1 August in 34th Division's attack near Beugneux. He was buried in the Beugneux British Cemetery, which contained the graves of thirty-six British soldiers (mainly of the 1st/5th Argyll and Sutherland Highlanders) who fell that day. The courage and tenacity of the 34th Division, fighting alongside the French, was commended by General Mangin:

Then during the whole day of the 1st of August, side by side with your French comrades, you stormed the ridge dominating the whole country between the Aisne and the Ourcq which the defenders had received orders to hold at all costs. Having failed to retake the ridge with his last reserves the enemy had to beat a retreat, pursued and harassed for twelve kilometres. All of you, English and Scottish, young soldiers and veterans of Flanders and Palestine, you have shown the magnificent qualities of your race: courage and imperturbable tenacity. You have won the admiration of your companions in arms. Your country will be proud of you, for to your chiefs and you is due a large share in the victory that we have gained of the barbarous enemies of the free. I am happy to have fought at your head, and I thank you.

38

The War in the Air

John Ritchie Johnstone
Lieutenant, Royal Air Force

At the beginning of the Great War, British air power employed about 2,000 personnel split between the Royal Naval Air Service, the air arm of the Royal Navy, and the Royal Flying Corps, the air arm of the army.

The different components were brought together in 1918. In 1917 Lloyd George had appointed a committee consisting of himself and General Smuts (whom we last met pursuing Lettow-Vorbeck in East Africa, but who was now a member of the War Cabinet in London) to consider how the air part of the war should be run. Its remit was to report on two issues: arrangements for Home Defence against bombing and, secondly, air organisation generally, including the direction of aerial operations. In practice Smuts had sole responsibility and his report of August 1917 recommended the fusion of the various elements into the Royal Air Force. His report was remarkably prescient, and foresaw the likelihood that air warfare would revolutionise conventional military and naval thinking. The Royal Air Force came into being on 1 April 1918.

A Scottish industrialist, William, later Lord, Weir, one of Lloyd George's 'men of push and go', director of munitions in Scotland, and later controller of aeronautical supplies, became

President of the Air Council soon after the RAF was created, and Secretary of State for Air. In that capacity he received a message from George V at the end of the war: 'The birth of the Royal Air Force, with its wonderful expansion and development, will ever remain one of the most remarkable achievements of the Great War.'

Indeed, the expansion of the service *was* remarkable. By the end of the war, the RAF was the largest air force in the world and had 280,000 personnel, 700 airfields and over 23,000 aircraft. The life expectancy of a pilot was even shorter than that of a junior army officer on the Western Front. In April 1917, for example, the average life expectancy of a fighter pilot was ninety-two flying hours. But this did not deter thousands of volunteers, keen to experience the thrills of the new experience offered by combat flying.

One of those was **John Ritchie Johnstone**, the son of a Glasgow iron merchant who ran his business from St Vincent Street. Ritchie, as he was known, was born in the west end of Glasgow and educated at Glasgow High School. The family later moved to Pollokshields, a well-to-do suburb on the south side of Glasgow, not far from where Lord Weir's company would turn out de Havilland DH9 biplanes during the war years. When Ritchie left school in November 1914 he became a law student, apprenticed to Finlayson, Auld & McKenzie, whose chambers were in the same street as his father's office.

His law books were set aside. On 14 April 1917, Ritchie became a cadet in the Royal Flying Corps at Farnborough, gaining his commission as a second lieutenant on 25 October 1917. He qualified as a pilot and became a Flying Officer on 27 February 1918. He was nineteen years old. When the RAF came into being on 1 April 1918 he automatically moved up a rank and became a full lieutenant. On 16 July 1918 he was assigned to 255 Squadron of the new Royal Air Force, based in Pembroke, South Wales.

He was very quickly transferred to a new squadron – 244, based at Abergwyngregyn, which was understandably normally abbreviated to 'Aber', a tented camp near Bangor, in the north of Wales. He died before the paperwork regarding his move had caught up with him and his service record shows him still with 255. His new squadron was equipped in part with aircraft taken from his former one.

Both squadrons were engaged in anti-U-boat operations, flying the Airco DH 6, a biplane designed by Geoffrey de Havilland as a training aircraft. It was a two-seater but most patrols were solo, as it was insufficiently powered to carry both an observer and a bomb. It had a number of nicknames – the 'skyhook', 'crab', 'clockwork mouse', 'flying coffin', and 'dung hunter'. The plywood cockpit was thought to resemble either a coffin or an outside privy.

At 06.00 on 14 August 1918 – just five days after his first patrol – Ritchie took off from Aber on an anti-submarine patrol. He never returned. It is assumed that he ditched somewhere off the coast of Wales. The following day a Captain Tuck was sent out for two hours on an unavailing search patrol.

On the day that Ritchie died, 255 Squadron had its first kill, when Lieutenant Peebles attacked a submarine at periscope depth, releasing his 100-pound bomb and seeing air bubbles and an oil slick.

Ritchie Johnstone had died in his first month of active service, and almost certainly did not get close to the average prevailing life expectancy of ninety-two flying hours. From Bangor he flew just four sorties, a total of just seven and a half flying hours. He was still five weeks short of his twentieth birthday.

Ritchie's name is on the Hollybrook Memorial in Southampton, built to commemorate almost 1,900 servicemen and women of the Commonwealth land and air forces who were lost at sea.

Ritchie's connection with Bridge of Weir is through his

parents, who moved to Rocklea, Bonar Crescent, around the time of his death. They joined Ranfurly United Free Church, their membership recorded at the kirk session meeting of 11 October 1918. Although not on the village war memorial, probably because he never lived there himself, his name is included on Ranfurly Church's memorial tablet to the sons of the congregation, which was unveiled on 24 October 1920. His father James was by then a church elder and served as such until his death on 24 November 1924.

39

The Hundred Days

There were two pivotal moments in the course of the great drama that began with the unleashing of the *Kaiserschlacht* and ended with the signing of an armistice in Foch's railway train in the Forest of Compiègne some time between 19.00 and 20.00 on 10 November 1918. The first was that dramatic conference at Doullens, when the Allies finally united behind one Supreme Commander. The second was a meeting between Haig and Foch on 16 May 1918. The role of Foch in contributing to the final victory must not be minimised. He told Haig that if there were not a German attack within the next few weeks, he wanted the retreat in the face of the *Kaiserschlacht* to stop. The Allies were to go on to the offensive.

But Haig had himself sensed that the Germans had shot their bolt, that their onslaught was checking, that it was time to move from the defensive. Further, what Foch had in mind on 16 May was a preponderantly French project; but Ludendorff now changed his plan. Rather than sticking to attacking the Allies at their weak point, the hinge between their armies in Picardy, he switched to the Reims front and attacked the French on the Aisne and the Matz. It was a bad decision that altered the dynamics of the war.

Now it was France, rather than Britain, which was bearing the brunt of the German attack. France's military vitality was already sapped to an extent from which she had still not recuperated by the end of the war. In the meantime, the British Army recovered its strength for a much more active role, and the key part in delivering victory.

By the middle of July, Haig was clear that the opportunity for a major offensive might be close; in the event that offensive was British, and British and Dominion armies delivered the victory. We are now moving into the final section of the Great War: the battles of the Hundred Days,* one of the great feats of British arms. During the Hundred Days Britain took 188,700 prisoners and captured 2,840 guns. France took 139,000 prisoners and seized 1,880 guns, the Americans 44,142 and 1,481 and the Belgians 14,500 and 414. With an army smaller than that of France, Britain took 49 per cent of all prisoners captured by the Allies and 53 per cent of all guns.

This, by far the greatest victory that Britain has ever won, is a victory of which most people are unaware, and Haig is not remembered as the man who delivered it. The Germans saw what was happening. 'Haig', said one of their reports at this time, 'is Master of the Field'. Foch acknowledged the achievement: 'Never at any time in history have the British Army achieved greater results in an attack than in this unbroken offensive.'

At Staff College Haig had been told – and he never deviated from the doctrine – that any battle went through three separate phases: the initial contact; the wearing-down when dominance was achieved; and breakthrough. It might be thought that his experience across so many contacts and wearing-downs where there had been no breakthrough might have eroded his confidence, but it did not, and in his Final Despatch he made a point of saying how right he had been. He did so by choosing to see the whole war as one gigantic battle, its outcome, the breakthrough, being the Hundred Days.

---

* There were in fact only ninety-five days, but history has preferred a hundred, which has more of a ring to it.

And unappealing and unimaginative as the doctrine sounds, it may have been right for its time. Experience of industrialised warfare, total war between modern nations in arms, is limited to just the two world wars of the twentieth century. The first was won by the wearing-down on two fronts, particularly the Western Front, coupled with economic blockade; the second was only won after wearing-down on the Russian Front, area bombing on the west, and again economic blockade. Smart weapons and superior technology *may* be the key in a future conflict; we cannot know and hope not to find out.

The history of the First World War is bleak and dispiriting partly because it seems just to go on and on, without any battle (other than those of the Hundred Days) proving decisive. Men seem to have died to no purpose. None of the Bridge of Weir deaths made an individual contribution to victory. All that can be said – and it is something profoundly important – is that cumulatively the battles and the deaths mattered. It is because of them that Europe did not come under the rule of Prussian militarism. It is Haig's statue and not Ludendorff's that stands on the Castle Esplanade in Edinburgh and on Whitehall.

In the Hundred Days the learning curve, the amalgam of various trends and new tactical thinking, came together to favour the intelligent use of small, multi-skilled units, relying far less on the rifle than before, adapting their movements to the terrain in which they found themselves. These tactics were those which Britain used throughout the Second World War and indeed for twenty-five years more. Preparation and rehearsal were meticulous and took place in full-scale training areas behind the lines. Security was strictly enforced, camouflage was used and misleading diversionary tactics took place. It all savours much more of the Second, rather than the First, World War.

J.M. Bourne summarises very well the revolution over which Haig presided:

In August 1914 the British soldier might have passed for a gamekeeper in his soft cap, puttees and pack. He walked into battle. He was armed with little more than a rifle and bayonet. For support he could call only on the shrapnel-firing field guns of the Royal Artillery. His commanders were often elderly and unfit, with little relevant pre-war experience of any level of command above the battalion. By September 1918 he was dressed like an industrial worker in a safety helmet, with a respirator protecting him against gas close to hand. He was just as likely to be armed with a Lewis gun, grenade or rifle grenade as a simple rifle. He was trucked into battle. His appearance on the battlefield was preceded by a deception campaign based on sophisticated signals intelligence. He was supported by a high-explosive artillery barrage of crushing density, by tanks, armoured cars, machine-guns, smoke and gas. Enemy guns were identified and attacked using leading-edge technologies of sound-ranging and flash-spotting, in which specially-recruited scientists played a key role.

On 8 August 1918, the Battle of Amiens – the opening battle of the Hundred Days – was fought and won by Britain in a matter of hours. It was said that this was 'the day we won the war in a morning'. Of course that was very far from the case. The Hundred Days was a hard-fought campaign in which losses were very high, against an enemy that was far from defeated, but it was a campaign that consisted only of victories. It was Haig, rather than Foch, whose mind was directing events. Foch was generous. He recognised Haig's stature, describing him as 'the greatest general in the world'. He wrote to Haig:

My dear Field-Marshal
Your affairs are going on very well; I can only applaud the resolute manner in which you follow them up,

without giving the enemy a respite and always extending the breadth of your operations.

And all of this was done by an army starved of resources, whose commander was constantly reminded by Henry Wilson, the Chief of the Imperial General Staff, that he would be held personally accountable for failure. Haig replied to Wilson with his own appraisal of the Cabinet: 'What a wretched lot! And how well they mean to support me! What confidence!'

In London the official War Office view was that the final push would take place in July 1919. Even Foch, as late as 7 October 1918, agreed with that. Other Cabinet members – even the ebullient Churchill – thought that the war might not end until as late as 1921. Haig had constantly to battle against this pessimism. He went to London on 9 September to impress on Lord Milner how things had changed: 'Within the last four weeks we had captured 77,000 prisoners and nearly 600 guns! There has never been such a victory in the annals of Britain, and its effects are not yet apparent.'

Haig was not a great strategist. He was certainly not the greatest general to command British armies. But if not the greatest, he was still *a* great general, and his was the vision and drive that created victory in 1918. The tone of his address to his Army Commanders on 22 August was very different from the 'backs to the wall' Order of the Day: 'I request army commanders will, without delay, bring to the notice of all subordinate leaders the changed conditions under which operations are now being carried on . . . To turn the present situation to account, the most resolute offensive is everywhere desirable. Risks which a month ago would have been criminal to incur ought now to be incurred as a duty.' While losses in the Hundred Days were high, it was Haig's achievement that he ended the war perhaps two years earlier than it would otherwise have ended, saving countless lives in the process.

This narrative will end with the stories of the men who died on that Great Advance, because it was that advance which ended the war, pushing the Germans back to where it had begun. But before that, we step aside a little from a strictly chronological approach to record a death in another theatre, and two that occurred after the war ended.

40

The Italian Front

John Higgins
Lance Corporal, 8th Battalion, King's Own Yorkshire
Light Infantry

In 1914 Italy, like Germany and Austria-Hungary, was a member of the Triple Alliance, the Central Powers who faced the Allies of the Triple Entente: France, Russia and Britain. But she wobbled. She harboured long-standing ambitions to recover territory lost to Austria in the course of the Napoleonic Wars. She also had an affection for Britain, who had favoured her reunification. Accordingly, Italy refrained from declaring war on the Entente Powers in August 1914.

Both sides courted her, but the Entente finally won, and the Treaty of London was signed on 26 April 1915, committing Italy to begin fighting the Central Powers within a month. Biding her time and identifying the winners was a good idea. She got it wrong in the next war.

Her fighting was concentrated in the north-eastern corner of the Italian peninsula, frequently on different stretches of the Isonzo River. There were no fewer than eleven battles of the Isonzo between June 1915 and September 1917, all of them ultimately inconclusive despite losses of around a million men. Much of the fighting was conducted in the Alps. In late 1917 the Germans reinforced the Austrians and in October a combined force launched the Battle of Caporetto. The battle resulted in substantial territorial gains for the Central Powers and pushed the Italians twenty miles back to the River Piave.

In November 1917, the British and French sent reinforcements. Their supply of war *matériel* and resources was vital. Moreover, in early 1918 the Germans withdrew their forces to concentrate on the Spring Offensive on the Western Front. The Austrians attempted to finish the Italian war with a two-pronged attack in June 1918, but despite suffering heavy losses in the Battle of the River Piave the Italians had the better of it.

By October 1918, the Italians had received more reinforcements from the Western Front, including the British 23rd Division. The Battle of Vittorio-Veneto was launched in eight thrusts along a 100-mile front. By late October, three bridgeheads across the Piave were secured, and some 300,000 Austrians had surrendered. The Austrians sought peace terms and an armistice was signed on 4 November 1918.

John Higgins was the brother of Peter Higgins, who died on the Loos Front in 1916, one of the two sons and five daughters of Peter, senior, from Ireland and Ellen Murray, a local girl. While Peter had gone into the tannery, the younger brother, John, became a postman. His real love was golf and he, like several others in this account, was good enough to become a professional. He began his career as assistant professional at Ranfurly Castle Golf Club, winning the Glasgow and District Professional Golf Association's autumn competition in 1911, pipping another Bridge of Weir professional, Edward Shedden, whose war has been described, into second place.

John moved to Walsall as club professional and married Lilian Smith there in 1915. He enlisted with the King's Own Scottish Borderers. He was promoted Lance Corporal and by the time of his death he had been transferred to the 8th Battalion of the King's Own Yorkshire Light Infantry. The battalion, part of 70th Brigade, 23rd Division, had already seen two years on the

Western Front when it was transferred to Italy. John was killed in action on 28 October 1918 while attached to the 68th Brigade, in the Battle of Vittorio-Veneto, on the day his battalion crossed the River Piave.

An account relates:

> The distance from the island's east shore to the far bank of the river was from 1,000 to 2,000 yards of a rapidly (ten knots) flowing river with about six islands before arriving at the far bank. Ferried to the island were the 68 and 69 Brigades of the British Twenty-third Division. Rapid as the current was [the bridge] still remained functional. Crossing was on foot with arms linked and feet dragging.

Whether a victim of drowning or a bullet, John died at the River Piave. He is buried in Tezze British Cemetery on the north side of the river. Consolidating the bridgeheads over the Piave was decisive for the Allies. The armistice with Austria came just one week after John Higgins was killed.

41

Two Deaths After the War Had Ended

Robert Jackson
Sapper, 37th Miscellaneous Trades Company, Royal Engineers

William Cairns
Private, 1st/5th Battalion, King's Own Scottish Borderers

The armistice with Austria was signed on 4 November 1918; the even more important armistice with Germany took effect one week later. But the story of two Bridge of Weir men who died after that date remains to be told.

Robert Jackson grew up in Glasgow, the youngest of the ten children of William Jackson, a house painter from Greenock, and Margaret Whyte. Robert followed his father's trade in Glasgow; his connection to Bridge of Weir is through his marriage, on 14 June 1910, to Elizabeth Hay Andrew, an assistant in a grocer's shop. They were married in her parents' two-roomed flat in Claremont Place, where Elizabeth had grown up as one of seven siblings.

Elizabeth was the sister of the Henry Andrew (see Chapter 32) who died early in 1917 after being invalided home from Salonika, and of the John Andrew (see Chapter 37) who was killed on 23 July 1918, in the course of the *Kaiserschlacht*. There were many such tragic intersections in a small community.

Elizabeth and Robert Jackson soon had two children, William born in 1911 and Janet in 1915. In his thirties with a family, Robert did not volunteer for the war, but he attested on 3 December 1915.

He was called up on 26 July 1916, and became a sapper in the Chief Mechanical Engineer's department of the Depot Railway Troops based at Longmoor in Hampshire. The rail networks in Britain and Europe saw unprecedented levels of use during the war, moving troops and *matériel*. The railways were effectively nationalised. 'Jellicoe Specials' took wagons of coal from South Wales to Grangemouth and on to Scapa Flow to feed the dreadnoughts. After the shells crisis of 1915, National Filling Factories like the one outside Bridge of Weir were built on rail routes across the country to bring raw materials in and take filled shells out.

Railway lines and railheads were built in France. The final connections to the front line consisted of a network of 1,300 kilometres of narrow-gauge light railway better able to cope with constrained alignments and steeper gradients.

By 1916 200,000 tonnes of ammunition were transported to the Front every week entirely by rail. The railways also had to get daily rations to 2.5 million men and feed for horses. Daily postal deliveries kept troop morale up and mail too was carried by rail. It was a complicated exercise of logistics and supply for which the Commander-in-Chief was ultimately responsible, along with huge other practical burdens that included road transport on top of his purely military function.

In March 1917, Robert Jackson was transferred from Longmoor to 37th Miscellaneous Trades Company in France where he continued his transformation from house painter to railway engineer and reached the 'Superior' level of proficiency.

On 3 November 1918, Robert was admitted into Rouen Hospital in northern France. The medical notes read: 'Onset. Headache, general pains, cough and pain in chest'. It was influenza, 'Spanish Flu'. The Spanish flu of 1918/19 was a particularly severe strain; acute pneumonia often developed and could kill anyone, even healthy young adults, within a day or two. Despite the 'Spanish' tag, virologists have deduced that the outbreak may well have originated at the notorious troop staging camp at Étaples in northern France. The flu pandemic was to result in more fatalities than the war itself, with an estimated 50–100 million deaths worldwide between 1918 and 1920.

Robert deteriorated rapidly, developed broncho-pneumonia and died in hospital within a fortnight of being admitted, on 16 November 1918, the day before his daughter's third birthday. Elizabeth received news of her husband's death a week after the Armistice was signed.

William Cairns grew up in Glasgow, one of six children. His life was difficult. His father died young and the children were largely left to fend for themselves. By 1911 the two youngest girls were inmates of the Maryhill Industrial School for Girls. William became a baker but he enlisted in the Seaforth Highlanders as soon as war was declared in August 1914. The fact that he survived four years of war had much to do with the fact that his army career was chequered and that he saw limited overseas service. As early as December 1914, he was discharged from the army for misconduct with 'bad military character' on his service record.

But by May 1915 he had wangled his way back in, this time to the Army Service Corps as a baker. This time he lasted six months before being sentenced to 118 days' detention in December for disobedience and striking a superior officer. He returned to duty in March, only to be discharged on 28 April 1916 as being no longer physically fit for war service. The medical report said that he had 'chronic bronchitis originated in childhood in Glasgow'. One has the sense that the army was looking for a way of getting rid of a man it had difficulty in dealing with. His pension entitlement was meanly and meticulously calculated as 361 days minus 94 days for detention served.

But William seems to have liked the army more than it liked him. Undaunted, and presumably without having his service record checked, he succeeded in joining up for a third time and was back in the Army Service Corps by the time he married Elizabeth Ward on 12 March 1918 in Bridge of Weir. Elizabeth was a domestic servant and lived at Ladeside. His service records tell us a little about her husband's appearance. We know that William Cairns was five feet six inches tall and had a vertical scar over his right eye – perhaps a clue to the more colourful episodes in his army career – and tattoos on both wrists, a sword and a boxer.

William was in post-war Flanders in 1919, by then with the 1st/5th (Dumfries and Galloway) Battalion, King's Own Scottish Borderers as part of 34th Division. The Division had been in Cologne at the beginning of 1919 as part of the Army of Occupation. He died in hospital, on 11 August 1919, at Wimereux in the Pas-de-Calais region of northern France.

His cause of death was recorded as septicaemia. We may never know how William sustained his wound. His history suggests that it was as likely to have come from a brawl as from a more heroic injury. Whatever caused his septicaemia, William Cairns, the willing but maverick soldier, was the last of the seventy-two on Bridge of Weir's memorials to die. He was a bad boy. Armies always attract bad boys, and some of them turn out to be the best and bravest of soldiers. William did not have the chance to die in action, but his persistence in seeking out service when others often sought to avoid it speaks of one face of courage. It is appropriate that Bridge of Weir's fallen should include, along with those who died more heroically, this scarred and tattooed rascal, a typical component of armies over the centuries.

Having stepped aside from our timeline, we now return to it, to the Hundred Days that ended the war, and the men who died in bringing it to an end.

42

The Men Who Fell in the Great Advance

William Smart Kerr
Corporal, 7th Battalion, Black Watch (Royal Highlanders)

Robert Moodie Browning
Gunner, 26th Heavy Battery, Royal Garrison Artillery

John Gray
Captain, 2nd Battalion, Argyll and Sutherland Highlanders

William Blackley
Signaller, 6th Battalion, Highland Light Infantry

Hugh Fulton
Second Lieutenant, 9th Battalion, Highland Light Infantry

William Neil
Lance Sergeant, 13th Battalion, Black Watch

William Smart Kerr was born in Edinburgh, the son of William Kerr, a journeyman joiner from Stirlingshire, and his wife Alice Wood from Lancashire. William was working in Chorley at the time of the 1891 census. By 1901 the family had settled in Paisley. By the time William, junior, was fifteen he was a Post Office messenger, the traditional entry route to the postal service for a young lad. He did well. In 1911 he was appointed assistant postman in Paisley, and was promoted to postman in 1913, at the age of eighteen. He was allocated to Bridge of Weir and was working there when the war began. His 'genial and obliging disposition' made him popular in the village.

William volunteered for the Black Watch, initially enlisting in the 9th Battalion and later being transferred to the 7th. He survived over three years of action on the Western Front, and was promoted corporal. The 7th was part of 51st (Highland) Division, which after fighting in the Champagne area in July 1918 was transferred to Roclincourt near Arras, to take part in the British offensive on the River Scarpe.

At 04.30 on 24 August 1918 the battalion mounted an assault on the tactical features of Greenland Hill, Hausa and Delbar Wood and the Hyderabad Redoubt on the north slopes of the River Scarpe. The redoubt was on the summit of a crest overlooking Arras, and of considerable importance. The Germans launched several counter-attacks but failed to re-take it. Shells containing mustard gas were by then a feature of the German tactical armoury and Corporal Kerr was a victim of gas poisoning. The Regimental History speculates that the Germans, having decided to retire, were glad to fire off as much ammunition as they possibly could. Although he survived long enough to be taken to a casualty clearing station, the pernicious effects of the gas had entered his system and he died on 29 August 1918. The genial and popular postman was one of five Post Office employees from Bridge of Weir to serve, and the second one to be killed in action. He was twenty-three.

Robert Moodie Browning was the eldest of a family of four born to James Robert Browning, a picture-frame maker from Kilbarchan, and Marjory MacGraw, from Fortingal, Perthshire. The family steadily moved up the social ladder in Bridge of Weir from a flat in Gryffe Place, on to Neva Place, and by 1911, they had made it to Dunardrie, an eight-roomed villa in Ranfurly. James and both sons were in the family business. Robert, aged twenty-four, was employed as a clerk and James junior as a commercial traveller.

Robert served as a signaller in the Royal Garrison Artillery. He was with the big guns. He died of wounds on 13 September 1918 and is buried in Hendecourt-lès-Cagnicourt between Arras and Cambrai in the Pas-de-Calais.

John Gray was the only son of one of the wealthiest men in Bridge of Weir. His father, also John, came from farming stock in Renfrewshire but went off to the colonies and did well for himself in Burma, becoming an eminently suitable target for 'the fishing fleet' – the annual armada of young unmarried women who had made no match in the UK, but knew that there was less competition and a ready-made supply of bachelors in the colonies. The fleet of 1887 included the twenty-four-year-old Amelia Elizabeth Hopper from Gillingham, and John, by then forty, wasted no time in recognising her charms; they married in May that year. They wasted equally little time in starting a family and Marguerite (Rita) and Cecilia (Cissie) were born in Rangoon. Amelia then returned to Kent and in April 1891 was in Gravesend in the home of her Aunt Rebecca, pregnant with John.

By 1901 John, senior, had made enough money as a Burma rice merchant (the family describe it as his Klondike experience) to retire to Airlie, a grand villa in Prieston Road, Bridge of Weir. Young John was sent to Glasgow Academy, where discipline was at least on one occasion too strong for his father's liking; he took exception to his son's being caned by a martinet arithmetic master. John survived that ordeal and became a law apprentice with McLay, Murray and Spens in Glasgow, whilst taking classes in Scots Law and Conveyancing at Glasgow University.

The Gray children were sporty. They enjoyed winter sports and hill-walking and were accustomed to taking holidays in

Scandinavia and Switzerland. In July 1914, John was on holiday in Switzerland, acting as chaperon to his sisters Rita and Cissie (whom, as a VAD nurse, we met in Chapter 20), when their father, with a better sense of what lay ahead than the Cabinet, sent a telegram instructing them to return home at once, and through Italy, not France. They ignored the precaution and their train journey home took them past refugees already fleeing from the mobilising armies.

John was already in the Territorials and he enlisted as a private in the 9th HLI as soon as war was declared. He received his commission in the 5th (Territorial) Argyll & Sutherland Highlanders in November 1914. The 5th Argylls served in Gallipoli from July 1915 and Egypt from 1916 until April 1918, taking part in Allenby's successful campaign in Palestine.

John rose to the rank of captain, although reverting to lieutenant when he was posted to France, joining the 2nd Battalion of the Argylls on 30 April 1918. By September, the battalion was at Villers Guislain near Cambrai, advancing on the Hindenburg Line. Villers Guislain had exceptionally strong defences of concrete pill-boxes and machine-gun posts manned by the 14th Jaeger Regiment of Germany's Alpine Corps, a crack unit. On 21 September John's battalion was ordered to bomb the trench system known as Leith Walk while 19th Brigade made a frontal attack. The battalion war diary states:

> The 19th Brigade attack was made under a barrage and was only partially successful. 'B' Coy's attack reached its objective, and Lt. Gray who headed the assault was seriously wounded and subsequently died in trying to establish touch with the 19th Brigade south of LEITH WALK . . . Eventually at about 10 a.m. when no signs of the 19th Brigade were seen, 'B' and 'D' Coys withdrew to their original positions after having suffered about 25 casualties.

No immediate benefit was derived from John Gray's valiant and determined effort, although the German Army's general retreat in the face of the Allied offensive allowed the St Quentin Canal to be crossed and the Hindenburg Line in the vicinity was occupied on 4 October.

William Blackley was born in Greenock in 1885, the son of a stonemason originally from Twynholm in Kirkcudbright and his wife Anne Campbell. By 1891 the family was in Bridge of Weir. Anne had died before William was fifteen. His younger sister Annie was a residential inmate at Paisley Industrial School in 1901 (at the age of twelve), the best her father could do for her. William was a telegraph messenger by the age of fifteen and a postman at twenty-five. In 1911 he married Helen Fichlie, a domestic servant from one of the Ranfurly villas. A young postman had a good opportunity for sizing up pretty maidservants. Their daughter Annie was born on 19 June 1912, and Agnes on 23 July 1914.

Despite his wife and young family, William volunteered in early November 1914 for the Black Watch. He lasted a week before being discharged on medical grounds. In the opinion of the Medical Officer, his poor physique and bad teeth did not suggest that he was 'likely to become an efficient soldier'.

This did not deter William. By August 1915, standards had fallen (or perhaps he had been building himself up and having his teeth fixed), and he was accepted into the 6th HLI as a signaller. Sixth HLI was part of 157th Brigade, in 52nd (Lowland) Division which had fought in Gallipoli, Palestine and was in France from March 1918.

In early October 1918 the Division was preparing to break through the Hindenburg Line at Cambrai. William was killed during a changeover of front-line forces, always a dangerous exercise. He was one of two Other Ranks killed by intermittent shelling during the night of 4 October. He was the third of the Bridge of Weir postmen to be killed. He left a widow and two daughters aged six and four.

Hugh Fulton was the younger brother of Archie Fulton, who had been killed on 18 November 1916, the last day of the Battle of the Somme. Hugh, inspired by his brother's example or by the example of so many of his schoolmates in the High School of Glasgow, volunteered for active service in September 1915 when he was still seventeen, and by 5 April 1916 he too was in France, fifteen days short of his eighteenth birthday and more than a year before he was supposed to be old enough to serve overseas.* He was by no means unique in that. A young volunteer willing to swear to a false age was likely to be accepted by the recruiting officer. It is estimated that over 250,000 underage soldiers fought in the British Army during the First World War. Hugh probably saw action on the Somme, Arras and Third Ypres. He received his commission on 29 January 1918, becoming a second lieutenant at the age of nineteen.

Hugh was attached to 18th Cameronians (Scottish Rifles) shortly after they arrived in France in July 1918. By then, barely twenty, he already had well over two years' combat experience in some of the toughest engagements of the war.

In October 1918 the battalion was engaged in the final advance east of Béthune and north of Lens, with 16th Division. His death is the main entry for the battalion war diary of 9 October:

> Acting on a prisoner's statement that the enemy were retiring, No. 3 Coy. sent out a daylight patrol on BILLY BERCLAU–CANAL ROAD. Patrol met with heavy hostile M.G. fire during which 2/Lt. FULTON, C.S.M. WILLIAMS and 1 O.R. were killed.

Hugh and his two colleagues paid a heavy price for misleading intelligence.

---

* The rules changed, but at this stage in the war the minimum age for enlistment was 18, and the minimum age for service overseas was 19.

His parents were initially informed he was missing, and then that he was wounded and taken prisoner. This later news appeared in the *Paisley and Renfrewshire Gazette* two weeks after the Armistice and must have raised high hopes that he would soon be reunited with his family. The final confirmation of his death would have been a cruel blow.

William Neil was born in Cadder, Lanarkshire, the second of seven sons and two daughters born to a ploughman, also William, and his wife Margaret Roy. William, senior, was another, like the Millar family, who turned his skill with horses from ploughing to carting, and later moved on to mechanical transport. By 1911 the family was living in Cornmill House, by the banks of the River Gryffe in Bridge of Weir, between the tannery and the leather works. William, senior, was by then a carting contractor and coal merchant. Two of his sons, Alexander and Hugh, were also carters, presumably helping their father, but William, junior, became a house painter. He was twenty-one when he volunteered in October 1914 and joined the Black Watch.

His surviving records contain an anomaly. His medal index card has him first reaching France in September 1915 with 10th Black Watch, but the local newspaper records his return home in May of that year after suffering from gas inhalation in the defence of Ypres. The engagement in which he was gassed was probably the Battle of Aubers Ridge on 9/10 May. He reported back for duty on 10 June, 'feeling fit and eager to be engaged in any part in the zone of fire' and was rewarded with rapid promotion. He was a lance sergeant by 19 June.

If William was indeed with 10th Black Watch at the relevant time, he will have spent only two months in France before being shipped to Alexandria and onwards to Salonika, where 13th Black Watch, with which William was to spend his last months, arrived in October 1916. He survived operations there, and both 10th and 13th Battalions returned to France in June/July 1918 to participate in the final advance to victory.

The 10th was disbanded on 15 October. A unit was usually disbanded when it had had such a bad time that it was severely reduced in numbers or morale. Tenth Battalion certainly had a terrible time in Salonika, chiefly because of disease. It had scarcely settled in France before disease struck again – this time 'Spanish' flu. Fifteen men a day were being sent to hospital. Eventually what was left was sent to reinforce other battalions. William went to 13th Black Watch.

His new battalion went into the line at Vendhuille about six miles south of Cambrai. Action followed, relieved by brief periods of rest, and William participated in a series of advances as the Germans fell back, still fighting fiercely. On 8 November the battalion was ordered into the line again outside Semousies. The Germans were protecting their retreat with some token shelling and machine-gunning, but Semousies was liberated at 02.00 when the Germans suddenly abandoned their positions. Here William's war ended. After surviving more than three years he was killed three days before the cessation of hostilities. There is, objectively, nothing worse about a death on the last day of the war rather than the first, and yet it seems inescapably poignant.

Semousies is about 25 kilometres due south of Mons, where the British Expeditionary Force saw their first action in 1914, where the Great Retreat, rather than the Great Advance, took place, where South Wales Borderer Thomas Spink of Bridge of Weir began his long march south. It was four years before William Neil retraced Thomas's steps in the final days of the Allied advance to victory that took the armies close to where they had begun their convulsive struggle.

43

The Memorials

News of the Armistice reached Bridge of Weir on the day itself, Monday, 11 November 1918. One of the teachers rushed out of the school and started to ring the school bell, but, unused and untested for so long, the rope immediately broke. The same happened to the local constable at one of the kirks. The Armistice was only a truce, not surrender, and although the truce held, the peace that followed was flawed and broke down in less than a generation. The failure of the bells was prophetic.

Bridge of Weir soon began to reflect on how the dead should be remembered. What was decided on did not emerge spontaneously in a mood of idealistic unity. The war had not destroyed the ordinary human capacity to debate and disagree. Money did not pour in unasked. There is even some tantalising evidence of a local grudge.

On 16 January 1919 a meeting was held in the Parish Church Hall to discuss a suitable memorial. On the motion of County Councillor John McLeod, Mr W.M. Fleming, JP, was appointed chairman. It was agreed that 'necessary steps be taken to provide a suitable memorial or memorials to commemorate the magnificent work done in the Great War by the boys of Bridge of Weir'. A committee of ladies and gentlemen was charged with reporting to a further public meeting. Office bearers were appointed: Mr Fleming as convener and Chairman; Mr James Porteous, Clydesdale Bank, as Honorary Treasurer; and Mr John Buchanan as secretary. Several suggestions were made as to the most suitable form the memorial should take, all of which were to be considered by the newly formed committee.

On 22 February an anonymous letter in which an element of personal feud is evident was printed in the *Gazette*:

> Sir, I was gratified to learn that some of the leading people of the village had taken up the question of erecting a memorial to the natives who had fought the war. In my opinion, this memorial should take the form of something that would prove useful and beneficial to the inhabitants . . . I would strongly recommend that it should take the form of a public hall. Such a hall would be the means of enabling the people to find some relaxation, as a library could be run in connection there-with, and the hall could be utilised for local entertainment.
>
> In closing it has forcibly struck me that if Dr Barbour of Edinburgh, who is largely interested in Bridge of Weir, could find it practicable to grant the public use of the Freeland Hall, such an act of his would be some slight token of proof of his sincere gratitude to the men of the village who have fought, and in numerous instances laid down their lives, in order to protect not only their homes but the doctor's broad acreage as well. – Yours etc 'Native'.

The next meeting, in the Church Hall on 26 March, was well-attended The committee summarised the suggestions received including a public hall in which the people could relax or read, perhaps even use as a library. But the proposal that a purely symbolic memorial be erected at some suitable location within the village was put before the meeting by the chairman, and a discussion took place as to the merits of such a memorial.

A number of different views were aired and reported in the local press. Mr Gilmour proposed that a simple monument be erected to commemorate our dead heroes while Mrs Fullerton thought that the boys who had been spared to return should not be forgotten, and suggested a combined memorial. The Reverend A.M. Shand, the Church of Scotland minister, thought that a public park would be a suitable tribute, adding that a monument might be erected in such a park to 'perpetuate the memory of the lads who had fallen'.

After considerable discussion the chairman got his way, and it was resolved that a memorial of symbolic nature should be erected. A sub-committee was appointed to go into the matter and report back.

The discussions were long and thorough and a unanimous decision was not reached until December 1919. The Glasgow and South-West Railway Company had offered, at a nominal price, a triangular piece of ground opposite the Ranfurly Hotel and between Johnstone Road and Kilbarchan Road. The sub-committee unanimously agreed to recommend to the General Committee that the site be accepted and to submit 'a memorial design showing a scheme of treatment embodying a reproduction of the Barochan Cross'.

The Barochan Cross, a boldly decorated Celtic Christian monument of some two metres in height, stood for 1,000 years in an open field near Houston and is now housed in Paisley Abbey for its preservation. It is made from sandstone and dates from perhaps AD 900. A tentative interpretation of its four elaborately designed panels is that it may have been constructed in celebration of a victory gained by the Britons who lived by the Clyde in those days. It was thus a suitable choice of memorial to another victory a millennium later.

A rough estimate of the cost was put at £1,500. It was agreed to adopt these recommendations, and the sub-committee was empowered to communicate these facts to the public and also to proceed with the erection of the memorial, as sketched by Mr Andrew Balfour, FRIBA. Andrew Balfour was the architect whose son George had been killed at the Somme at the age of nineteen. Andrew Balfour had thus a poignant personal interest in the memorial as well as a professional one.

The committee hoped that now a definite plan had been agreed, everyone would join in the 'sharing of the great deeds done by the boys'. By this stage the sum of just £470.0.6d had been collected, less than a third of the required total, and an appeal for more donations was made in order that there might be no more unnecessary delay in completing the memorial.

By 18 February 1920, £860 had been donated by 153 subscribers. An average donation equivalent to roughly £500 per head in today's money was a generous response, but the total number of donors was very small. In order to widen support, a canvas throughout the village was planned, with a personal approach to all those willing to subscribe. Until arrangements were completed for this, it was recorded, it was hoped that those who had delayed in sending in their subscriptions would now do so at their earliest convenience and so allow the memorial committee to proceed.

By the end of 1920 a list containing the names of the local men who had fallen was displayed in three locations in the village to give all interested parties an opportunity to examine the rolls and ensure that all the names which should be included were contained, and to notify any omissions or corrections without delay.

On 25 June 1921 the *Paisley and Renfrewshire Gazette* reported:

This handsome memorial, which has been erected by the residents of Bridge of Weir, is to be unveiled and dedicated on Sunday first, at one o'clock, by Lieutenant-General Sir Francis Davis, KCB, KCVO [General Officer Commanding-in-Chief, Scottish Command]*. A guard of honour, buglers, and pipers of the 6th Battalion

---

* The newspaper spelled the officer's name wrongly. He was none other than the Lieutenant-General Davies who had ordered an enquiry into the failed attack on the Vineyard at Gallipoli and who had so severely castigated 1st/6th HLI for their conduct.

Argyll & Sutherland Highlanders, will be present at the ceremony by kind permission of Lieutenant-Colonel S. Coats, DSO Commanding 6th Argyll & Sutherland Highlanders.

The Memorial, which takes the form of a Granite Cross after the style of the 'Barochan Cross', is erected at the junction of Johnstone and Kilbarchan Roads and in front of the Parish Church. The ground has been tastefully laid out, and with the surrounding freestone walls and iron railings makes a pleasing and imposing picture as it can be seen from the different approaches. The front of the Memorial carries the names of those who made the supreme sacrifice, some 69* in all.

The unveiling and dedication of the Bridge of Weir War Memorial took place on 26 June, when the weather conditions were perfect. The service opened with the singing of the 2nd Paraphrase, *O God of Bethel*, led by the joint choirs of the three churches, who were accommodated at the rear of the memorial. *O God of Bethel* was sometimes referred to as Scotland's unofficial national anthem. The Scottish churches, remembering their time of persecution, identified with the tribulations and wanderings of Israel.

Then the Reverend A.M. Shand, MA, Bridge of Weir Parish Church, engaged in prayer, after which he read the names of the fallen. Mr Shand's name has been mentioned several times. He was appointed assistant minister in 1898, and was ordained minister of the parish in 1899. In 1917 he was attached to the Paisley Presbytery Hut in France, and wrote to the *Paisley and Renfrewshire Gazette* to tell them of his experiences – 'I . . . can honestly say it is the hardest month's work I have done in all my life. I am up at reveille every morning – 5.30, and have only once got to bed before 11, and am on foot all day'. He admired the men that he met, and in particular their modesty and reticence.

---

* A seventieth name was subsequently added; two others are recorded on church memorials only.

After the prayers Lieutenant-General Davies unveiled the memorial and gave a stirring address to the large audience assembled. Pipers of the 6th Battalion Argyll & Sutherland Highlanders played the Lament,* followed by the Last Post by the buglers of the same battalion. Mr Shand engaged in the prayer of dedication and the Reveille was then sounded by the pipers of the battalion. Those present sang Hymn 477, *Our God, our help in ages past.*† The choice of hymn, as of the paraphrase, is interesting: it is based on Psalm 90, reflecting the Church of Scotland's emphasis on psalm and paraphrase for its sung worship. After the Benediction was pronounced by Mr Shand, the National Anthem was sung.

Wreaths of flowers in profusion were placed round the memorial by relatives and friends of the fallen. Detachments of the Boy Scouts and the men belonging to the local branch of the British Legion were present, all of whom received a personal word from Lieutenant-General Davies before dispersal. The arrangements were carried out most successfully, reported the *Paisley and Renfrewshire Gazette.*

The deaths recorded on the Cross not only touched the immediate families, but, because so many had died in a close community, they left a chasm at the heart of that community. What effect did this have on life in the village? At a superficial level, less than might have been expected. Even during the war,

---

* The Regiment, now a battalion in the Royal Regiment of Scotland, does not have an official Lament and it's not known what was played. At funerals and other solemn occasions the two pipe tunes that the Argyll and Sutherland Highlanders normally play are *The Flowers of the Forest,* the inexpressibly poignant melody which remembers the destruction of the army and the flower of Scottish manhood at Flodden in 1513, and the scarcely less haunting expression of the pain of separation, *Lochaber No More.*

† In 1738 John Wesley changed the first word to 'O', but here it was sung as Isaac Watts had originally written it.

study of contemporary documents shows that the mundane detail of daily life received as much attention as ever, and when the war ended people very much wanted to put an anomalous experience behind them. Those aspects of ordinary life that had been on hold resumed. In April 1920, for example, a start was made on building new cottages between Ladebank Terrace and the Old Corn Mill, and opposite the Mimosas.

The demographic effects of the war were not as dramatic as might have been expected. About 6 per cent of the male population of the village (3 per cent of its total population) died. The impact was greater in the age group of the soldiers: marriageable males decreased by about 16 per cent. But all the same, the male/female split of the population in 1921 was almost the same as in 1911.

Seventeen of the seventy-two men who died are known to have been married. Six of the seventeen widows remarried, nine died without remarrying, and nothing is known about the remaining two.

The effect of the war on women's employment was not as marked as might be supposed. The Restoration of Pre-War Practices Act of 1919 gave returning soldiers priority over women. That did not affect women already in employment; nonetheless in 1921 the proportion of women in gainful employment was less than in 1911.

Agriculture had flourished during the war and been modernised by the use of machinery. After the war there was a major agricultural recession. That and mechanisation meant that returning farm-hands struggled to find employment. Under a government scheme, small-holdings were set up for returning soldiers. Examples of these are still to be seen on the north-east of the village. They made little impact on the problem of agricultural unemployment.

Some returning ploughmen found employment in the increasingly motorised transport businesses like that of the Millar family which were replacing the old self-employed carter.

In August 1920 a large wooden and iron garage was built on land adjoining Hope Hall for a Mr McKenzie, a motor-car hirer.

The memorial was not the only physical reminder of the war. Princess Louise Scottish Hospital for Limbless Sailors and Soldiers (later Erskine Hospital and then just Erskine), Scotland's principal hospital for wounded servicemen, was established in 1916 at Erskine House, just a few miles from the village. In the year to October 1919, 5,500 patients were treated, mostly supplied with prosthetic limbs. Some returned to the community; some, alas, spent the rest of their lives in the hospital.

Ranfurly Hotel, once the golfing establishment over which Fritz Rupprecht had presided, then the hostel for the Belgians, and now overlooking the Barochan Cross Memorial, had been acquired before the war ended by the British Red Cross Society and converted into a hospital for wounded servicemen, Ranfurly Auxiliary Hospital.

But buildings and memorials were not needed to remind the post-war community of what they had gone through. The village was well aware of what the war had meant. Many had fought through it. This book is about those who did not come back, but most of those who went to fight did come back. We do not know how many men of Bridge of Weir survived the war. The best estimate is that around 452 men from Bridge of Weir went to the war and 380 returned.*

---

* There is an active and heated debate about the national death rate. An initial calculation, based simply on the relative populations of Scotland and the UK, considerably understated the number of deaths. A subsequent adjustment was inflated by exceptionalist views. It now seems likely that about 690,000 men were mobilised in Scotland, and that about 110,000 of them died. That would imply a death rate of 15.94 per cent, and on the basis of that ratio, 452 men from the village would have fought and 380 would have survived. But these figures are based on the national experience. More locally, 457 men are known to have gone to war from the neighbouring village of Kilmacolm and seventy-seven died. The ratio in that case was 16.85 per cent. Adoption of the same ratio would suggest that in Bridge of Weir 427 men fought and 355 came back. The difference is significant and interesting but the last figures may be flawed,

In addition, the nurses and volunteers and bereaved had shared in the convulsions of these years. They were no doubt principally concerned to put the war behind them, but there was also a fund of shared experience which needed no articulation. A whole raft of ex-servicemen's associations was established to support the returning soldiers. Largely due to Haig's efforts they finally came together in the British Legion. In February 1921 a local branch was established following a meeting held in Freeland Hall. The incidence of what is now called post-traumatic stress appears to have been much lower after the Great War than after more recent conflicts, and it has been surmised that this is due to the fact that veterans returned together into civilian life, and found mutual support, and a sharing of their experience, even at an unspoken level. That comradeship was available in the British Legion Hall, and the pubs and clubs and churches and golf courses of the village.

The fact that the village had the resilience to regroup and recover, and peace in which to do so, is in many ways the most fitting memorial to the men who died. It is no doubt what they would have wanted. It is essentially what they fought for, in the modest, reticent fashion that their minister, Mr Shand, had noticed.

They did not fight in order to have their names on a memorial, and in 1919, no memorial was needed to remind people of what had happened. But now, as the years have passed and continue to pass, it reminds us of sacrifices that were made, sacrifices of which we might not be capable, sacrifices that must be remembered.

Let those who come after see to it that their names be not forgotten.

---

because Kilmacolm had a higher ratio of officers to other ranks (33.8 per cent against 16.7 per cent), which would be expected to affect mortality. Although Bridge of Weir had a lower percentage of officers than Kilmacolm, it can be assumed to have more than the national average, and a death ratio of around 16 per cent may be as accurate an estimate as will ever be reached.

Bridge of Weir Memorial Website

A website has been established in association with this book (www://bridgeofweirmemorial.co.uk/), and readers are referred to it for further information about the seventy-two, together with additional photographs, details of sources and suggestions for further reading. The website is being added to and updated and will in itself constitute a further and evolving memorial to those who died.

Appendix:
Military Formations

The smallest unit in the army, and the one that represented the ordinary soldier's immediate family, was the platoon, consisting of about fifty men. Platoons were grouped together in companies, and four companies into a battalion: sixteen platoons came to be the normal strength of a battalion. A regiment was composed of a number of battalions, the number varying throughout the course of the war, and if the platoon was the soldier's immediate family, the regiment was his extended family and the unit to which he owed his loyalty and which felt responsible for his well-being.

But at an operational level battalions were more significant, as they could be swapped around and used as the building blocks for the larger formations that fought the great battles of the war. Around four battalions formed a brigade (about 4,000 or 5,000 men), and three, or perhaps four, brigades composed a division. The division was the largest autonomous unit in the army. It had its own field artillery, consisted of about 19,000 men, and was usually commanded by a major-general. At division level the nature of command changed. A battalion was run by its commanding officer very much on a hands-on basis, and even at brigade a good commander took the pulse of his command on a daily basis. The division, however, was too big for that. It was an all-arms, self-contained fighting force, and the divisional commander was a remote presence.

Above divisional level units were slightly abstract concepts. A corps was in essence just a nucleus, the staff that administered two or more divisions (though the corps was real enough to have its own additional artillery). It was more or less stationary: corps did not move about as divisions did, and functioned to a degree as an administrative link between divisional and army headquarters. An army was similarly a nucleus, the staff (about 100 officers) that controlled two or more corps.

At the beginning of 1918 there was an important reduction in the strength of the battalion and in the number of battalions forming a division.

Acknowledgements

To find the origins of this book we have to look back, to a time long before the book had ever been thought of, to the curiosity of a small group of enthusiasts who wanted to know something of the men whose names are recorded on the Bridge of Weir war memorials. The first debt we have to acknowledge is accordingly to the energy and activity of these volunteer researchers: Sandy Andrew, Alan Bennie, Mary Jane Bird, Joanna Crawford, Dick Hughes and especially Janet Birch, Margaret Howison and Susan Macdonald.

Few historians know more of the First World War than John Hussey, or have done more to illuminate the history of that war, correcting long-held and unthinkingly accepted myths and misapprehensions. He read this work in draft, made many helpful observations and shared invaluable insights. We are grateful to him, as are all those who study the history of the Great War.

We are glad to have this opportunity of recording our gratitude to George Blair; the former Bridge of Weir History Society; members and benefactors of Bridge of Weir Memorial Society; Diana Burns; the Commonwealth War Graves Commission; Cork Muskerry Golf Club; Lieutenant Colonel Alaistair Cumming, the Highlanders' Museum; Freeland Church, Bridge of Weir; Alan Gilmour; Melvin Haggerty, former Head of History, Paisley Grammar School; Brenda Hardingham; Houston & St Fillan's Church, Houston; Imperial War Museum; Jeff Jefford, RAF Historical Society; Marion Lacey; Fiona and Duncan McEwan; Chris Mackay, Head of History, The High School of Glasgow; Mitchell

Library, Glasgow; Jonathan Muirhead, Bridge of Weir Leather Company; National Archives; Old Ranfurly Golf Club; Paisley Central Library Heritage Centre; Quarrier's Homes Archives; Ranfurly Castle Golf Club; the Registrar General for Scotland; Renfrewshire Council; Royal Commission on the Ancient and Historical Monuments of Scotland; St Machar's Ranfurly Church, Bridge of Weir; University of Glasgow Archives; Walsall Golf Club; Simon Wood, Head of History, The Glasgow Academy; and the Reverend Suzanne Dunleavy and the Reverend Kenneth Gray, custodians of three of the memorials, who deserve special mention for the encouragement they have given.

Contact was made with some of the families of the men who died, and we hope that their recollections are faithfully reflected. The website includes photographs and mementos provided by the families of Henry and John Andrew, Richard Arroll, Frederic, Lyle and Speirs Barr, Malcolm Brodie, James Brooks, John Brown, John Clark, John Gray, John Holmes, William Houston, William McClure, William McKenzie, Robert and William Millar, and James Woodrow.

Our thanks to Dawn Broadley, who transformed illegible manuscripts, evilly ill-formatted typescripts and muttered dictation into a thing of beauty and a joy, if not forever then at least for our publishers. Helen Bleck was an inspired copy editor and at Birlinn Hugh Andrew, managing director, and Andrew Simmons, editorial director, were supportive and patient.

Our greatest debt, however, is to the seventy-two men who quietly went to war and gave their own lives so that the life of their country might go on undisturbed. They deserve remembrance.

WR
GM
PB
Bridge of Weir, July 2016

Index

Names of the Bridge of Weir fallen are in bold.